Let Their Light So Shine

Let Their Light So Shine

MORMON LEADERS IN NEW ZEALAND
Volume 3

edited by
SELWYN KATENE

First published in 2021 by Huia Publishers
39 Pipitea Street, PO Box 12280
Wellington, Aotearoa New Zealand
www.huia.co.nz

ISBN 978-1-77550-633-1 (Hardback)
ISBN 978-1-77550-654-6 (Paperback)

Edition copyright © Selwyn Katene 2021

Individual chapters copyright © their authors and the whānau of the subject
Back cover photograph courtesy of Matthew Cowley Pacific Church History Centre, Hamilton.

This book is copyright. Apart from fair dealing for the purpose of private study, research, criticism or review, as permitted under the Copyright Act, no part may be reproduced by any process without the prior permission of the publisher.

A catalogue record for this book is available from the National Library of New Zealand.

Contents

	FOREWORD *Charles A. Rudd*	vii
	PREFACE *Peter Lineham*	ix
	INTRODUCTION *Selwyn Katene*	1
I	A Man of Courage: Matene Rutatenga *Waana Celeste Watene*	5
II	Lord I Would Follow Thee: James Rongotoa Elkington *Jeanette Grace*	19
III	A Life of Service: William Roberts *Michael Roberts*	35
IV	He Kaimahi o te Tangata: Puti Tipene (Steve) Watene *Karina Elkington (née Watene)*	57
V	Ahorangi: Pateriki Te Rei *Marie Waaka (née Te Rei)*	77
VI	Humble Converts: Ian Garry *Peter Garry*	89
VII	From Sheep Farmer to Shepherd of Souls: Kenneth Molony Palmer *Jennifer Beth Roberts (née Palmer)*	101
VIII	A Record of Service: Nitama Paewai *Api Te Rina Paewai*	121
IX	One Called and Prepared: Geoffrey R. Garlick *Barry Garlick*	141
X	Honest Ben: Ben Couch *Derek Couch*	157
XI	E hoa mā (my friends) – 'In the service of the Lord …': Douglas J. Martin *Douglas J. Martin Jr*	173
XII	A Product of His Environment: Te Puoho Katene *Callum Katene*	195
	CONTRIBUTORS	215
	GLOSSARY	219
	INDEX	222

Foreword

Charles A. Rudd

At pivotal times in history the Lord has raised up capable men and women to perform His work in specific areas of the world. They have become His leaders. They have been inspired to achieve and to perform 'good works'. These noble and great ones were chosen and appointed to their stewardships before their missions on earth began (Abraham 3:22-23).

James Elkington was one of them. A paramount chief of the Ngāti Koata tribe, stake patriarch and patriarch of the Elkington, Hemi, Selwyn and Hippolite families of D'Urville Island, he presided over those families now numbered in the thousands, many of whom have served the Lord in various capacities for more than a century.

Another was Aucklander William Roberts, a first-generation member of the Church who was 'led by the Lord's hand' to accept the gospel in the early 1950s. He was blessed with key executive leadership roles, when most needed by the Church, as it experienced significant growth throughout the latter half of the twentieth century and transformed into a mainstream New Zealand religion.

People have always desired to be led by strong leaders with vision and conviction. Mentors of faith, humility and integrity have always been sought after. Such is the case in the lives of those portrayed in *Let Their Light So Shine*. Each was a special servant in his or her own way and a beloved leader in the eyes of others. They were humble saints who sought to do the will of the Lord. Some were strong in leadership style while others provided powerful influences by simple example.

Many of those profiled in this book were personal friends of my father, Elder Glen L. Rudd, a former missionary to New Zealand, president of the Hamilton New Zealand Temple and member of the Quorum of Seventy. He knew them well and loved and sustained them as they served the people of New Zealand. I grew up hearing their names and stories of courage, testimony and leadership. Some of them visited our family and stayed in our home.

On 7 November 2014 my father wrote the following:

> Almost 75 years ago or more, I landed in New Zealand to begin my first mission, and I traveled all over New Zealand. President Cowley was a brand-new mission president and I became his traveling companion for quite a lot of my mission. However, I rode my bike five or six thousand miles anyway in addition. I did love the people. I stayed in their homes, ate their food, and was a part of their family life.
>
> When I think of all the great Maori people I lived with 75 years ago, and incidentally, I've been in New Zealand 28 different times on several different Church assignments, I am so grateful for all of my many assignments in New Zealand and for having known so many of the people. President Cowley was a great blessing to me, not only as a mission president, but for the next 15 years until he died.
>
> I am 96-1/2 years old, so I won't live much longer, but I have a wonderful collection of Maori and New Zealand history and I think it will stay with my family for a good long time to come.[1]

My father had the great privilege of helping Mere Whaanga during the last two or three years of her life. She and her husband Hirini Whaanga had migrated to Utah in 1894 and my father had taken care of her grave and Hirini's grave for more than sixty years in the Salt Lake City cemetery. He knew that they were good people and that he was a part of them.

As the years progressed and each of these great people passed away, they left a beacon of light for others to follow. Throughout New Zealand glows the light of testimony and truth instilled in the lives of their posterity and friends.

During my recent service as a Mission President in Aotearoa (New Zealand), I was a personal witness of that influence. A study of their lives will continue to inspire us. Because of their work, love and service, the brightness of the gospel will continue to shine as expressed so well in the stories and perspectives of the twelve faithful pioneering New Zealand saints.

Charles A. Rudd
Chair, New Zealand Missionary Society
Salt Lake City, Utah

NOTES

1. Correspondence to Selwyn Katene from Glen L. Rudd dated 7 November 2014

Preface

Peter Lineham

It is a privilege to write in commendation of this fascinating collection of biographies of the generation of leaders of the Latter-day Saints in the post-war years. Two significant earlier books have introduced the life stories of the first and second generations of Latter-day Saints in Aotearoa. The fine work of descendants in writing those accounts reflects the importance for Mormons of genealogical work, and of that striking blend of Māori and Mormon respect for their forbears. Both books have done their authors and editor proud.

The present book includes a different mix of people, some of them Pākehā, some Māori. Although the earlier books include great figures within the church – Whaanga and Meha for example – the present book includes a generation of more public figures, especially Watene and Couch. It reflects the renewed mission of the church to Pākehā and the age of the creation of a second mission, the first stake and the New Zealand Temple and the Church College of New Zealand. All the biographies touch on references to these momentous years. They also are interesting because of the authentic voice of the converts and the role of dreams and prayer. There is a fascinating interweaving of links with the general authorities of the church and contacts with Utah. The shape of the Mormon community in New Zealand changed a great deal in those years, as the chapels were erected through the labour missionaries and the once-dominant marae testimonies were succeeded by new ways of outreach and testimony. But the outsider is bound to be impressed by the dynamics of the Mormon family, of the high level of interweaving of Māori and Pākehā within the Mormon community, of the ways in which sport played such a dominant role in the reshaped Māori community, and the ways in which hard work, especially manual labour, shaped people's ethics and qualities. So much is summed up in the remark of George Katene in 1940 quoted in Chapter Twelve: 'it is time to grow out of our shells and expand our modes of living so that we will be of more benefit to our neighbours.' The role of calling to church office and responsibilities played a significant part in the converts' lives, but so did community service. A theme of a later book could include more of the voices of women, more of the challenges of interethnic families and communities, and more understanding of what Mormons brought to politics. In these family stories I have some hints of how rich the story could be. I warmly commend this book to a wide readership.

Peter Lineham MNZM

Emeritus Professor of History, Massey University

Introduction

Selwyn Katene

Let your light so shine before men,
that they may see your good works,
and glorify your Father which is in heaven.[1]

The Coromandel Ranges, on the east coast of New Zealand's North Island, were known for their isolation, dense bush, steep hills and deep gullies. In July 1886 the winter was wetter and colder than usual. Just one month previously, Mount Tarawera, about 250 kilometres away, had erupted, killing about 120 people. Earthquakes were still being recorded around Rotorua and other areas of the North Island, including one on 14 July. For Elder William Gardner, a thirty-seven-year-old missionary of the Church of Jesus Christ of Latter-day Saints ('the Church') from Utah, alone and lost, without any companions, 15 July must have felt like the end of everything. After a miserable night and day spent limping 10 miles through the thick bush looking for signs of life, he saw a light shining in the window of a Māori home. The people there fed him and dried him off and then listened to his gospel teachings.[2]

The family Elder Gardner taught were Mita and Kataraina Watene. The light shining in their window, which had guided him to safety, had burned for many a long year, and brought to their home and their whānau (family) the true Church for which they had been searching. This light continued to burn even after Mita and Kataraina Watene were converted to the Church. Consequently, it became a family tradition to always burn a candle in their front window to cast a beacon of light in the night to any lost wanderer (see Chapter One).[3]

Let Their Light So Shine is the third in a series of books about early New Zealand leaders in the Church.[4] It is intended to showcase these leaders as a 'light in the window', a candle on a 'candlestick [giving] light to all in the house', a 'light [for] the world ... set on a hill [that] cannot be hid'[5], and a beacon of hope for people seeking inspiration, guidance and faith-promoting stories. Each chapter is written by their descendants, recording the experiences of twelve influential pioneering leaders who dedicated their lives to Church, community and family.

Let Their Light So Shine celebrates the many individuals and families who contributed to the advancement of the Church in New Zealand.

This book shines the spotlight on twelve leaders – Matene Rutatenga, James Elkington, William Roberts, Steve Watene, Pateriki Te Rei, Ian Garry, Kenneth Palmer, Nitama Paewai, Geoffrey Garlick, Ben Couch, Douglas Martin and Te Puoho Katene – and their roles and perspectives as leaders in the Church, community and family.

The following table provides some basic information on the twelve leaders:

NAME	BIRTH/DEATH	PLACE	ETHNICITY	LEADERSHIP
MATENE RUTATENGA	1802–99	Hauraki	Māori	Rangatira (chief)
JAMES ELKINGTON	1898–1985	D'Urville Island	Māori	Patriarch/tribal leader
WILLIAM ROBERTS	1907–94	Auckland	European	Stake/Mission/Temple President
STEVE WATENE	1910–67	Hutt Valley	Māori	Member of Parliament
PATERIKI TE REI	1912–95	Rotorua	Māori	Bishop/Ahorangi
IAN GARRY	1915–97	Ngaruawāhia	European	Branch and Temple President
KENNETH PALMER	1918–88	Auckland	European	Stake and Mission President
NITAMA PAEWAI	1920–90	Kaikohe	Māori	GP, Mayor, Stake Presidency
GEOFFREY GARLICK	1924–2010	Auckland	European	Stake President
BEN COUCH	1925–96	Wairarapa	Māori	Member of Parliament
DOUGLAS MARTIN	1927–2010	Hamilton	European	First Quorum of Seventy
TE PUOHO KATENE	1927–2010	Porirua	Māori	Patriarch

Two previous books[6] provide similar commentary:
- In *Turning the Hearts of the Children* the twelve leaders include Hirini Whaanga, Raihi Ngawaka, Whatahoro Jury, Ngahuia Chase,

Percy Going, Hohepa Heperi, Te Rawhiti Paerata, Stuart Meha, Wetekia Elkington, Sidney Christy, Polly Duncan and Turake Manuirirangi.
- In *By Their Fruits You Will Know Them* a further twelve leaders include Henare Potae, Rangikawea Puriri, Pere Wihongi, Pepene Eketone, Haana Wineera, Alice Halbert Mataira, Henare Hamon, Whautere Witehira, Mereana Hall Bean, Pera Ihimaera Smiler, Whakahe Matenga and Sydney Crawford.

The spiritual experiences and conversion stories of these forbears were based on fundamental gospel principles such as faith, repentance, baptism and receiving the Holy Ghost. If motivated by the inspirational and character-building messages of these pioneers, there is an obligation to seek, record and share one's own experiences so that the futures of our tamariki (children) and mokopuna (grandchildren) are well-assured.

Remember, you are descended from greatness.

E kore koe e ngaro, he kākano i ruia mai i Rangiātea
You will not be lost, for you are a seed descended from Rangiātea

NOTES

1. New Testament, Matthew 5:16
2. Gardner, W. (1895) *Missionary Journal*. Retrieved from https://history.lds.org/missionary/individual/william-gardner-1846?lang=eng
3. Watene, Waana (2020) 'A Man of Courage: Matene Rutatenga' (see Chapter One)
4. Katene, Selwyn (ed.) (2014) *Turning the Hearts of the Children: Early Māori Leaders in the Mormon Church*, Vol. 1, Steele Roberts Publishers, Wellington; Katene, Selwyn (ed.) (2017) *By Their Fruits You Will Know Them: Early Maori Leaders in the Mormon Church*, Vol. 2, Steele Roberts Publishers, Wellington
5. New Testament, Matthew 5:14
6. Katene (2014); Katene (2017)

REFERENCES

Gardner, W. (1895) Missionary Journal. Retrieved from: https://history.lds.org/missionary/individual/william-gardner-1846?lang=eng

Katene, Selwyn (ed.) (2014) *Turning the Hearts of the Children: Early Māori Leaders in the Mormon Church*, Vol. 1, Steele Roberts Publishers, Wellington

Katene, Selwyn (ed.) (2017) *By Their Fruits You Will Know Them: Early Maori Leaders in the Mormon Church*, Vol. 2, Steele Roberts Publishers, Wellington

I

A Man of Courage

Matene Rutatenga (*c.* 1802–99)

Waana Celeste Watene[1]

Uncertain of the name given him at birth, various records held by the Church of Jesus Christ of Latter-day Saints have listed him as Matene Rutatenga and also as Matene Te Ngā. Matene is the transliterated word for Martin, and he received this name upon being baptised into the Anglican Church.

As a chief of Ngāti Maru (Hauraki) he was not exempt from peril, tragedy and danger. Having lived during a turbulent period in New Zealand's history, he knew both battle and defeat.[2] He fought in many skirmishes including the battle of Te Waiweruweru, Te Tōtara Pā and the 1863 Waikato Land Wars,[3] and lived to the age of ninety-seven years.

This chapter will feature two prominent events in the life of Matene Rutatenga: first his courageous leadership of his whānau, hapū and iwi, and second his conversion and baptism into the Church of Jesus Christ of

Latter-day Saints, including how his whānau came to join the Church and contribute to its growth. Matene's legacy of courage and endurance will permeate throughout.

Whakapapa (Genealogy)

Descending from Hotunui, the father of Hoturoa, captain of the Tainui canoe, and as a direct descendent of Marutūahu, Matene Rutatenga's ancestral legacy cascades down through twenty-one generations. The following lineal chart presents his line of descent from Marutūahu, from whom originates the iwi, Ngāti Maru.

Marutūahu = Paremoehau (1)
Tamatepō = Rangiriri
Rauakītua = Rongomai
Puha = Puke
Te Rākau = Waipaepae
Miria = Te Puhi
Te Maunu = Rangiteauria
Tuwhakauhoa = Tarakihi (2)
Te Tiki (f) = Rongotūkiterangi
Matene Rutatenga = Riripeti Te Kohu
Kataraina = Mita Whareroa Watene
Pirimona Watene = Whakamura Whatuoho Hetaraka
Hōri Pirimona Watene = Ani Matengaukino Morris
Floyd Aratama Watene = Ringihia Te Aroha Eketone
Waana Celeste Watene

Born *c.*1802 to parents Rongotūkiterangi and Te Tiki, Matene was one of three children: Pātara Rangiteapake, his older brother, then him, followed by Arapera, his only sister. After the death of Pātara, Matene married Pātara's widow Riripeti Te Kohu, accepting the responsibility of helping to raise their only child, Hoani Nahe. Together Matene and Riripeti Te Kohu had five children: Kataraina, Hana, Raiha, Hori and Waana Moengahau.

Some years later, Riripeti Te Kohu died, after which Matene married Apikera and had another two children: daughters Papu and Te Aue. In 1898, at the age of ninety-seven years, Matene joined the Church of Jesus Christ of Latter-day Saints and lived a further sixteen months before he died on 27 December 1899.

Battle of Te Waiweruweru

According to Toke Watene (n.d.), in 1819, at the age of seventeen, Matene was one of eighty young warriors who fought against the Northland tribe Ngāpuhi in their ill-fated attempt to take siege of the impregnable stronghold pā (Māori defensive settlement) of Ngāti Maru at Te Tōtara, in Hauraki. Matene and his companions stole their way through the bush, battling their opponents to retrieve water for women and children held captive within the pā. Returning to the pā with water-soaked cloaks and mats, they wrung the remaining water into their parched mouths. This battle was known as Te Waiweruweru, otherwise known as the Battle of Dripping Garments.

Fall of Te Tōtara Pā

In 1821 Ngāpuhi returned to Te Tōtara a second time under the command of their chief Hongi Hika to try to overtake the pā.[4] The young Matene was again called upon to join this infamous siege, known as the Battle of Te Tōtara Pā. Matene led some women and children to a place near Tairua called Takatakahia. On returning to Te Tōtara, he along with others tried to convince Te Puhi, the highest ranking chief, to abandon the pā but Te Puhi refused.[5] Departing the desolate remains of Te Tōtara, a sad Matene remembered looking back and seeing the glare of many fires as the ovens were made ready and hearing the chanting and stamping of hundreds of Ngāpuhi warriors dancing their haka (war dances) in triumph of their work of death.[6]

A New Era

Such destruction and desolation culminated in Ngāti Maru relocating to live among the Waikato people of Ngāti Korokī and Ngāti Hauā offering temporary residence between Maungatautari and Kirikiriroa (Hamilton). Within a few short years Ngāti Maru spread themselves throughout the area, creating much concern for the aforementioned iwi (tribes). To counteract such intentions, several intertribal assaults took place; the final one known as the battle of Taumatawīwī (1830) where the defeated Ngāti Maru were escorted back to their homelands in Hauraki. Although there is no record to suggest that Matene took part in this battle, it is highly probable that he did.

From this point onwards the impact of Europeanisation was to result in major changes within Māori society throughout the country. In 1840, a significant and historical event took place in the Bay of Islands with the signing of Te Tiriti o Waitangi, a pact between the British Crown and Māori chiefs, and the founding document of New Zealand. The 1850s saw the establishment of a newly formed settler government introducing legislation that stripped tribal leaders of their mana motuhake (chieftainship) and resources belonging to Māori, and introduced raupatu (confiscated lands).

More specific to the Hauraki region was an influx of settlers in search of the precious ore 'gold' that lay plentiful within the Coromandel hills and tribal lands of Ngāti Maru. The 1860s marked an era of civil unrest and turmoil exacerbated by land wars and further land confiscations. A Māori pan-tribal unity was created by several iwi called Te Kīngitanga (the Māori King Movement) in an effort to avert the sale of Māori lands. Retaliating, the government launched into war commencing in Taranaki, followed by Waikato and moving throughout the North Island.[7]

This upheaval impacted on Matene, and his chieftainship, evidenced by his active involvement in the 1863 Waikato land wars.[8] At the turn of the century the Māori population was in decline due to the wars and European-introduced diseases. But the resilience of Māori, coupled with inspired leadership from tribal leaders including Matene, resulted in significant changes as Māori sought to hold fast to their culture while embracing the positive aspects of European life. Religion was one avenue that chiefs pursued in an attempt to improve the socioeconomic circumstances of their people.

Conversion

In 1888 Matene's daughter, Kataraina, and her husband, Mita Whareroa Watene, were baptised into the Church of Jesus Christ of Latter-day Saints and confirmed members by Elder Joseph Burgess. Yet, the story of their conversion began some two years prior. The story is told by Matthew Cowley, then President of the New Zealand Mission, of one young missionary, Elder William Gardner, and the lonely and treacherous conditions he endured to bring the light of the gospel to Kataraina and Mita Watene. Great-grandson, Floyd Aratama Watene, recounts the story:

> He was not receiving any encouraging news from his home and particularly at this time, he was alone without a companion in the Coromandel Ranges. It appeared that Elder Gardner was wandering … on these ranges for many days and nights sleeping under bushes … It so happened during these wanderings that he found his way to the Kirikiri valley … some thirty-five miles south of Coromandel … With no road or guide but dense bush all around, forging hills and deep gullies, for a few days and nights, Elder Gardner had actually

lost his way till he came to the Kirikiri Stream in the Kirikiri Valley. So he decided to follow that stream until it came out at the Kirikiri Settlement and by that time it was dark. He kept on walking and came ... to the ... Watene family home and saw a light shining from one of the windows. Elder Gardner was very tired and ... debated whether or not he should go and knock at the door. But he did not for he pushed his way along into the night and got lost again in the bush. The next day, it appeared that he had wandered back into the Kirikiri bush again and finally came upon the Kirikiri Stream ... He again followed the stream and the following evening came up to the same house and saw the same light shining out to him. But this time he felt sure that he must call in and knock at the door. He did, and stated to the people that he was a missionary of the Church of Jesus Christ of Latter-day Saints and asked whether he could come in. He was gladly welcomed to the home. The next day was a big day for the Watene family and also for those who congregated there. A meeting was called and quite a large gathering of people from the settlement came to hear the message of the gospel given by Elder Gardner with the help of an interpreter. The story goes that many hearts were converted to the gospel including Mita Watene, and other members of the family.[9]

Of this incident, Elder Gardner wrote in his diary on 15 July 1886:[10]

After one of the longest and most miserable nights I ever spent, day finally dawned but the timber was too thick that it was 7 o'clock before I could see or dare venture in any direction. I humbly asked the Lord to lead me out of the bush and I thanked Him for the preservation of my life through the night. I started; the scenery all looked strange and I could not find my tracks [from] the night before. I hunted around but was very careful not to get turned around or bewildered and I marked trees to guide me. I finally found my tracks; it was impossible to follow them through the grass and shrubs. Every bush was hanging with water and I was soon drenched to the skin. I worked my way in the direction I thought [I] came. My right knee failed me and I had a job to get down the mountain, but I asked the Lord to give me strength, perform my labours and the pain left me. I heard a stream of water running in the direction of the canyon below and I worked my way down through the mass of timber and found the creek and waded down it till it led out of the timber on the trail that I had went up the day before. There I knelt down and thanked the Lord for my deliverance. I followed about a mile to Maori kainga [settlement] where the natives soon gave me some food. I took off my clothes and dried them to get warmed up good and I felt better. In the evening I visited amongst them and preached to them and they were much interested in my teachings and they seemed to sympathise with me on account of my exposure and they said if I had not been a servant of God I never would have got out alive. I had walked 10 miles.

Mita and Kataraina Watene.

Elder William Gardner, missionary 1884–87.
Retrieved from https://history.lds.org/missionary/individual/william-gardner-1846?lang=eng

The 'light' shining in the window as told by President Matthew Cowley was, as recorded by the Watene whānau and passed down from one generation to the next, the guiding influence that brought the true Gospel of Jesus Christ to them.

As a point of note, 'light' also relates to the name Te Rama o Hauraki, which by interpretation means the 'Lamp of Hauraki', the whare tūpuna (ancestral meeting house) in Kirikiri at Mātaiwhetu Marae. This name gives reference to early Christian missionaries who came to that area preaching the gospel. In his book *A Study of the Stars or Mataiwhetu Marae*, the author, Hōri Pirimona Watene, provides a commentary regarding the origin of this name 'Te Rama o Hauraki':

> ... the name Rama was highly respected by Ngāti Maru in remembrance of a certain leader among them in the early days who introduced the Light of Christianity into the district. He was Te Poari, who married a chieftainess named Meteria.[11]

However, it would appear that, despite the many religions being preached at that time, Mita felt there was something amiss. His people had been in darkness for a long while, despite the introduction of Christianity some years earlier. This is illustrated in the following account provided by James Rukutai Watene, great-grandson of Mita and Kataraina Watene:

> Mita a very astute person was knowledgeable in the Bible. One evening whilst reading the Bible he was overcome by the urgency that he should light a candle in his front window each evening as it was to be a sign for the true Church to come.[12]

Mita and Kataraina Watene's house.

The light in the window, which he burned for many a long year, would bring to their home and their whānau the truthfulness he had been searching for. This candle continued to burn even after Mita and Kataraina were converted to the Gospel of Jesus Christ as taught to them by Elder William Gardner. Consequently it became a family tradition to always burn a candle in their front window to cast a beacon of light in the night to any lost wanderer. 'The Watene home became a refuge for the missionaries from that time, and a branch was organised there in 1888.'[13]

Matene's Conversion

Despite his conversion to the Church in 1898, ten years after his daughter Kataraina, Matene was the first generation of the Watene whānau to join the Church of Jesus Christ of Latter-day Saints.

Returning to New Zealand later as mission president, William Gardner renewed contact with the Watene whānau. Unfortunately his visit coincided with the passing of Taramana Hei Watene, Kirikiri's first branch president until his passing. He was Mita and Kataraina's son, and Matene's grandson – who himself at the same time suffered ill health.

As Taramana's life drew to a close and in spite of Priesthood blessings, president Gardner was of the view that Taramana 'wished us to dedicate him to the Lord, but we could hardly do so. He seemed very anxious to go but we told him he must wait the Lord's own due time … and he seemed content to do so.'[14]

In 1895, president Gardner wrote in his journal:[15]

> The people were gathered under the big willow tree by the Church where we held our Conference last year. They had him nicely laid out dressed in white as he had dreamed of seeing people dressed in white. He had a very nice coffin. The Saints and all who were present were feeling well over the dying words of their dear Bro. He had settled up all his business and gave instructions how his property was to be disposed of. Told his wife it was his desire that she should

Australasian Mission President William Gardner, 1893–96.
Courtesy of the Matthew Cowley Pacific Church History Centre

marry his brother Wilson (Wirihana) or if she married anybody else to be sure and be married or she (would) never come to where he was. He also called for his grandfather and told him that his dying request was that he should join this Church, be baptised for said he, 'This is the Church of Christ.' He said, 'You can take the smartest and wisest man you can find in all these other Churches and one of their little ones can confound them.' He said to his grandfather, 'Matene, if you don't receive the Gospel I will stand before the judgment bar of God as a witness against you. Therefore be in a hurry to grant my request as my breath is failing me.' The old gentleman said; 'If you get well, I will.' Taramana said, 'I have been called to preach the Gospel to the spirits who have died without a knowledge of the Gospel. The Elders will preach the Gospel to you people.' He said, 'I desire that when William Gardner returns that he will give my wife and children a Father's blessing that they will be preserved in the truth. My dying exhortation is, "Be firm to the covenants you have made. Be kind to the Elders, both in good circumstances or in poverty for they are the servants of God."' Mita, Taramana's father spoke up and said, 'Matene your tupuna won't join the Church' for all his children had died in the Church of England. Taramana was smiling and his wife asked him what he was (looking) at and he said he (had) seen their little daughter playing around his wife (and) sent loving messages to her. Then he passed away as if going to sleep. His wife and mother had cut their hair and braided it on to some of their greenstone war clubs or meremere and laid them on the coffin … We comforted the widow and relatives. They were all feeling comforted by the dying words of Taramana to them. Both Saints and outsiders had copied this and that was all the conversation. They fixed us some dinner and we visited and comforted the people. We had prayer by the coffin under the weeping willow tree.

(L–R) The Anglican and the LDS Church at Kirikiri, Thames.

Taramana Watene was laid to rest at Te Tōtara Pā on Thursday 26 September 1895, and his grave was dedicated by President William Gardner.

Of Taramana Watene, Andrew Jenson, Assistant Church Historian, who visited New Zealand in 1895 wrote:

> His fine dying testimony was read in public throughout all Maoridom long afterwards. [He was] one of the most faithful Maori Elders who ever joined the Church.[16]

Jenet Watene-Spencer wrote regarding the conversion of Matene Rutatenga:

> After Taramana's death, Matene Tenga greatly mourned the loss of his favourite grandson. They had a special kinship. He could not abide the thought of never seeing him again. True to his word Matene was baptised in the Kirikiri stream by Elder N. P. Westenskow on August 21, 1898 and confirmed a member of the Church of Jesus Christ of Latter-day Saints by Elder A. E. Asper.[17]

Matene's experiences afforded him acts of selflessness, love and sacrifice – aroha ki te tangata, manaaki ki te tangata. Love and service rendered to his people – a willingness to put others' needs ahead of his own – was his mark. As a young warrior, he became a leader of accountability, exercising responsibility for the protection and welfare of vulnerable women and children. As a kaitiaki (guardian), his role was to protect and preserve whānau relationships, ensuring the preservation of whakapapa, through the transmission of oral and written accounts – ngā taonga tuku iho.

Gazing into the eyes of Matene one sees an astute rangatira (chief). Although his eyes speak of uncertainty and mistrust, they also speak of mana (prestige), agility, prowess, wisdom, intelligence, experience, courage and survival.

From his youth, in his teens, he courageously fought in battles. Throughout his adult life he led his whānau, hapū (sub-tribe) and iwi. Then in 1898, as an elderly man, he converted to the Church of Jesus Christ of Latter-day Saints. Matene Rutatenga is an honoured and revered tūpuna (ancestor), leader, chief and patriarch of the Watene whānau. His example inspires a zeal for all his descendants to declare boldness, integrity and bravery during difficult times. His faith to tread in unknown and troublesome paths can be a light and guide for all. His fortitude encourages one to erect spiritual palisades in offering protection against adversity. His selflessness inspires aroha – love unfeigned, kindness, respect and charity; the pure love of Christ.

This is the legacy he has left for his descendants, who continue to provide strong leadership throughout New Zealand, beginning with Matene Rutatenga, Mita Watene and Taramana Hei Watene, Toke Watene (Hauraki district president), George Watene (New Zealand Mission secretary),

Steve Watene (Member of Parliament), Floyd Watene (labour missionary) and many others.

Tēnei tōku mihi aroha ki a koe, e te rangatira. Nō reira, tēnā koutou, tēnā koutou, tēnā tātou katoa.

NOTES

1. Waana Celeste Watene is the third great-granddaughter of Matene Rutatenga
2. Mair, G. (1923) *Reminiscences and Maori stories*, Brett Printing and Publishing, Auckland
3. Watene, T. (1940) Matene Te Nga, *Te Karere,* New Zealand Mission, The Church of Jesus Christ of Latter-day Saints, Auckland
4. Smith, P. (1910) *Maori Wars of the Nineteenth Century,* Whitcombe and Tombs Limited, Christchurch
5. Mair (1923)
6. Watene-Spencer, J. T. A. (n.d.) Watene Whareroa Wharemāhīhī
7. Jones, P. T. (1959) *King Potatau: An Account of the Life of Potatau Te Wherowhero the First Maori King,* The Polynesian Society, Auckland
8. Watene (1940)
9. Watene, F. A. (1985) *Journal*, Zoom Printers, Hamilton
10. Gardner, W. (1886) *Missionary Journal.* Retrieved from https://history.lds.org/missionary/individual/william-gardner-1846?lang=eng
11. Watene, H. P. (1979) *A Study of the Stars or Mataiwhetu Marae,* Thames
12. Watene, J. R. (n.d.) *Mita Watene*
13. Newton, Marjorie (2012) *Tiki and Temple: The Mormon Mission in New Zealand 1854–1958*, Greg Kofford Books, Utah, p 52
14. Gardner, W. (1895) *Missionary Journal.* Retrieved from https://history.lds.org/missionary/individual/william-gardner-1846?lang=eng
15. *Ibid.*
16. Newton, p 52
17. Watene-Spencer, J. T. A. (n.d.) Watene Whareroa Wharemāhīhī

REFERENCES

Gardner, W. (1886) Missionary Journal. Retrieved from https://history.lds.org/missionary/individual/william-gardner-1846?lang=eng

Gardner, W. (1895) Missionary Journal, Retrieved from https://history.lds.org/missionary/individual/william-gardner-1846?lang=eng

Iles, A. J. (1889) Photograph of Matene Te Nga, Thames. Retrieved from https://www.google.co.nz/search?q=matene+te+nga&rlz=1C1DVJR_enNZ729NZ732&source=lnms&tbm=isch&sa=X&ved=0ahUKEwiIsYOk0pDYAhUGJZQKHaH-Ciw4ChD8BQgLKAI&biw=1229&bih=607#imgrc=Keycg7aNu9e5NM

Jones, P. T. (1959) *King Potatau: An Account of the Life of Potatau Te Wherowhero the First Maori King,* The Polynesian Society, Auckland

Mair, G. (1923) *Reminiscences and Maori Stories*, Brett Printing and Publishing, Auckland

Newton, Marjorie (2012) *Tiki and Temple: The Mormon Mission in New Zealand 1854–1958*, Greg Kofford Books, Utah

Rikihana, T. (1986) *Tangi a te ruru*. Retrieved from http://www.folksong.org.nz/te_hokinga_mai/

Smith, P. (1910) *Maori Wars of the Nineteenth Century*, Whitcombe and Tombs Limited, Wellington

Watene, F. A. (1985) *Journal*, Zoom Printers, Hamilton

Watene, H. P. (1979) *A Study of the Stars or Mataiwhetu Marae*, Thames

Watene, J. R. (n.d.) *Mita Watene*

Watene-Spencer, J. T. A. (n.d.) Watene Whareroa Wharemāhīhī

Watene, T. (1940) 'Matene Te Nga', *Te Karere*, The Church of Jesus Christ of Latter-day Saints, Auckland

Madsen Bay, D'Urville Island
Courtesy of the Matthew Cowley Pacific Church History Centre

II

Lord I Would Follow Thee

JAMES RONGOTOA ELKINGTON (1898–1985)

Jeanette Grace[1]

Whatsoever Ye Shall Ask of Me in Faith Shall Be Given Unto Thee …

Wetekia, overwhelmed by the cravings of pregnancy, desired a fish. She went down to the beach at Ohana, Rangitoto ki te Tonga (D'Urville Island) to get the little dinghy that was left there for fishing. It was gone. Driven by her craving she waded into the tide and implored God to give her a fish. She promised to dedicate the child she carried to his service. A stingray appeared at her feet providing the means to satisfy her craving. From that time forth she was steadfast in her resolve that this child would serve the Lord.[2] Thus was the path set for James Rongotoa Elkington, the gentle giant who walked with the Lord his God all the days of his life.

James was born on 21 June 21 1898 on Tinui Island, the third child of Wetekia and Ratapu (John) Elkington and the first of fourteen children born to them to survive infancy. His iwi connections include Ngāti Toa Rangatira, Ngāti Koata, Te Atiawa and Ngāti Tama.[3]

Whakapapa (Genealogy)

Roma Hoera Ruruku was the son of Te Ruruku, chief of Ngāti Koata, who migrated south in the early 1820s from Kāwhia along with Ngāti Toa. After the battle at Waiorua on Kāpiti Island in 1823, Ngāti Koata took possession of D'Urville Island, where Te Ruruku's descendants still live.

James's mother, Wetekia, was a keeper of whakapapa (genealogy), purakau (stories) and taonga. A strong familial relationship existed between Wetekia, her father Roma Hoera Ruruku and Princess Te Puea Herangi at Ngaruawāhia. This resulted in the gifting of a cloak and two mere (Pare-Hauraki and Pare-Waikato), to Roma and Wetekia by Te Puea. They were the physical manifestation of the blood ties between the whānau and the respect and affection they held for each other. James's sister Polly carried the name Pare-Hauraki. On his paternal side, James's great-great-grandfather was Nohorua, the tohunga of Ngāti Toa Rangatira, and descendant of Hoturoa, captain of the waka Tainui.

When this child of faith and illustrious whakapapa was born his iwi had long been dispossessed of the property and leadership that had fostered their prosperity. Whānau lived off the sea and remnants of land supported their survival. Like many of his contemporaries as a young boy he helped his father take care of their extensive whānau gardens. He learned at the knee of his mother Wetekia, and was guided and taught by his grandfather and other family members. He grew tall and strong and his mother true to her word instilled in her son a deep and enduring faith in the Saviour and the Church of Jesus Christ of Latter-day Saints.

Wetekia was a matakite (visionary) and seer and so her children were raised in an environment of constant prayer and faith. One day, James was out fishing with his grandfather Roma Hoera Ruruku when a terrible storm arose. Roma directed his grandson to go and stand at the front of their dinghy and raise his arm. He said, 'as long as your hand is out I will have calm water.' James, who was just a young boy, did so. The waves did not break over their boat and his grandfather was able to row them to shore in the smooth passage that appeared in front of his grandson's outstretched arm.[4] Such things were not considered unusual or impossible.

Train Up a Child in the Way He Should Go …

James was taught to work long hours at a very young age; he was obedient and capable. When he was twelve years old he secured paid employment in Nelson picking hops and doing other odd jobs to help out the family. One day the family was visited by an American. It turned out to be mission president Orson D. Romney, who was on a tour of the New Zealand mission to speak to members about a new Church school for boys that was being built in Hastings. The family was asked to consider sending James there.[5] The benefits to be obtained from an education in a Church school were too compelling. The Māori Agricultural College (MAC) was opened by the Church in 1913, and was the first of its kind to be built outside America.[6]

At the age of fourteen James was able to travel to MAC for his college education.[7] It would be easy to assume that he would have been lonely, surrounded entirely by strangers far away from home. However, his grandfather, Roma, and uncle, Turi Ruruku, very likely visited James at hui tau (annual Church conferences of the New Zealand Mission), which were held at or near Hastings. James would also have been familiar with some of the missionaries who were teachers, and the spiritual activities of daily living he had learned in his own home. James quickly applied himself to his studies and was a 'top student'.[8] At the December 1914 end-of-year activities, 'Hastings draper Matt Johnson presented a gold medal to the best student, James Elkington of French Pass.'[9]

The resources available at MAC must have been amazing to James, who had been raised in remote, isolated areas with few facilities and resources. He was in the MAC school band and played a steel double guitar. He was also a rugby enthusiast and loved to tell people that the famous All Black George Nepia attended MAC. Generally, James was a quiet young man; however, if he felt something was wrong he was not afraid to meet it face on. One evening when an altercation threatened, he stood in the doorway and told the group of irate young men that passage to beat the other boys would be over his dead body. The fight did not proceed.[10]

James Elkington as a student at the Māori Agricultural College, Hastings, 1913.

When James completed his schooling, he was asked to stay on at MAC as a teacher. One day a young woman walked past a window at the college as James and the principal were talking. 'James,' the principal said. 'You don't have a girlfriend, do you?' 'No,' was the quiet reply. 'You are going to marry that girl.' The principal called Huitau into the room, where shy James could barely speak, so she did most of the talking.[11] At the age of nineteen on 31 January 1917, James married Huitau Mere Meha from Waipawa, Hawke's Bay.

Huitau was also born into a family of faith and distinguished ancestry. Her father, Arapata Meha, and mother, Mere Te Hau, were baptised into the Mormon Church in 1885. Arapata, a prominent member of Ngāti Kahungunu and Rangitāne tribes, was a successful sheep farmer and landowner, and Mere hailed from Ngāti Rakaipaaka. 'Before [her brother] Stuart was born it was prophesised that he would save his ancestors; this was later seen as a prediction of the Mormon practice of baptism for the dead'.[12] He not only fulfilled this prophecy but also became an accomplished translator of Mormon scripture and a genealogist.

James and Huitau Elkington.

Huitau was an educated, talented woman and nurse. James, much to her distaste, referred to her with pride and relish as 'my missus'. He marvelled, without covetousness or envy, at the difference between the home she had been raised in and the humble abode he came from at D'Urville Island.

As For Me and My House We Shall Serve the Lord

In 1921, when Elder David O. McKay of the Council of Twelve Apostles visited New Zealand and appeared at the hui tau at Waahi Pā, Huntly, missionaries from the Reorganised Church of Jesus Christ of Latter-day Saints (RLDS) appeared and began arguing about doctrine. 'When they refused to leave after the owner of the property ordered them off, James Elkington picked one of them up, and dropped him over the fence.'[13] The next day, the RLDS missionaries appeared again and were 'apparently once again deposited over the paddock fence.' 'Elder McKay rewarded security man James Elkington (a former star of the MAC Rugby team) with a big hug.'[14]

James had planned to try and establish a farm with Huitau in Taranaki but he was asked by Church leaders to return to Rangitoto ki te Tonga as his people needed the support he and his wife could provide. Ever obedient to the servants of the Lord, James took Huitau and their four children, Olive, Sam, Herbert and Rangikauia, back to the island home of his childhood.[15]

James was able to secure a loan from the Department of Māori Affairs and his construction skills were put to good use. During this time the schoolhouse was moved from Whareatea Bay to Haukawakawa. A Mormon missionary, Elder Julius V. Madsen, helped to rebuild the school and houses at Haukawakawa and from that time to the present day many whānau members have known the Bay as 'Madsen'.

The 'top house' was built for James's family on his Uncle Turi Ruruku's land. Other homes at Madsen included the 'big house' where James's parents, Ratapu and Wetekia, lived; the 'middle house' where James's brother Son (Turi) and his wife Nui lived; and the 'far end' where another brother Rangi and his wife Lucy lived. Before they built James's place (the top house), the family lived in a tin shack.[16]

James and Huitau worked hard to make their island home beautiful, productive and comfortable, a sanctuary for their whānau. Daughter Terewai[17] recalled her mother planting peach, quince, apple and plum trees, staining the floors with condys crystals and producing snow-white sheepskins that contrasted with the shining richly coloured floors. She remembered her mother preserving fruit. She also dried and stored food for the lean winter months.

Huitau had a favourite peach tree and the children, who now included John, Madsen, Terewai and Emron, were forbidden to pick fruit from it. If fruit fell from the tree, however, they were allowed to eat it. Terewai recalled, 'if we were out with Dad and those peaches were ripe he always managed to accidentally shake a branch or two as he passed.'[18]

Terewai also talked about her father taking them to gather tītī (muttonbirds):

> Dad would only take small women and children to gather muttonbirds because they nest in the same nest year after year and heavy careless people could stand on the nest/burrows and destroy them. We would return to shore and our aunties and uncles would pack the first kerosene tins for the whanau in Porirua. The second batch were for whanau in Nelson and the last were packed for us for Christmas and special occasions.[19]

Every Sunday the whānau laid their work aside and observed the Sabbath. Minute books in possession of the Ruruku whānau recorded the attendance, roles and responsibilities of whānau members each week at their Church meetings. Attendance at Hui Tau, such as those James would have participated in when he was at MAC, were also an important part of whānau life.

James was elected as the first president of the MAC Old Boys Association at a Hui Tau in 1927.[20] The purpose of the Association was to maintain communication among themselves to support local missionaries and to promote the college. During World War Two the missionaries were withdrawn from New Zealand; however, tumuaki Matthew Cowley stayed with the support of the seven Māori High Priests, and MAC staff and students.

> The majority of the alumni assumed important leadership roles during the absence of the missionaries such men as James Elkington and Stuart Meha are but a few of the men who contributed greatly to the leadership of the Church in New Zealand.[21]

As was the case for many others, James's Church work was undertaken while simultaneously juggling his whānau obligations and work responsibilities. James worked as a contractor, lighthouse keeper and farmer. He was also in charge of D'Urville Island's home guard during the war. The children on the island were taught to semaphore and often, when middle aged, his daughter Terewai and her cousin Frank Hippolite had a lot of fun communicating in the non-verbal language. The children on the island were as brother and sister, and uncles and aunts were as parents. Emily, Patricia, Huiarotu, David and Jamesina boosted the number of children in James's whānau and Jamesina recalled their childhood as inclusive, magical and full of fun.

Even so all the children were taught to work and had different jobs. Emron, Jamesina, David and Huia gathered firewood, Patricia cooked, Terewai cleaned.

Madsen and Kay both took turns at manning the lighthouses. John worked beside his father and Olive was her mother's right hand. The twins, Sam and Herbert, who had previously worked with their father and grandfather as axemen, left to serve missions for the Church, then took up military service. James won a contract to clear land for the Crown; however, his older sons were away at war, and the others were working. To his chagrin he had to co-opt his daughters as his labourers. Olive, Kay and Emily became Tom, Dick and Harry on the payroll ledger. Fulfilling whānau responsibilities wove the family tightly together, in body and spirit.

Jamesina recounts:[22]

> Sam was not in the army long but Herbert was sent overseas with the military. On one occasion Mum and Dad were to travel with other whanau members by boat to Nelson. On the morning they were leaving Olive told Daddy that Herbert had come to her in a dream in the night and told her that their parents must not go through the French Pass. Nevertheless Daddy decided that he and Mum would go on the trip, however as they neared the Pass he insisted that the boat turn back and take them to the settlement on shore. After strong debate the boat which was nearing the entry to the turbulent waters of the Pass altered course. A great roaring wind suddenly came out of nowhere, Daddy said their boat would have sunk if they had been in the Pass.

Sadly, Herbert died overseas in Tunisia on 8 May 1943, a casualty of war. In a letter to James, Huitau and family, mission president Matthew Cowley wrote:

> There is little that I can say to give you comfort in such a time as this. Time will heal the wound and bring him back to you. He is separated from you for a season, but you cannot lose him. The sealing power of the priesthood will make him yours forever. You have been blessed with a large family and now God has only exacted a tithe of what he has given you. God expected much of you when he blessed your home with so many children, and you have failed neither God nor your children.[23]

Once more the Church asked James to take his family to support his other whānau; this time the call was to Takapūwāhia. Huitau's health was failing so the call to move came at a good time. The whānau left their beloved Madsen and moved to Porirua.

James and his son John had been lucky enough to enter a carpentry training programme that was being offered to soldiers returning from World War Two. As there were insufficient numbers for the programme, James and John were able to attend classes together. They established Elkington and Sons Company and foresaw secure and enduring employment opportunities for all the boys.

James and his older sons John and Madsen obtained work building houses for the Department of Māori Affairs. They were able to build a home for themselves on land given to them by James's father's half-brother Ringi Horomona. James and his family quickly got involved in marae, Church and community activities at Takapūwāhia. Huitau was called as the Relief Society President and some of James's roles, over time, included choirmaster, counsellor in the District Presidency, secretary to the Whakapapa Committee and Porirua branch president.

Weeping May Endure for a Night, but Joy Cometh in the Morning

Huitau was born during the 1892 Hui Tau and she died in 1946 as members from Porirua were travelling to a Hui Tau. James missed his companion of twenty-seven years, working from dawn till dark six days a week, and on the seventh throwing himself into Church-related activities.

> On Sunday May 29th, our choir, under the leadership of our branch president, brother James Elkington, was invited to attend a service at Johnsonville. Before a congregation of Methodists and Presbyterians, the choir rendered three anthems and sang three congregational hymns. We were complimented and thanked by the minister and in his own words he expressed it as being an eye opener to him, and he felt sure to many of the congregation.[24]

While some of James's older children had married, they continued to live with their father in the family home until they built homes of their own, helping to alleviate his loneliness. Their activity in the Church also kept their home filled with whānau and friends. Olive served as the Primary President, and Sam served as the Sunday School President with his brother Madsen as a counsellor and his brother Chiefy (Emron) as the secretary. 'Under the direction of Bro James Elkington a party of young people was taken to Plimmerton to assist in a concert which was held to raise money for a dance hall in that area.'[25]

James was also busy advocating for a Church school as a replacement for MAC, which had suffered earthquake damage in 1931.

> Mission President and future member of the Quorum of the Twelve Apostles of the LDS Church, Matthew Cowley met with members of the MAC Old Boys Association including the association's President at the time, James Elkington and a letter went to Church head-quarters in Salt Lake City, Utah, requesting that another Church school be established in New Zealand.[26]

The Church was aware that there was a growing need for more Church buildings across the Pacific. When James was asked by his District President to go and build chapels in Northland, he sent John instead as he needed to keep their business going. John served without pay on the building of two chapels and participated in the repair of several others before he returned home.[27]

James then left John in charge of the business and went to serve the Church in Auckland and overseas. He was asked to assist the Church in the Kingdom of Tonga.

> At the mission conference of September 15, 1950 the first labour missionaries were called to help build Liahona under the supervision of professional builders like Emile Dunn, Lionel Going, James Elkington, Charles Wolfgramm and Archie Cottle. This became the genesis of the Church's labour missionary programme that built hundreds of chapels and other buildings throughout the Pacific and elsewhere.[28]

During this vibrant time of sacrifice and hard work a seminal event occurred for James. Once more it involved an American (George R. Biesinger). Elder Biesinger suggested that James ought to marry Elsie Chirney (née Wolfgramm). Elsie was a beautiful, accomplished part-Tongan member of the Church. James said, 'She wouldn't look at me.' Unbeknown to both men, sister Rangi Davies (née Chase) had been encouraging her good friend to re-marry. Elsie is said to have told sister Davies, 'there is only one man in this country I would marry and that is James Elkington, but that won't happen.'[29] In 1951, the Porirua reporter for the mission newsletter *Te Karere* announced, 'Congratulations to Bro. and Sis. James Elkington on their recent marriage ...'[30]

James and Elsie Elkington.

James adored Elsie. She was a sweet, strong, faithful, talented and supportive woman, a wonderful cook, and their home was a haven to all who entered it. They were delighted by the birth of their daughter Rangi Liahona and delighted with each other, a state of affairs that was to last all their lives.

When the decision was made in the 1950s to build a temple, co-educational college and chapels throughout New Zealand, Church members from across the country and Pacific region committed themselves fully to the building programme. 'This programme of trained men from America and local members donating their time to build the school became known as the Labour Missionary Programme.'[31]

In 1951 James's sons, John and Madsen, with four other carpenters from Porirua donated their three weeks of holiday to building the Auckland Chapel.[32]

Rangi Liahona Moleni, daughter of James and Elsie Elkington.

At the 1952 hui tau at Korongota, Hastings, mission president Sidney J. Ottley explained the proposed labour missionary programme:

> A model of the college was displayed; and James Elkington, who had helped build the Church College in Tonga, described how the system worked there. Workmen were needed; they would be set apart as labour missionaries, and their home branches would provide food and one pound per week pocket money for each missionary, all of whom would be trained in various trades.[33]

Te Karere reported, 'Everywhere the whole-hearted support is coming. Brother George Chase has proffered the use of his trucks. Brother James Elkington has written a wonderful letter pledging the help of himself and his fine family.'[34]

This strong faith was exhibited through the service of Church members as well as labour missionaries. James explained, 'the Americans are the only people on the face of the earth that could have pushed this project to its completion, but the Polynesian people are the only ones that could have taken the pushing.'[35]

In total, James and his family contributed forty years of man hours in construction work for the Church working on both the temple and the Church College of New Zealand. This was not without some sacrifice, as their fledgling construction business, Elkington and Sons, was subsequently discontinued in favour of their serving the needs of the Church.

James played a leading advisory role during the Church building project, including the supervision of chapels. Construction of the Kaikohe chapel began in April 1953 with Jim Elkington supervising.[36] When the first branch was organised in 1953, James's son John was called as its branch president. He later became construction supervisor for the Church throughout New Zealand and the Pacific region.

Many labour missionaries became proficient tradesmen as a result of their missions, and they were able to support each other to build their own homes.

These homes are still standing in communities that remain strongholds of the Mormon faith.

Legacy of Leadership

James joined the staff at the Church College of New Zealand (CCNZ) in 1958, teaching the Māori language and establishing the school's Māori Cultural Group. The record *Great Songs of the Maori* is an example of the group's calibre.

> It is not surprising of course that some of the best Maori choral music has been recorded by groups from boarding schools where there is time to give the students the necessary grounding and discipline in the vocal arts. On this disc the sacred music is the best. The music is sung without any striving for effect and the balance between the various sections of the choir is good throughout. There is a particularly fine version of Evan Steven's 'Song of the Redeemed', better known in Maori as 'Kia Kotahi Katoa', and the young singers tackle the complex part-singing with vigour and confidence.[37]

James was also called as a Church stake patriarch in 1967. On days that he was giving patriarchal blessings to worthy Church members he and Elsie would fast and pray in preparation for the blessing. Elsie then typed all his blessings verbatim. James enjoyed his role as patriarch because it aligned with his love of whakapapa, and genealogy. James was firmly of the belief that Māori were the blood descendants of Israelites who had crossed into the Americas and then entered the Pacific.

James's patriarchal role also extended to his wider whānau, which included his siblings' children the Hippolites, Hemis, Selwyns and others. The Elkington whānau hosted the missionaries on numerous occasions, including the Maglebys at French Pass on 31 January 1931, and Matthew Cowley later.

In later years, James and Elsie were dorm parents in Elva Dorm for young women students at the CCNZ. James was renowned for referring to people, including students and family members, as 'matey'; whether you were in big trouble or about to be praised could only be told by the way the word 'matey' came out of his mouth. He loved the Saturday night movies shown at the school, particularly if they were cowboy movies. He baked delicious-smelling loaves of fresh bread and a raspberry spider was a treat he especially enjoyed. He loved boiled wheat. He would soak the wheat overnight and then boil it in the morning for his breakfast. Elsie would grate coconut and cook tasty chicken dishes in the cream, then place it before her grateful husband who ate with relish and declared his food fit for a king.

James Elkington and whānau with President Matthew Cowley of the New Zealand Mission at D'Urville Island. (L–R) Turi Ruruku, Turi Elkington, Pene Ruruku, James Elkington, Matthew Cowley and Arthur Elkington.

Legacy is all About Ohana (Extended Family)

In 1971, at the age of 74, James left CCNZ to become Māori Advisor at Brigham Young University in Hawaii. This meant that James and Elsie were close to their beloved daughter, Rangi Liahona, her husband Fisi Moleni and their children. He also once more worked alongside his son John, his wife Waitohi and their children. John had gone to Hawaii to help complete the building of the Polynesian Cultural Centre, and also served on its board.

Eventually James and Elsie returned to New Zealand and retired, though they were active at Church and temple attendance. They lived in John and Waitohi's home in Temple View and at times live-in support was provided by Olive, David, Jamesina and James, and Liahona and her family. The little children brought joy and laughter to the elderly couple.

James created a beautiful garden and members of the Temple View community would know that Uncle Jim had passed by, in the early hours of the morning, when they opened their doors and found garden produce on the doorstep.[38] James maintained a repository of whānau whakapapa and he wrote many stories that had been handed down by his mother and other whānau members. They are said to be archived in the Hamilton Library.

A comment was made one day that the Church had taken his life and he had nothing to show for it; he did not even own his own home. That was true;

he gave his life to the Church and in so doing gained great strength of character, wisdom, generosity of spirit, humility and serenity. He was, and is, loved by thousands of people, not just those with family connections. His descendants for the most part are faithful, loving and kind, leading as he did in many different ways.

He would have been quietly gratified at the number of his descendants who have served Church missions and that his daughter Rangi Liahona's testimony was shared worldwide.

> My parents accepted Joseph Smith as the prophet of the last dispensation, and so do I! They were pioneers of the Church of Jesus Christ of Latter-day Saints in the islands of the Pacific.[39]

James is reported to have said, 'I have been a lucky man, for I have been loved by two beautiful women.'[40]

> James died peacefully at 11.40pm in his son John's home in Temple View June 1st 1985. He was a quiet unassuming man whose love for the Gospel governed everything that he did, esteeming every person as himself constantly living his personal motto of 'Doing unto others as he would be done by.'[41]

NOTES

1. Jeanette Grace is the grandaughter of James Rongotoa Elkington
2. Kett, Jamesina (2019), personal communication
3. Tu Tangata (1 August 1985)
4. Kett (2019)
5. *Ibid.*
6. Hunt, B. (1977) *Zion in New Zealand: A History of the Church of Jesus Christ of Latter-day Saints*, Church College of New Zealand, Temple View, Hamilton, p 33
7. Tu Tangata (1 August 1985)
8. Tu Tangata (1 August 1985)
9. Baldridge, Kenneth W. (1971–73) interview
10. Elkington, Harold (2019) personal communication
11. *Ibid.*
12. Lineham, Peter J. (1998) 'Meha Stuart', Te Ara – The Encyclopedia of New Zealand. Retrieved from https://teara.govt.nz/en/biographies/4m50/meha-stuart
13. Newton, Marjorie (2012) *Tiki and Temple: The Mormon Mission in New Zealand, 1854–1958*, Greg Kofford Books, Salt Lake City, Utah, p 164
14. *Ibid.*, p 166
15. Kett (2019)
16. *Ibid.*
17. Grace, Terewai (2004) personal communication
18. *Ibid.*

19. *Ibid.*
20. *Te Karere* (1958) Newsletter of the New Zealand Mission of the Church of Jesus Christ of Latter-day Saints, Auckland
21. Hunt, p 88
22. Kett (2019)
23. Cowley, Matthew (20 May 1943) Letter from New Zealand Mission president to James Elkington
24. *Te Karere* (1949)
25. *Te Karere* (April 1947)
26. Retrieved from https://www.sporty.co.nz/macrugby/History/NewTab1
27. Baldridge (1971–73)
28. LDS Church History Sites in the Kingdom of Tonga. Retrieved from https://www.arcgis.com/apps/Cascade/index.html?appid=91350121200d6432883536279c777b1eb
29. Kett (2019)
30. *Te Karere* (1951)
31. Hunt, p 107
32. Te Karere (1951)
33. Newton, p 242
34. *Te Karere* (1949)
35. Thacker-Biesinger, Wendy (2017) *More Than Bricks and Mortar: An Account of the New Zealand Labour Missionary Programme*, DMT Publishing, Utah, p 92
36. Newton, p 245
37. Retrieved from http://teaohou.natlib.govt.nz/journals/teaohou/issue/Mao58TeA/c40.html
38. Katene, Kahuwaero (2020) personal communication
39. Moleni R. L. Retrieved from https://www.josephsmith.net/article/new-zealand?lang=eng
40. Kett (2019)
41. *Tu Tangata*, 1 August 1985

REFERENCES

Hunt, B. (1977) *Zion in New Zealand: A History of the Church of Jesus Christ of Latter-day Saints*, Church College of New Zealand, Temple View, Hamilton, https://scholarsarchive.byu.edu/cgi/viewcontent.cgi?article=5813&context=etd

Lineham, Peter J. (1998) 'Meha Stuart', Te Ara – The Encyclopedia of New Zealand. Retrieved from https://teara.govt.nz/en/biographies/4m50/meha-stuart

Moleni, R. L. Retrieved from https://www.josephsmith.net/article/new-zealand?lang=eng)

Newton, Marjorie (2012) *Tiki and Temple: The Mormon Mission in New Zealand, 1854–1958*, Greg Kofford Books, Salt Lake City, Utah

Polynesian Cultural Centre Home Page 'The Polynesian Cultural Centre Legacy is all about Ohana (family) 22 Nov 2017.' https://www.polynesia.com/blog/legacy/

Te Ao Hou. Retrieved from http://teaohou.natlib.govt.nz/journals/teaohou/issue/Mao58TeA/c40.html)

Te Karere. Retrieved from https://journal.interpreterfoundation.org/remembering-and-honoring-maori-latter-day-saints/

Thacker-Biesinger, Wendy (2017) *More Than Bricks and Mortar: An Account of the New Zealand Labour Missionary Programme*, DMT Publishing, Utah

Tū Tangata (1985) Issue 25, 1 August. https://paperspast.natlib.govt.nz/periodicals/TUTANG19850801.2.38

III

A Life of Service

WILLIAM ROBERTS (1907–94)

Michael Roberts[1]

William Roberts was a child immigrant with his parents from Manchester, England, in 1910, settling in Northcote in the city of Auckland. Norma Johnston was a third-generation New Zealander, born in Dunedin, her grandparents having migrated from Scotland and Ireland. Their story is like many others of that era. They went to school, they got jobs, found romance and love, got married and struggled to make sense of a world at war. But it was the concern for the languid malaise of the excessive post-war years of celebration and socialising that drove them to look for some deeper purpose in life. With the coming of the Church to their small neighbourhood, their lives were turned upside down and they embarked on a journey of service to God and to those around them. This would become a lifelong pursuit of love and devotion to the cause of truth.

Early Years

William Roberts was born in Levenshulme, Manchester, England on 25 June 1907, the only son of William Parry Roberts and Jessie Roberts (née Chaplin). His father fought in the Manchester Regiment in the Boer War, returning home to England in 1902. He felt drawn back to South Africa and, three years after the birth of his son, he left England with plans for his wife and child to join him there once he was established. However, upon arrival in South Africa, he was disappointed with the economic conditions he found there and decided to continue on to New Zealand. He cabled his wife, instructing her to change her travel plans and to join him instead in Wellington, New Zealand.

Although only three years of age, young William reported a number of vivid recollections of that early journey on board the SS *Arawa*: the hissing steam from the great locomotive as their train pulled out of Waterloo Station with its glassed-in roof, the young native boys diving for coins in the blue waters of the bay at Tenerife in the Canary Islands, a ride in a horse-drawn hansom cab in Cape Town and finally the contours of the hills around Wellington as they came into the harbour at their journey's end.

Reunited, their little family made their way up the North Island to the North Shore of Auckland, establishing their family home in the borough of Northcote. Two years later, his younger sister Elsie was born on 30 November 1912. His father, a journeyman printer, found work in the printing trade and became a community stalwart, notably as the longest-serving superintendent of the Northcote Volunteer Fire Brigade.[2]

Education and Early Employment

Young William attended Northcote Primary School for eight years and then went to Auckland (Boys) Grammar School.[3] He passed his matriculation exams, but was interested in an outdoor life and decided not to go to university. He was initially attracted to a career in either engineering or architecture, but, because there were so many people qualified in that area, he decided to become a surveyor. As surveyors travelled frequently, it was not practical to go to university. His first job was with a private land surveying and engineering firm. He greatly enjoyed the work, but after some frustration with his employer, who was somewhat erratic in paying his employees, he managed to secure employment as a civil servant working for the Lands and Survey Department of the New Zealand Government.

In his early years in government employment William learned the tools of the job as a survey draftsman and computer[4] doing survey examination and title examination work. Later he became interested in land administration (especially Māori land). He represented the various government departments in the Māori Land Courts of the country. It was this work that brought him into close contact with the Māori people and their culture and tradition which he admired greatly. For fifteen years he was land purchaser for various government departments, experience that would stand him in good stead in later Church assignments.

As a young man William was active in sport (rugby, soccer, tennis, sailing, golf) and other outdoor activities (tramping in the bush, mountain climbing), and cultural pursuits, including music (violin, piano) and painting.

William had been aware of a young girl, Norma Johnston, who had attended the same primary school as he had in Northcote, and later went to Auckland Girls Grammar School. After finishing school, they commuted on the ferry boat together across from Northcote to downtown Auckland for work. Often they would be late for the passenger ferry and catch the car ferry, which left shortly after. Normally the only two passengers not in cars, they would often talk to the captain. The commuting trips were where their friendship blossomed to romance. On 2 April 1935 they were married in the Radio Chapel by an interdenominational minister.

Early Encounters with Organised Religion

William had developed a dislike for organised religion in his teenage years. He was christened as an infant in the Church of England in Manchester, but when the family arrived in Northcote, he remembered going to the local Methodist Sunday School at the age of fifteen. He reported: 'While our Bible class teacher was teaching us about the scriptures and giving us some Bible training, he was slowly poisoning his wife. In fact, he was later proved to be guilty, and he was duly hanged for his misdemeanour.' He recounted further, 'at the same time the secretary of the Sunday School decamped with the funds, and the superintendent of the Sunday School robbed the Church of many thousands of pounds in a bogus contract that he drew up with them.'

Needless to say, these events did nothing to bolster William's flagging enthusiasm for organised religion. He noted, 'I decided then and there that perhaps the Methodist Church was not my particular calling, and left.' This did not mean he lost his faith in God. In his own words, he 'never at any stage thought there was anything but a creator and that God was at the helm of everything.' He recalled times during his military service in World War Two when he found himself 'praying on many occasions for life to continue.' When he was away from active deployment, he never missed an opportunity to go to the simple Church services that were available to them in the military camps.[5]

World War Two

When the war broke out in 1939, William and Norma had been married for about four-and-a-half years. At that time, they had no children. Seeing that he would inevitably be called upon to serve in the military effort in some way, he joined up with a training unit and for six months trained with a reserve unit in New Zealand. In mid-1940, when the military was beginning to draft units into service overseas, he volunteered for overseas service. He was finally called into overseas preparation training at the beginning of 1941.

He described their feelings at the imminent prospect of departure in the following manner:

William and Norma just before his departure for overseas military service in World War Two, early 1941.

> I think Norma had considerably more courage than I gave her credit for. She has always been a courageous one in a quiet way. I've always admired her for this great quality. When it came time to say goodbye to her, I think she showed these attributes, but it was a sad parting.[6]

Their convoy travelled from New Zealand to Egypt via Sydney, Freemantle and Singapore before finally arriving in Suez in early May 1941. After an initial training period, they were deployed with the New Zealand Division in the Western Desert under the leadership first of Lieutenant-General Bernard C. Freyberg and later Field Marshall Bernard L. Montgomery of the British 8th Army. They were to spend the next two-and-a-half years fighting in some of the toughest engagements of the war, relieving the siege of Tobruk and fighting in the first and second battles of El Alamein, finally culminating in the surrender of the Axis forces in North Africa. During this time William was seriously wounded in a Stuka dive bomber attack. He was hospitalised for several months and then given leave to recuperate in the Holy Land for some time. Once rehabilitated, he was called up for officer training, which lasted for about six months.

Finally, in late 1943, the New Zealand Division moved with the British 8th Army across to Italy, and over the next year and a half traversed Italy from its southern tip all the way up to the north. His time in Italy included the fourth Battle of Monte Casino, where their victory gave entry into central Italy and Rome. During this battle William served as aide to his colonel, who was the observer-in-chief. They were positioned on a ridge overlooking the battle scene but were protected by a rocky outcrop. The enemy knew they were there but couldn't dislodge them from their position. Their role was to observe the battle and feed information back to their headquarters. They observed the taking of the railway station, which signalled the end of the battle. The news reports that appeared the next day were almost word for word taken from the reports they had sent through. They pressed on northward and into the Po Valley near Faenza.

With the end of hostilities in sight, the New Zealand Army administration adopted a policy of giving home leave to those who had been in active service for more than four years. William was relieved of duty and made his way south to Taranto where they shipped out to Egypt. Eventually, they embarked on a ship home. The night before they embarked, one of the men went out of bounds against orders and contracted smallpox. They only realised that he had contracted smallpox after the ship had sailed. He died the day after they sailed and they buried him at sea. This meant that the rest of the company was in quarantine without shore leave on the way home. When the ship arrived back at Auckland, New Zealand, instead of disembarking, they had to spend three days out in the bay waiting for someone to come and clear them to come ashore, while Norma was 'running up and down the beach watching the ship to see what was happening.'[7]

William arrived home to find that Norma's auburn hair was now streaked with grey, and he realised that she had suffered with him in his experiences. He later recalled:

> I left in the early part of 1941 and didn't see her again until April or May of 1945. When I left her she was a brown-haired girl. When I got back home her hair was going grey, especially on my account because of the worry she had at not receiving news during the time that I had been wounded. I soon realised that there were marks of the war in many areas.[8]

They had not had any children before he went to serve in the war, and on his return they decided to start a family. For a while it seemed as though they could not have any children, and were in the process of arranging an adoption, when Norma fell pregnant with their elder son John, who was born in July 1947. He was followed by a second son, Michael, born in April 1950.

Post-War Years and Conversion to the Gospel of Jesus Christ

In the years following the end of the war, people tried to pick up the threads of relationships, work and their lives in general. For many, the way to forget the horrors of war was to socialise and have lots of parties. It was as if they had become so relaxed that they didn't want to engage in anything of an arduous nature. For William and Norma, life began to feel a little empty because it lacked the serious intent of the war years. Norma began to read the Bible daily, seeking for meaning and purpose in life. She had been doing this for some months when in early 1951 the Auckland Mission President sent missionaries to tract their area on the North Shore of Auckland to see if it might be a fruitful area for missionary work. They had tracted (door-to-door proselytising) all day and met with nothing but refusals.

In the latter part of the day they came to the street where William and Norma lived. The neighbours had spread the word that the Mormons were in the area and people should not open the doors to them. Norma, however, was curious. She looked out the window and had seen the missionaries in earnest discussion. Later it turned out that they were debating whether to call it a day and catch the bus and ferry back to the city, or to continue and finish the street, which meant they would get home an hour later. Their decision was to carry on, and they knocked on her door. She decided that if they knocked on her door, she would let them in. She was a devout Presbyterian, although she did not believe all of their teachings. In particular she struggled with the doctrine of the Trinity and the nature of God. She had been taught that God was an unembodied spirit who was everywhere and nowhere, that he was so large that he could fill the universe and so small that he could fit in her heart, and that he was without body, parts or passions. She could not identify with such an abstraction. She believed that God was kind and loving and personal like her own father, only perfect. She was especially close to her father because her mother had passed away when she was seven. When the missionaries knocked on the door, she asked them what the Church taught about the nature of God. When they explained the doctrine of the Godhead and the nature of God as a loving Heavenly Father, it resonated with her, and she asked them to come back when William would be home from work.

They began to meet weekly with the missionaries, receiving the discussions known then as the Anderson Plan. Norma was converted quite quickly, but William held out for many months. After dinner while washing the dishes with the missionaries, he would delight in asking difficult questions to test the seriousness of their intent and the depth of their commitment. Gradually, he became impressed with their earnest intent and their patience with his questions and he felt his heart changing. Finally he agreed to be baptised, on the understanding that he would be a back-row observer, and would not be asked to fill any positions of responsibility. With this caveat, he and Norma were baptised one fine Saturday morning at 6 a.m. on 8 March 1952 in the waters of Waitemata Harbour in Auckland.[9]

Early Church Involvement

When they were first baptised, there was just one small branch of the Church in Auckland, a ferry ride away across the harbour. They met in a small rented hall at the top of Queen Street. On Saturday nights it was used by other groups for socials and when they came for Church on Sunday morning, the first task was to open the windows to get rid of the cigarette and beer smell, sweep out the cigarette butts and tidy up the beer bottles from the night before. After about a year, they established a small dependent Sunday school back across the harbour in Devonport with a few families and the missionaries. Norma was called to serve as the secretary to that first Sunday School. Again, they were using a small hall, the old Labour Hall in Fleet Street, which they rented just for Sunday meetings. Soon their little group began to grow, with some less active members from other places coming back into activity and new families and individuals being converted through the efforts of the missionaries.

The men were attending a priesthood class conducted by Elder Gary Ursenbach, one of the missionaries. One week Elder Ursenbach announced that he was returning home and they needed a new teacher for the class. He gave William the lesson manual and told him that he would be teaching the class from the next week. That was William's first real job in the Church. They adopted a book called *Programme of the Church of Jesus Christ of Latter-day Saints*[10] by Elder John A. Widtsoe of the Quorum of the Twelve Apostles as their text. William was quite attached to that book because, in his words, 'it gave me my first insight and vision of the Church.'[11] Their dependent Sunday School became a dependent Branch with Tony Marquis, a man who had been converted in England and migrated to Auckland, as Branch President, Oscar Broederlow, a Samoan brother, and William serving as counsellors. By 1955 they had outgrown the small Labour Hall in Devonport. They found a bigger hall, the St John's Ambulance Hall in Takapuna, which was more suited to their needs. A district Elder's Quorum was created with Oscar Broederlow as president and William as one of his counsellors. Eventually William was called as a counsellor in the District Presidency, serving under President Matthew Chote, the man who had conducted their baptismal service back in 1952.

North Shore Branch circa 1953.

The Church Construction Programme

Around this time, under the guidance of President David O. McKay, a large building project, grand in scope and anticipating rapid growth in the Church in New Zealand, had been commenced in New Zealand. In 1950 President McKay, then Second Counsellor to President George Albert Smith, called George R. Biesinger and his wife Audrey to come to New Zealand and head up the Church Construction project in New Zealand and the South Pacific. Land had been acquired in Hamilton for the construction of the Church College of New Zealand, and Scotia Place at the top of Queen Street, Auckland, to build a chapel. The construction project also provided trade training under the supervision of skilled construction supervisors for many young Church members while they served as labour missionaries. In 1955 President McKay, now president of the Church, came to Auckland to dedicate the Scotia Place chapel and to observe progress on the construction of the College at Hamilton. While he was there he met with Wendall B. Mendenhall, who had been given a special assignment to find possible temple sites in New Zealand and the South Pacific. As a result of this discussion they decided to purchase the land adjacent to the College site, where the temple now stands. Six months later, Elder Wendell B. Mendenhall was called by President McKay to head up the new worldwide Church Building Department.

William recalled a time when the prophet, President McKay, was touring the site in 1955 with the then New Zealand Prime Minister, Sidney Holland. The Prime Minister asked President McKay when the project would finish and school would begin. President McKay responded:

> Well, the project will be finished perhaps in a couple of years, but the school has already begun. These young men here who are giving all their time to the Church have never been able to do the things they do now. They're bricklayers, they're carpenters, they are plumbers, they are plasterers, they are painters. Not one of them had any experience in this work, but now they are experts. When this project is finished, they'll be getting out into business of their own account. So the school has already begun.[12]

Many of the local members provided supplementary assistance in the building efforts on public holidays, annual work leave and Saturdays. William participated with others in this effort, making the eighty-mile trip to the building site from Auckland after work on Friday night. He recalled work on the first of the buildings built – the Kai Hall – where they would all eat:

> We had to pour a concrete floor nine inches deep, eighty feet wide and 160 feet long. We poured that in one day, and that takes a bit of doing. Those boys were running even when we finished at nine or ten o'clock that evening. I said to them, 'We're nearly finished. You don't need to run so hard.' They said 'Yes, but we have to go to the dance at the MIA after this.' I could scarcely move one foot from beyond the other. Such was the vitality of noble youth.[13]

Two years later in 1957 the school was completed and the first intake of students commenced their studies. William was invited to become a member of the Advisory Board of the College. He served in this role for nearly twenty years, most of that time serving as the Chairman of the Advisory Council. In 1958 the temple was completed and President McKay returned to dedicate the Temple and the College. The cultural celebration preceding the dedication and the multiple sessions of the Temple dedication ceremony took place over three days from 20 to 22 April 1958 and the Latter-day Saints poured into Temple View in their thousands from all over New Zealand. The night before the festivities were to begin, the Labour Missionaries and other helpers were still working on putting the finishing touches to everything and finished at about midnight.

William recalled:

> They worked right until midnight the night before to get it ready for the dedication. From then on until two or three o'clock in the morning all those who had laboured so valiantly and so faithfully on that occasion were grouped in the temple. They did not want to leave the building. It was with

great reluctance that they finally decided to leave the building and get ready to attend the dedication. They wanted to stay there all the time, so great was the Spirit. They were very spiritually minded and were very susceptible to the Spirit that was there. They were great days.[14]

Stakes: The Strength of Zion

In May 1958, the month following the dedication, the Auckland Stake was organised under the direction of President Marion G. Romney. This was the first stake to be organised outside of the American continent. George R. Biesinger was called to be the stake president, with William Roberts as his first counsellor and Stanford W. Bird (also in Church Construction) as his second counsellor. Presidents Biesinger and Bird were based in Hamilton and William lived in Auckland, eighty miles away. The stake area was very large, extending from north of Auckland down to Rotorua and Tauranga. William was ordained a High Priest by President Marion G. Romney as part of the organisation of the new stake. Norma and William were blessed to be able to enter the temple at the beginning of June 1958 and to be sealed for time and all eternity to each other and to their two sons.

The work of the new stake now began in earnest. Only President Biesinger, President Bird and others who were called from the United States to work in Church Construction or at the school had any experience at all working in Stakes and Wards. For everyone else it was all new and they were on a steep learning curve. What they lacked in experience they more than made up for in enthusiasm. Later, when William was being interviewed for the James D. Moyle Oral History Programme, he recalled the financial struggles of the members to meet the financial requirements of the Church building programme. In those times, in addition to paying tithing, members were asked to contribute to budget (to pay for operating expenses) and the building fund. While the bulk of the funding came from the tithing fund of the Church, a certain percentage had to be contributed by local members. Until that contribution was met the buildings could not be dedicated. He noted:

> We developed early on a Polynesian cultural programme that performed in Maori, in Samoan, and in Tongan on the ships (passenger liners) in the port and at special concerts. They earned quite a bit for the stake and for the Church. They put that into the building fund. With that, together with the assignments that the wards received and responded to, we never failed in our commitments and our buildings were dedicated as soon as they were finished. That speaks volumes for the faith of the people. We developed ten buildings in that area.[15]

The special concerts were mainly in two areas. One was an annual participation in the Auckland Easter Show over the years of intensive chapel building. The stake members would build a 'Polynesian village' at the showgrounds with different cultural displays and stalls and a stage to perform on. Members would work every year to make food and other cultural items to sell. Later on, they would run Sounds of Polynesia concerts, over several nights each year, in the newly built Auckland Stake Centre. Again, the combination of cultural performance and Polynesian cuisine was a great attraction and a great contributor to the building fund. Of course, the involvement in such a great enterprise was a tremendous fellowshipping tool for the members and a great missionary opportunity to showcase the Church to their friends.

William had great love and respect for President McKay. He was asked by people why New Zealand had received so much – the school, the second temple outside of North America, the first stake outside of North America and as one of the first areas of focus of the Church Construction Programme outside of North America. His answer was, 'I wouldn't try to presume to read the mind of President McKay at that time, but I know that he knew the needs of the people. He knew that it would be a great blessing to them.'[16]

Growing Leadership

After only two years, the original Auckland Stake had grown to the point where it was ready to be divided into two as the Hamilton Stake and the Auckland Stake. William was called to be the stake president of the reorganised Auckland Stake. He chose as his counsellors Geoffrey R. Garlick and Matthew T. Chote. While the Hamilton Stake still had the benefit of stake-experienced members working at the school and in the Construction Programme, Auckland was now dependent on local converts stepping up to the mark.

The reorganisation stake conference was held on 5–6 November 1960. President Spencer W. Kimball, then Elder Kimball of the Quorum of the Twelve Apostles, was assigned to preside at the conference and to reorganise the stake. He and Sister Kimball came and stayed in the Roberts home for the week leading up to the stake conference. William spoke of that time:

> He (Elder Kimball) didn't know what conditions we were operating under. I think he expected every member of the Church there to have a telephone. That wasn't so in those days. We were getting messages out by bicycle and some even on horseback and having messages taken out on foot to many parts of the stake area so we could get brethren in to interview them. They all came in on schedule and on time, but I don't think President Kimball knows to this day (1977) just how we got the news to them.[17]

Auckland Stake Presidency with Elder Glen Rudd circa 1963. (L–R) Mathew Chote, Geoffrey Garlick, Elder Rudd, William Roberts.

Elder Kimball was untiring in his efforts to prepare the leaders of the new stake. They would work in the stake office most nights until late. When they got tired, Elder Kimball would say, 'Let's have a rest.' They would lie down on the carpeted floor of the office for five or ten minutes and then get back to work. One night they didn't get home until 1.30 in the morning. William reported:

> When we arrived home, Sister Kimball chided him (Elder Kimball) for being so late. Sister Kimball approached Sister Roberts the next morning with an abject apology, telling her that she had no right to speak to her husband the way she did the night before. We had a work to do, he had a great responsibility, and he had to see it out. She had no right to make the comment she did, and she felt very sorry for making it. Sister Roberts said to me, 'I loved her for the human touch she showed on that occasion.'[18]

At the conference, Elder Kimball gave extensive training to the priesthood and auxiliary leaders regarding their callings. William commented that he gave the stake a great start-off and they never looked back. A few days after the organisation, Elder Kimball met in a social setting in the Roberts home with the members of the high council and the bishops and their wives. He spoke to them for over an hour about the members of the Quorum of the Twelve

Apostles, each with their different gifts and talents and how they worked together harmoniously to benefit the Church.

It was apparent that this lesson was well learned. William said of the stake leadership:

> We counted round the table and discovered that we had thirteen different nationalities represented in the group of leaders there. I remember saying to the group at the time, 'What a wonderful thing it would be for the United Nations to have the kind of influence to meet (under) that we have enjoyed.' With all the years of our associations together, we never had any unkind words or anything that looked like contention. We seemed to resolve all of our problems in a very friendly spirit. We had several Samoans, we had Tongans, we had Maoris and we had Europeans, some born in India, Australia, England, Canada and the United States. You can imagine that in frank discussions you might have some difficulty of communication, but it was never so. Even with all the different inflections and the different idioms that we introduced into our discussions, there was always a wonderful spirit which lingers in my memory.[19]

The assistance from Church headquarters came not just in material terms, but in leadership training. In those days stake conference was held quarterly, and it involved two sessions on Saturday and two sessions on Sunday.

The brethren back in Church headquarters were anxious for the new stake to succeed and sent a succession of general authorities and auxiliary general board members to attend stake conference and give training. The stake members never felt neglected and always received kind encouragement. Usually they had general authority visits at two of the four stake conferences per year, and, on special occasions, general board members would come and tour through New Zealand giving instruction and help. Each of the auxiliary organisations would have monthly leadership meetings, usually on weekday nights, but when the general board members came it was always special to be able to receive their training.

Sometimes, the general authorities came at great personal sacrifice. William tells the story of Legrand Richards, a member of the Quorum of the Twelve Apostles:

> He was very, very ill ... in considerable pain, but he refused to give in. In the morning he delivered one of his wonderful addresses. When he finished he sat down thoroughly exhausted, and his face was like parchment. We practically carried him from the rostrum down into the stake office. We had him lie down on the couch there and we made him comfortable. I think he had a little sleep. I didn't want him to come back to the afternoon session, knowing how much he was suffering. We were to meet at two o'clock. About ten to two I just put my head into the room to see if he needed anything, and he was struggling

to his feet. He knew what time it was. He wasn't going to be beaten. He said, 'I came here to attend conference, and that's what I'm going to do,' despite my urgent plea to him to rest. He said, 'I won't be able to take too much interest in the proceedings. Just let me know when it is my turn to contribute to the meeting.' He sat there with his head on his chest, obviously in pain. ... (toward the end of the meeting) I asked him how he was. He said, 'Do you want me to speak?' I said, 'No, not unless you are well. We enjoy just having you here.' He said, 'Help me up.' I helped him to his feet and to the rostrum. He rallied himself, got his great spirit working, and gave a wonderful address. At the end of that he just completely collapsed. We carried him away and sent him back home on the plane that night. We discovered afterwards that he went straight to hospital and had a serious operation following that journey.[20]

Nowadays, it is the normal practice for new convert adult males to be ordained a priest in the Aaronic Priesthood as soon as possible after their baptism and confirmation. However, in the days of the original Auckland Stake, often it would be some time after their baptism that they would be ordained as a deacon and, after a suitable time had passed, as a teacher and eventually as a priest. One of the early leadership training mechanisms was the Senior Aaronic Priesthood Programme. They ran Senior Aaronic schools where new converts, less active members, people who had the Aaronic Priesthood but needed to be prepared to receive the Melchizedek Priesthood and be ordained elders were prepared for the responsibilities of the higher priesthood.

William had a great testimony of the value of these schools:

We had projects for them. We ran schools on a regular basis. I can remember one time in Huntly when two of our students arrived at one of those schools. They were inebriated. They were right outside the pale of the Church, as far as the Word of Wisdom was concerned, and arrived in a rather garrulous condition. We persevered with them and one of them became a bishop later on, and a great bishop he was too.[21]

New Challenges

In 1963, after forty years of government service (including his war service years), William was able to retire from his position in the Department of Lands and Survey and take early retirement at the age of fifty-six. Because of his work experience in the Department of Lands and Survey, he was able to qualify for a real estate licence, and he set himself up in business as a real estate agent, pursuing this business for over three years. This was to stand him in good stead when in 1967 he was asked to become the real estate representative for the Church in the South Pacific. In this role he was responsible for negotiating the purchase of chapel sites, school sites and mission homes, and maintaining the records of the Church real estate holdings throughout the South Pacific Area including New Zealand, Australia and the Pacific Islands. By the time he retired in 1976, he was managing approximately 500 property files.

About the same time as he was called to serve as the Church real estate representative, he was called to set up the translation programme in the South Pacific by Bishop Victor L. Brown, the Presiding Bishop of the Church, and Brother Tom Fyans, the head of the Church's Translation Services Department, who were both in New Zealand. That evening they asked him to manage the programme, which involved setting up translation teams in the various Polynesian and other languages and setting up a printing office and distribution centre in Auckland. When William explained that he had just been asked to represent the Church in real estate matters in the South Pacific they reasoned that while he was going around setting up this translation programme he would be able to do his real estate work at the same time.

Roberts family attending Auckland Stake Green and Gold Ball at Takapuna Chapel circa 1967. (L–R) Michael, William, Norma, John.

William later reflected:

> For those following six or seven years I was really busy ... I was grateful for that assignment to work in the Church, because I know that our work was directly responsible, to a large degree, for the development that took place afterward. I don't think that we would have had stakes in Samoa, Tonga or Tahiti but for the translation programme. It helped us to get the instructions from the Church into a language that they understood, including all the books of the Church, the auxiliary manuals, the Church manuals, and of course the standard works.[22]

They set up a printing office with eventually up to fifty staff. He studied other printing operations and noted that often there was sometimes jealousy or perhaps non-cooperation between the various trade skills involved in the running of a printing shop. He remembered thinking, 'Well, the main thing in setting up a printing office where you're relying on one another would be to have people who had the right attitude and the right frame of mind for their work and that they'd all want to help each other.' So he selected the staff from the ranks of school teachers, painters and people who had worked in all sorts of jobs other than printing. He said:

> It paid off handsomely, because they had the right attitude. They were going to find out all they could about their new job, and this they did. In the end these printing friends of ours told us, 'When any of your men are tired of working for you, would you let us know? We want them to come and work for us.' That's the kind of skills we developed.[23]

In October 1969 William received a call to be a regional representative of the Quorum of the Twelve in New Zealand (a responsibility similar to that of the Area Seventy today), having served nine years as stake president. He wasn't replaced as stake president until February 1970. He used to joke about sending letters as a regional representative to himself as a stake president and not receiving very satisfactory answers on occasion. New Zealand was divided into four regions or geographic groupings of stakes. Towards the end of his time as a regional representative, Western Samoa and American Samoa were added to his area. In this role he would travel around the regions holding training sessions with stake leaders. His son, Michael,[24] had not long come home from a mission and would sometimes accompany him to these sessions in a secretarial role. He remembered one training session involving the work of the priesthood executive committee in the wards. William had made a working model of an engine with cogs made out of old sellotape spools mounted on a thick piece of cardboard and thick rubber bands to demonstrate how the executive committee was the engine room of the ward. When he cranked the central cog (the executive committee), the action was transmitted to the outer spools to make them all rotate in unison. It was a powerful image teaching a simple gospel principle on the need for ward leadership to be united in purpose.

By the mid-1970s William had retired from being the manager of the Distribution Centre and this role had passed to Ken Palmer, also the subject of a chapter in this book. William continued with his work as real estate representative and as regional representative right up to April 1976.

Near the end of his term as regional representative, he was given the assignment to chair the arrangements for the Pacific area conferences in New Zealand and Samoa, both countries within his jurisdiction. President

Kimball, with his typical kindness toward the people, approved an unscheduled conference session in American Samoa where their plane landed. The night before his arrival, the rain was driving in so fiercely that it was penetrating the seals on the louvre windows. The local people had so much faith and were sure that it would clear up for the prophet. Sure enough, the next morning was fine and the all the people and the government hierarchy came down to meet him. In Western Samoa they could not get buildings large enough to house all those expected to come to the conference. They experimented with several possibilities, one of which included building a wire framework, and stretching a polyethylene tarpaulin over the top. When it rained, the rain pooled in the polyethylene, which stretched and doused the people beneath it, while the wind caught hold under it and threatened to tear it away. When the time came to assemble the people, they came from all over the island with big palm leaves, which they hurriedly thatched onto the framework. They established what was called the coconut tabernacle, providing shelter for about 6000 people. Both President and Sister Kimball were sick with influenza when they arrived, but he would not quit. There were three days of meetings in Western Samoa. The huge crowd gathered under the coconut tabernacle could see the rain clouds threatening in the hills around them, but the rain held off until a few minutes before the end of the last session. Then the rain came down. The people just sat there and took no notice of it. In spite of their condition, both President and Sister Kimball ignored their physician's, Dr Russell M. Nelson, advice to cancel the rest of the trip, and got on the plane to Auckland. President Kimball said, 'I came down here to do a job, and we're going to do it.' John Roberts, William's older son, wrote, 'They landed in New Zealand and President Kimball walked down the steps of the plane in front of all the cameras … and submitted to a news conference with the media there in Auckland, where, by Elder Nelson's description he gave brilliant answers to their questions. But when he went to bed, his temperature was high again.'[25]

For William, the highlight of the conference in New Zealand was the cultural evening themed 'Youth Garden', which they put on for President and Sister Kimball the following day in Hamilton. They had a 1300-voice choir and choreographed dancing. They wrote their own script, did their own choreography, wrote their own music and sang it beautifully. President Kimball was so sick that he was advised by his doctor not to attend the cultural evening. President Tanner had announced to the youth present that President Kimball was too sick to attend. He then called upon one of the young men to offer the opening prayer. The young man prayed, 'We are two thousand youth. We have been practising for six months to perform for thy prophet. Wilt thou heal him and deliver him here?' 'When the prayer finished, President and Sister Kimball's car drove into the arena and the youth and the assembled crowd cried out with a shout of joy.'[26]

One Saturday in November 1975 William was awoken at 5 a.m. by a phone call from President Marion G. Romney, a counsellor in the First Presidency. President Romney asked, 'Would you be able to get your affairs in order so that you could go on a mission?' William replied in the affirmative. 'Is your health good?' Again, the answer was in the affirmative. 'Can you get ready?' 'Oh yes,' was the reply. They did not find out where they would be going until May of 1976. Their call was to the England Leeds Mission. William was delighted to receive this assignment as it meant he could return to the country of his birth. He and Norma arrived in London on 29 June 1976 and after an overnight stay moved on to the mission home in Harrogate, officially commencing their duties on 1 July. Prior to their arrival, the mission had been split into two, leaving them with only 113 missionaries, with the expectation that their complement would reach 190 in the following twelve months.

William reported that the greatest impact in their lives came from their association with the missionaries:

> We find that our lives are interwoven with the missionaries. I've found that this above all else helps in the administration of a mission. One must become a sort of a father. Although the terms 'father' and 'mother' are not encouraged, this father and mother image is quite real … Their success is our success. It is the overcoming of challenges and the achieving of goals. When they rejoice, we rejoice with them, and when they're depressed we are affected, and we need to restore them.

After two years of the expected three, he received a phone call from President Kimball asking him how he felt Sister Roberts would enjoy being the matron of the Hamilton New Zealand Temple. In his typical understated dry sense of humour William reported to his family that he had worked out that he had to figure in the equation somewhere and he realised that he was being called as the president. They served for four years in that role and loved every minute of it. A highlight of their time in the temple was when President Kimball visited them at the temple and stayed with them in the temple home.

End of Life

With their younger son Michael being the only family still in New Zealand, William and Norma moved from Auckland to Hamilton in 1992 to be close to temple and family. At the time Michael and his wife Christine were in

Temple President and Matron of Hamilton New Zealand Temple 1978–82.

Hawaii on sabbatical leave from the university. A few days before Christmas they received word that Norma had suffered a stroke and slipped into a coma. They arrived home on Christmas Eve and were able to visit her at the hospital. She passed away the next day without regaining consciousness, but they felt it a tender mercy that she hung on until they arrived home.

William continued living on his own for about seven months, at which time he visited the doctor and received a diagnosis of acute leukaemia. The family fasted together and Michael gave him a blessing. As much as he wanted to promise his father that he would be made well, the spirit whispered that his time on earth was ending and he was being called home. All he could do was bless him to have faith in God's plan of happiness and to rejoice in the love, comfort and support of his loved ones as the disease took its course. When he was finished, he hugged his father and with tears streaming down his face, stammered, 'I'm sorry Dad.' Ever gracious, William replied, 'It's all right, son. I know my time has come.'

He came to live with the family and they watched him slowly withdraw from life. At first he would go out for walks around Hamilton Lake. Then, one day, he couldn't keep it up and had to be rescued in the car. From then, he was no longer able to go out driving in the car, but on good days he would sit outside in his favourite chair in the sun. Eventually, this became too much for him and he was confined to his Lazyboy rocker.

Visit from then Apostle Elder Russell M. Nelson in November 1993, a few months before William passed away.

During this convalescence he was visited by then Apostle, Russell M. Nelson, who was in town on assignment and had heard that William was nearby and in failing health. This was a tremendous boost to William's morale.

Finally, he was confined to bed and, as the pain medication dose was increased, he slipped into a coma and passed away on 14 January 1994. Michael and his family were present in his room when he passed away and, instead of the grief they expected to feel, felt nothing but gratitude for a life used up in the service of God and joy in anticipation of a happy reunion with his beloved Norma.

Conclusion

At the end of the final interview for the James D. Moyle Oral History Programme, William was in a reflective mood:

> Much of my life before joining the Church included thoughts and actions which I am happy to have expunged through the waters of baptism. However there are things which I cherish such as the loyalty of old friends. I remember the sacrifice and the service – even the sacrifice of the lives of young men, taken in the prime of youth – lives given in the service of their country and for freedom. The spiritual courage of these men I hope bring forth ways and means for them to enjoy eternal life. Some of my life seems to have been aimless, without any special design on my part, but with special guidance from a kind wise Heavenly Father (it became filled with purpose aligned with

His will). All my vocational training in life seems to have had some value in the Church assignments which have been given to me. Those have been stepping stones for my own development and progress, but happily they have been useful in contributing in the smaller byways of the great kingdom-building process of the Church.

For the first half of his life he and his beloved Norma were without the blessings of the restored gospel of Jesus Christ, but in the latter half of their lives they gave their whole hearts and lives to the building of the Kingdom of God here on the earth. The legacy of that service continues to bless the lives of their children, their grandchildren and their great-grandchildren.

NOTES

1. Michael Roberts is the son of William Roberts
2. He served in the Brigade for thirty-one years from 1915 to 1946, of which twenty-five years was in the role of superintendent (Swanson, undated)
3. While the term 'grammar school' refers to elementary education in the American system of education, New Zealand follows Great Britain in using it to refer to secondary education (high school)
4. In the pre-electronic age a surveying 'computer' was a person using mathematical skills (geometry and trigonometry) supplemented by line of sight to work out exact locations needed for legal descriptions, land ownership verification and construction accuracy
5. Reported to Charles Ursenbach, in a series of oral history interviews for the James Moyle Oral History Programme, 1976–77
6. *Ibid.*
7. *Ibid.*
8. *Ibid.*
9. This story is told in more detail in Rector, Hartman, and Rector, Connie (1973) 'The Last House', in *No More Strangers,* vol. 2, Bookcraft, Salt Lake City, Utah, pp 141–44
10. Widtsoe, John A. (1939) *Program of the Church of Jesus Christ of Latter-day Saints*, The Deseret News Press, Salt Lake City, Utah
11. Ursenbach (1976–77)
12. *Ibid.*
13. *Ibid.*
14. *Ibid.*
15. *Ibid.*
16. *Ibid.*
17. *Ibid.*
18. *Ibid.*
19. *Ibid.*
20. *Ibid.*

21. *Ibid.*
22. *Ibid.*
23. *Ibid.*
24. The author of this chapter
25. Ursenbach (1976–77)
26. *Ibid.*

REFERENCES

NZ Truth (15 May 1930) 'A. T. Munn on Trial for His Life.' Issue 1276. Retrieved from https://paperspast.natlib.govt.nz/newspapers/NZTR19300515.2.2

Rector, Hartman, and Rector, Connie (1973) 'The Last House', in *No More Strangers,* Vol. 2, Bookcraft, Salt Lake City, Utah

Roberts, William (1976–77) Oral History. Interviews by Charles Ursenbach. Harrogate, Yorkshire, England. Typescript. The James Moyle Oral History Programme, Archives, Historical Department of the Church of Jesus Christ of Latter-day Saints, Salt Lake City, Utah

Swanson, B. (n.d.) Northcote Volunteer Fire Brigade. United Fire Brigades Association. Retrieved from http://www.ufba.org.nz/brigade_files/1914/The%20Full%20Story%20of%20Northcote%20Fire%20Brigade.pdf

Widtsoe, John A. (1939) *Program of the Church of Jesus Christ of Latter-day Saints,* The Deseret News Press, Salt Lake City, Utah

IV

He Kaimahi o te Tangata

Puti Tipene (Steve) Watene (1910–67)

Karina Elkington (née Watene)[1]

This chapter is based on James Rukutai Watene's unfinished biography about his father Puti Tipene (Steve) Watene, entitled *He Kaimahi o te Tangata*. In the foreword he wrote, 'This book is dedicated to my mother Phyllis May Rukutai who said: "We don't write things about our tupuna, we leave it to others".' He wrote, 'well Mum I have waited long enough for the others and now I want to let people know about my Dad.'[2] James Watene was never given the opportunity to see his writings published. It is left to his daughter to now fulfil one of his dreams.[3]

Poroporoaki (Farewell)

> I expect to pass through this world once. Any good therefore that I can do or any kindness I can show to any fellow creature let me do it now. Let me not defer it or neglect it for I shall not pass this way again.[4]

On 14 June 1967 at approximately 11 a.m. a call came from the New Zealand Parliament to Phyllis May Watene that her husband Steve Watene, the Member of Parliament for Eastern Māori, had taken a turn and that she needed to be there. With a few phone calls to the Gear Meat Company in Petone to let the family know, Phyllis asked her son Tuhoea to take her to Parliament. It was about a twenty-minute drive away from home. In his own words Tuhoea said:

> When we drove into Parliament the Ministers and colleagues of Dad were waiting for us. The family were taken to the Māori Committee Room where my Dad laid at the foot of the Treaty of Waitangi. He looked asleep. Bill Nathan, a cousin and friend of the family, was there and other members of the Māori Committee. Mum was told that Dad had passed away. Mum who never showed a lot of emotion cradled Dad's head to her bosom and kissed and held him. It was very moving to see her on the floor with him.[5]

There lay not just a Member of Parliament, but a rangatira, a father, a grandfather, mentor and, more importantly, a faithful endowed member of the Church of Jesus Christ of Latter-day Saints. His spirit had now passed into eternity. It was not until many years later that the family came to realise the true significance of the contribution Steve Watene made to the people of Aotearoa New Zealand.

The *Evening Post* reported:

> The member of Parliament for Eastern Maori, Mr P.T. Watene collapsed and died in Parliament buildings today during a sitting of the Parliamentary Maori Affairs Committee. Mr Watene popularly known as Steve had been cross examining a witness on submissions he made on the controversial Maori Affairs Amendment Bill. Suddenly he slumped back in the chair, someone called 'get a doctor quickly,' and several people rushed to Mr Watene's aid. Ten minutes later a doctor pronounced him dead. The tragedy happened at 10.50am.[6]

The tributes flowed from far and wide as to what this man had meant to so many people. At his tangi held at Te Tatau o te Pō Marae in Petone, the then Prime Minister, the Right Honourable Sir Keith Holyoake said, 'Steve Watene was a true servant to the people, their voice and their shield, a vine that bound the tribes and a bridge between Pākehā and Māori.'[7]

The Right Honourable Norman Kirk, Leader of the Opposition at the time, had this to say about his friend and colleague: 'Although Steve had only been in Parliament since 1963 he had already made his mark. He was a great link between the Māori and Pākehā cultures, and he died in the service of his people.'[8]

The Chairman of the Māori Affairs Committee, Mr Allan McCready, expressed sympathy to the family, saying: 'I wish to express my deepest sympathy to Mr Watene's wife and family and to tell them that he died like a man.'[9]

Te Amorangi (A Leader in the Making)

The Church of Jesus Christ of Latter-day Saints, of which Steve Watene was a member, believe that all leaders are prepared in the pre-existence for their sojourn on this earth. They all have gifts and remarkable qualities. Steve was no different. He overcame physical disabilities. He did not come from a wealthy family in the material sense but was given more riches than anyone could imagine, especially from a spiritual and family viewpoint.

Steve was blessed throughout his lifetime. A visionary man, he always looked to the future as a way of preparing young men and women to take their rightful place in society. An innovator, where everything else failed, he would be creative and improvise. He was a renowned sportsman on and off the field, and an athlete who excelled in many sports including tennis, rugby and especially rugby league. He was loyal to his Church, union, community, country and in particular to his Māori people as a promoter of Māori culture and customs.

As a family man, he loved his wife, children and extended family. He cared for and helped meet other people's needs through his selfless service. He would leave no stone unturned to get the best out of and for the people who were without the necessities of life. He would often get out of his own bed and sleep on the floor for his guest or visitor and gave the best in the house for them even at the expense of his family.

A humble individual, he was more relaxed sitting on an old wooden box, peeling potatoes, than on a stage representing the government at endless meetings. Throughout his lifetime he was a councillor on a number of community boards. He was also a chairman on various committees throughout New Zealand and overseas. He led by example and expected others to do the same. As he would say, 'Whatever I ask you to do, I have done many, many times before.'[10]

The experiences of life were instilled in Steve at a very early age from his parents – Toke (1881–1955) and Rose Watene (1887–1964), and his grandmother Kataraina Watene (1838–1916) and other tupuna. His grandfather Mita (1830–1908) passed away before he was born.

Whakapapa (Genealogy)

The whakapapa of Steve Watene makes one mindful of how it plays an important part in the development of an individual. As you follow the line of descent you come to realise that his life was prepared for him before he was born. On his Māori side he was a direct descendant of Hotunui of the Tainui waka, which crossed the Pacific to bring his people to Aotearoa. On his Pākehā side Steve was Irish, a direct descendant of the Savage line.

The Savage family emigrated to America in the 1700s. In 1775, thirty-one members of the family were soldiers in the Revolutionary War.[11] His great grandfather, Benjamin Boscawen Savage had come to New Zealand from America and had been a trader up and down the East Coast of New Zealand.[12]

Whakapapa[13,14]

HOTUNUI (captain of the Tainui Waka)
Marutuahu
Tametepo
Tamatera
Whanaunga
Te Ngako
Taurukapakapa
Rauakitua
Mohao
Kairangatira
Pakira
Hineahi
Poutangi
Tokorau
Taramauroa

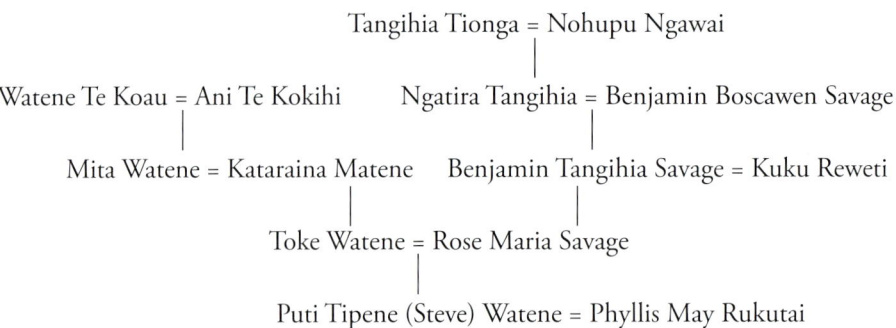

Te Timatatanga (The Beginning)

Steve was born in Kirikiri, Thames, on 18 August 1910. He was the only child of Rose Maria Savage of Te Arawa and Te Whānau a Apanui descent, and her second husband Toke Watene, a farmer of Ngāti Maru descent.

Steve's paternal grandparents were Mita Watene and Kataraina Matene, and his maternal grandparents were Benjamin Tangihia Savage and Kuku Reweti.

Steve had a half-brother from his mother's first marriage – William Taiwhanake Savage. His parents helped to whāngai (raise) more than fifty children. It was from this home that the Mormon Apostle Matthew Cowley (former mission president and missionary to New Zealand) found and adopted his son Tony (Watene) Cowley.[15]

When Steve was born there were many comments about how pretty he was. He looked frail and skinny, hence the name Puti, meaning pretty. His birth marked a major event for the Ngāti Maru tribe as an influx of religions into the area had made inroads among the Māori people. The Watene family were devout members of the Church of Jesus Christ of Latter-day Saints.[16] Steve's paternal grandparents, Mita and Kataraina Watene, were always aware of the promises and blessings that had been handed down from generation to generation for the eventual return of mana (respect) to the Ngāti Maru people. Kataraina was the daughter of the prominent Ngāti Maru chief, Matene Te Ngā,[17] also referred to as Matene Rutatenga, the subject of Chapter One in this book.

To the kaumātua (elders) of the time, Steve was the fulfilment of these promises. He became special to the kaumātua of the Iwi (tribe) and was often seen in their presence listening and learning the ways of the Pākehā as well as the ways of the Māori. He would say, 'A foot in both worlds keeps one's feet on the ground.'[18]

In Steve's own words.

> I was fourth generation baptised into the Church of Jesus Christ of Latter-day Saints. My father Toke would make me get out of bed morning and night and study the scriptures with him and my mother. We would spend an hour in the morning and an hour at night. He would give me scriptures to memorise and recite verbatim. In time I became very efficient in reading and understanding the gospel. Throughout my childhood we had American Elders – missionaries – stay with us. Our home was the area headquarters of the Church until 1925. Early Church reports from the Hauraki came from the branch in Kirikiri.[19] These Elders would also teach me of the many truths of the gospel. Whenever there was a hui or gathering at home, my duty was to sit and listen to all that was said whether it was in Māori or Pākehā. Time and time and year after year I would always be with my grandmother or my parents. My cousins who were bigger than me were jealous of this and would often give me a beating.[20]

The kaumātua would gather under the trees located near Toke and Rose's homestead in Kirikiri, Thames, and they would call Steve over from a very young age and have him sit on a log in the middle of them. They would draw a rugby field on the ground in front of Steve. They would put walnut shells down to represent players on the field and then strategise and create various situations and manoeuvres, which Steve had to solve. He said:

> Young as I was, barely 7 years of age, I would look at their plays and then go to bed at night and think about what I would do. As time passed, I would include the move into my evening prayers and while I slept, I would dream the moves. In the morning I would tell my father and he was always amazed that I could figure it out. As I grew older the moves became more difficult and my time to find solutions cut dramatically to the point that the answer would have to be instantaneous. To improve my recall a long stick was my re-prover for an incorrect answer. Very soon I was that good that the stick was never used.[21]

Māuiui (Sickness)

When Steve was eight years old, he was struck by infantile paralysis and rheumatic fever. The family was devastated that he should suffer such an illness. The doctors gave him little hope of recovery. He was not expected to live longer than a week. His mother Rose, a strong woman and convert to the Church, went to the Lord on bended knees and pleaded for the life of her son. She said:

> I had barely got to my feet when two elders of the Church came to the back door and asked her if they could help. I quickly asked them to come with me to the hospital and give my son a blessing, they agreed. When we arrived at the hospital my son was gasping for air and I cried out. The Elders came to my son and with oil they administered to him calling on Heavenly Father if it so be his will to make my son well and restore him to full health to fulfil his mission in life. For the first time I saw colour come back to his cheeks and he went into a deep sleep. I knew these Elders were an answer to my prayers.[22]

That same year Steve was baptised on 1 September 1918 in Kirikiri, Thames.[23]

Steve recovered but, unknown to him, he had a hole in his heart for the rest of his life. His mother gave specific orders that he was not to play any more sport and, more importantly, no rugby. Steve loved his rugby and pestered his father, Toke, to take him to games to watch. Toke did this; however, later he would be seen hiding his son's rugby boots in the blackberries down the road and then picking them up when they were off to watch a game. Steve played each weekend and when he was selected in the local representative team his mother found out. Rose was very upset and angry with Toke. His uncles, aunties and the kaumātua insisted that she should not stop him. Rugby came easy to Steve because he had been taught and schooled in the art of the game from a young age. His Uncle Pirimona Watene was a first-class player and would have been an All Black if he had not withdrawn his name from the team trials because his wife was having a baby.[24] Steve had been taught by the best and in later years it was to pay dividends.

Mātauranga (Schooling)

Steve's schooling days were exciting, and he was always involved in some sporting pursuit. In 1915 Steve attended Thames Kopu Native Primary School, now Matai Whetu marae,[25] which was on the top of the hill directly behind his homestead. He remained there until he was twelve. In 1923 he attended Thames High School. In his words:

> In 1925 I made the 1st and 2nd XV in rugby. I played tennis and won the championship. I enjoyed every sport that I could participate in. There were many times that I would sneak out of the house to play until my mother caught me. So that I would not get a beating my father took my punishment. He was not a big man and Mum was about six feet tall and weighing (in her prime) 15 stones (95 kgs) and very strong. My mother's beatings with a piece of wood had devastating results.[26]

At the end of 1925 Steve's grandmother Kuku Reweti died in Ōmāio in the Bay of Plenty. Out of respect to the memory of his grandmother he remained with his Aunty Amelia Bradley (née Savage) in Ōpotiki for a year. In 1926 he went to Ōpotiki High School and captained the 1st XV rugby team. They won the Bay of Plenty Secondary Schools championship for the first time. He was selected for the Bay of Plenty Secondary Schools representative team and they won the McIntosh Shield that year. A fellow footballer, who was a major transporter in Ōpotiki, in later years said 'it was Steve who took us through to win the Bay of Plenty Secondary Schools Championship for the first time. We have great admiration for what Steve accomplished in his lifetime.'[27]

In 1927 Steve attended the Māori Agricultural College (MAC) near Korongota in the Hawke's Bay, a predominantly Mormon community.[28] Many future athletes and rugby players attended the college, including George Nepia (All Black 1924–30) and Tom Dennis (Māori All Black 1926–27), and academic scholars like Wi Pere Amaru[29] and Joe Hapi.[30] It was there that Steve gained his education in the art of oratory that was to carry him into Parliament and other accomplishments in his lifetime. Opportunities to speak were part of what it was to be Mormon. Steve was also a member of MAC's 1st XV. He graduated from MAC in October 1927.[31]

In 1928 he was selected for the Prince of Wales Cup,[32] a rugby contest between Māori teams from the four corners of the country. Steve played fullback opposite the great All Black fullback at the time, George Nepia.

The local newspaper reported that Steve was 'the equal on the day of George Nepia.'[33]

Māori rugby great Tom Dennis said:

> I first met Steve on the rugby field, a young man playing for Auckland Maori (Te Tai Tokerau). He was playing fullback. We thought our team (Tai Rawhiti) from the East Coast had this side as we were stacked with many Maori All Blacks and we had George Nepia on our side. We were very sure of a victory. As the game progressed, each time we got close to Auckland's goal line Steve the youngest in the team kicked the ball right back to our goal line and out-played us all day. Steve with his tenacity, speed, and guile and his team beat our team. Steve was nothing short of magnificent.[34]

During his days in the Hawke's Bay Steve travelled up and down the East Coast, visiting all his relatives and friends. At Tokomaru Bay, Kaiser Paerata said of Steve:

> He would always visit late at night and I was only a young boy at the time. I would hear him call out for my mother 'Mum I am back' and then my mother would yell out Kaiser open the door for your brother. I liked it because he was a hero to the Coasters.[35]

Joe Hapi, one of Steve's friends from his days of attending MAC (who spent decades in the United States of America) said:

> Steve was one of my greatest adversaries when it came to oratory. I thought I was a good speaker and I could out-talk others until I met Steve. He was great and his words would roll off his tongue and he knew what he was talking about and he was certainly my equal if not better.[36]

The Right Honourable Hugh Watt (Minister of Māori Affairs in 1967) also attested to Steve's public speaking abilities: 'He was a brilliant orator on the marae and he could translate the thoughts of Māori people so that you and I could understand.'[37]

The Right Honourable Norman Kirk said, 'His speeches were always thoughtful and well informed, and he went to a lot of trouble to ascertain the exact truth of anything.'[38]

The Ultimate Teacher

After leaving MAC, Steve moved to Auckland in search of work. He worked as a clerk in the Native (Māori) Affairs Department's Māori Land Court. It was here that his whole perspective on life changed and took a new direction. His supervisor was James Rukutai,[39] who would be his future father-in-law. He guided Steve in the right direction, teaching him the intricate details of administration, tikanga (protocols) and politics.

James Rukutai taught him the art of negotiation, how to act and speak in public, even how to play better rugby and tennis. It was Rukutai who taught him about the new game of rugby league and instructed him to have a look at what direction he was heading in and what future he held as a second-string fullback to the great George Nepia, who was still in his prime. Steve continued to be overlooked by the All Blacks after he left school. James Rukutai said:

> Steve you must make a choice, either wait until George is old and of course you would have passed your prime or make a change now and become a pioneer in the game of Rugby League.[40]

Steve made the change to league. Switching codes from amateur rugby to semi-professional rugby league during this time wasn't a difficult decision, as players were attracted by the financial support league could offer its national representatives, noticeably during the Depression.[41]

Steve remained faithful and loyal to the rugby league code and is known as one of its great pioneers. The National Māori Rugby League Tournament, an annual event during New Zealand's Labour weekend holiday, is where teams from different Iwi rohe (tribal areas) play for the Steve Watene Memorial Trophy.[42] Since 2014, the Watene ki Hauraki team, made up of descendants of Steve Watene, have played in the tournament.

Steve and Phyllis Watene, 1966.

Whenever or wherever James Rukutai went, you could be sure Steve was close by, recording meetings, arranging agendas, preparing speeches and meeting important people in Māoridom. During this time, he met Phyllis May Rukutai, daughter of James Rukutai and a well-known local tennis player in Auckland. She was also working for the Native Affairs Department. Their courtship resulted in marriage on 20 September 1934. James Rukutai continued to counsel and guide Steve, whose work experience with the Native Affairs Department proved invaluable. Much of the focus of that work was dealing with urban Māori issues, the substandard conditions of rental homes and the poor work conditions for Māori. Many Māori were forced to live in inner-city dwellings, as these were the only affordable housing at the time. James and Steve would visit local Māori in and around Auckland seeking ways to meet their needs. Of Steve, the Right Honourable Mr Rata (Northern Māori) said:

> I remember Steve's work in the State Housing areas such as Tamaki. He realised the problems of Māori people who moved into such areas, and his influence was such that he is remembered with gratitude by many families.[43]

Steve once asked his father-in-law which political party was best for the Māori people. The advice that James gave Steve was that the party that he should give his allegiance to was the one helping Māori.[44] At that time in the 1930s–1940s the Labour Party courted Māori and showed that they were serious in trying to improve their social and economic circumstances. In 1932 an alliance between the Labour party and the Ratana Church was well supported by many Māori.

Steve became a member of the Labour Party and throughout his lifetime he referred to those early years as the start of his political life. As he moved around the country with his Māori Land Court duties, he met many Māori and built relationships of trust and respect. The kaumātua in each rohe (area) he visited would allow him to sit in their Iwi meetings and invited him to stay at their homes. With his sporting achievements and his work for the Native Affairs Department, his popularity grew with Māori across the country. The Right Honourable Sir Keith Holyoake recognised that the greatest tribute that could possibly be paid to him was the fact that thousands came from every tribe and every region of New Zealand to his tangi.[45]

Sportsman

Steve was selected for the New Zealand Kiwis in 1930, while only nineteen. He was one of sixteen uncapped players in the 1930 team that toured Australia, and he led the haka. He played for the Kiwis until 1937, captaining the New Zealand Rugby League team in three tests in 1936 and 1937, becoming the first Māori to captain a national side.[46]

After his retirement in 1937, Steve coached and selected representative teams, and served as an administrator up to national level. When England

Steve Watene when he played rugby league.

toured in 1950, Steve was chosen to provide the address as a token of respect for the late Māori leader, Tonga Mahuta, in appreciation for Tainui hosting the visiting English team:

> I thank the South Auckland League for affording me this opportunity as a representative of the Māori people to join in welcoming our visitors … In this Rugby league game of ours there is no room for the sniveller, the squealer, or the pointer, be he administrator, official or player, he must display a sense of impartiality, and a degree of tolerance to all who have contributed to maintaining this modern brand of football. And so today like in previous years we witnessed football played by specimens of mankind, perfect in physique, and in a manner we all enjoyed. The manliness was reflected in knocks given and taken and once again our visitors have shown us something new for the future.[47]

His address was described as illuminating.

Vocation

The Native Affairs Department wanted to promote Steve but his feelings for Māori saw him refuse promotion because he did not want to be tied to bureaucracy. He enjoyed the flexibility of being out and about in the regions. Nonetheless, he learnt much about government policy and its application. He met many Māori Land Court judges and on occasion there were issues the judges would seek his opinion about.

During the 1940s and 1950s Steve became involved in the integration of rural Māori into urban towns and cities, particularly in Auckland's Mount Wellington–Tamaki area. As well as helping to arrange state housing for the newcomers, he was instrumental in the formation of the Ngāti Muturangi Māori Club and in 1948 helped establish the Māori Community Centre in Fanshawe Street in Auckland, a forerunner of the Māori urban marae.[48]

By this time Steve had seven children and was struggling to support his family on a government wage. This led him to the waterfront, where he saw great possibilities. However, as time passed, working conditions became poor. It was a tough time and it took strong and courageous men to stand up to employers and the shipping companies. He became a Union delegate, then part of the Waterfront Union Executive.[49]

Steve and two others toured tribal districts on behalf of the New Zealand Waterside Workers Union to discourage Māori from volunteering as strike-breakers.[50] Steve's son James Rukutai Watene was only ten years old at the time and remembers the looks of anguish and frustration on the faces of his father, mother and his family:

> I felt the hell of no food and the sniggering sneers that were directed towards father. At school the Māori kids banded together to protect one another from the persecution and prejudice that was levelled at us. I learned and experienced from an early age what racism was in our society.[51]

Steve and many of his colleagues were blacklisted and were refused credit, shops were actively discouraged from selling food to them and money for the families was non-existent.

On 29 June 1951, Walter Nash, then-Leader of the Opposition, argued in Parliament:

> The government has taken steps to prevent help of any kind being given to the wives and children of waterside workers if their husbands and children's fathers are parties to a declared strike.[52]

He was referring to Regulation 8 of the Waterfront Strike Emergency Regulations 1951, which criminalised the act of providing material support to striking workers.[53]

Not to be defeated, Steve organised for food to be sent to the strike workers from all around the country. His contacts through work, iwi, community and members of the Church responded to his call for help, and food and provisions started to come in. By this time Steve had fourteen children to support and so the older ones were sent back to Kirikiri, Thames, to stay with his parents Toke and Rose Watene.

Steve knew that the strike was an honourable one. He believed going on strike set the course for better negotiations for the future in employer and union relationships. It showed that employees have rights for better working relationships and should not be ignored.

Service

In 1953 Steve was elected to the Mount Wellington Borough Council in Auckland, serving for three years. He was also a member of the Tamaki School

Committee. Watene Road in Mount Wellington was named in his honour after he left the borough.⁵⁴

Around 1956 the family moved to Petone, Wellington, where Steve became a hostel manager and industrial welfare officer for the Gear Meat Company. The company recognised him as perhaps the one man who could best look after the interests of its employees and that is probably the one reason, according to Sir Walter Nash, that there was less trouble proportionately in the freezing works at Petone than anywhere else.⁵⁵

He worked closely with trade unions and earned a reputation as a man of fairness and strong convictions. He was a member of the Petone Borough Council (1962–65) and chairman of its works committee. He served on the administrative committee of the New Zealand Māori Council and worked for the Māori Education Foundation. His commitment to education was spurred by his belief in its importance to the development of Māori self-determination.⁵⁶

During this time, he was also busy fulfilling his Church callings. He served on the district presidency and travelled around the district visiting branches and wards. His daughter Joanne Paora (née Watene) travelled with him to attend many Church meetings. Vic Parker served alongside Steve on the District Presidency, and regarded Steve as a man of influence that he admired for being principled and a Church stalwart.

As a hostel manager at the Gear Meat Company, Steve supported many young Māori men who had moved from all over the country to Wellington to work. He was known to load up his van on a Sunday morning and take them all to Church at the Lower Hutt chapel of the Church of Jesus Christ of Latter-day Saints with his whānau. It became a normal Sunday activity for these young men, some of whom were not Mormons, to go to Church. He also revitalised the Petone Rugby League Club and had all his sons and young men living at the Gear Meat Company hostel playing the game.

Steve held several positions in the Labour Party, from serving on and chairing the Māori Advisory Committee, to representing Māori on the National Executive Committee for six years.

He was elected the Labour Member of Parliament (MP) for Eastern Māori in November 1963 – New Zealand's first Mormon member of parliament. As a Mormon, he broke the stranglehold of the Rātana movement on the Māori seats, and he was known to hold different political and social views from the Ratana Labour members.

Steve was an effective MP, respected by both sides of the house, and a staunch advocate for Māori interests. He was acutely aware of the plight of his constituents and remained accessible to their concerns. A fierce opponent of

Māori land sales, he also vehemently challenged racist or patronising remarks in the House.

Deeply committed to New Zealand's founding document, the Treaty of Waitangi, Steve maintained a traditional view of the rights and duties embodied in the relationship between Māori and the Crown. He saw the Treaty as a guarantee of Māori parliamentary participation and supported increasing the number of Māori seats.

After his father's death in 1955 he had become a spokesman for Ngāti Maru in their claims over the Hauraki goldfields.[57] Sir Walter Nash said that one of his earliest memories was in regards to Hauraki. Steve knew something about the history of the Māori people and was concerned that they (Hauraki iwi) had sold the land out of which all the mines in Waihi later took gold. He believed that Māori were entitled to some share of that, which had been sold as land only.[58]

While he supported integration of Māori into New Zealand society, Steve also believed in Māori self-sufficiency. He urged that the country's wealth be spread evenly and expressed his concern about the widening gap between Māori and Pākehā. He saw the role of the government as creating an environment where people might thrive as a result of their labours, not as a welfare agency. He foresaw continued urbanisation and argued that, as well as education, Māori needed realistic employment opportunities.

Steve Watene in Tehran.

In 1966 Steve represented the New Zealand Parliament at an Inter-Parliamentary Union conference in Tehran, Iran. He was one of the first Māori to represent Parliament at such a level. On his way to Tehran he stopped off in Bountiful, Utah to visit his cousin Hinauri Tribole. It was reported in the local papers that he was particularly interested in visiting Salt Lake City and rerouted his trip there.

The following year, on 14 June 1967, he died at Parliament Buildings, Wellington. He suffered a heart attack while cross-examining a witness at a sitting of the Māori Affairs Committee on the controversial Māori Affairs Amendment Bill.[59] Steve had feared that the bill would lead to the continued alienation of Māori land, an issue at the heart of his mission as a MP. He was too young to die but if the end was inevitable it could not have been in more fitting surroundings.[60]

The then-Prime Minister Sir Keith Holyoake went down to the Māori Affairs Committee room to see Steve as he lay there. He later said:

> I have a memory of the scene which will always abide with me, he appeared so composed, so strong, so much at peace and at rest, and it seemed fitting that he should lie there in the room that is so important and so dear to all Māori … There he lay beneath the Treaty of Waitangi and the pictures of the past great leaders of the Māori people – Buck, Ngata, Carroll, and Pomare. How fitting an epitaph to a lifetime of service to the Māori people.[61]

Noman Kirk said:

> Both inside and outside of Parliament he was noted for his firm adherence to his Church and to Christian principles, a man to be admired in every respect, and particularly so because he allowed his faith to be his guide in his private life.[62]

The Right Honourable Mr Brown (Palmerston North) described Steve's sterling character:

> A man with high religious convictions, a man who could never deviate from the teachings of his Church, and a man that would stand by his word once it was given.[63]

Unveiling

The unveiling of the headstone in memory of Puti Tipene Watene was held at Te Puni Street cemetery, Petone, on the weekend of 14–16 June 1968. It was an occasion that prompted the attendance of approximately 2000 Māori and Pākehā, some of importance, the majority of humble status, who came to pay a final tribute to a man they respected and loved. The Māori Queen, Te Atairangikaahu, was especially invited to perform the unveiling; she was supported by about 200 followers of the Kīngitanga movement.[64]

Rugby League has also been important to our whānau. Steve's great grandson Dallin Watene-Zelezniak carries on Steve's tradition of being a faithful member of the Church and the captain of the New Zealand Kiwi Rugby League Team (2018). Dallin was also co-captain of the New Zealand Māori All Stars (2020), and his brother Malakai also played in the same team. Through the legacy of our tupuna, the descendants of Steve have continued those traditions.[65]

Steve was a faithful member of the Church of Jesus Christ of Latter-day Saints, a leader, a pioneer of the game of rugby league, a defender of the rights of Māori, a husband, a father and grandfather. He was the first Māori to captain a national sports team and the first Mormon to become a member of New Zealand's parliament.

Steve, Phyllis and their mokopuna.

The Church of Jesus Christ of Latter-day Saints has been an important part of the Watene whānau. Children, grandchildren and great-grandchildren of Steve have served missions, and have married in the temple. Eighth-generation Watenes, living around the world, are growing up in the Church.

The Right Honourable Hugh Watt (Deputy Leader of the Opposition) shared the following whakataukī in the session of Parliament after Steve's death (20 June 1967):

He toa piki pari, mate pari; he toa ngaki kai, ma te huhu tēnā; engari he toa tauā, mate tauā;
People who climb cliffs die on cliffs; the man who cultivates a garden dies silently in peace, but the warrior who dies in battle dies in honour.[66]

NOTES
1. Karina Elkington (née Watene) is the granddaughter of Puti (Steve) Tipene Watene
2. Watene, James Rukutai (1990), *He Kaimahi o te Tangata*, unpublished, Hamilton
3. *Ibid.*

4. Grellet, Stephen (1869) Retrieved from https://en.m.wikiquote.org/wiki/Stephen_Grellet. This quote was used as part of the funeral programme for Steve Watene on 17 June 1967
5. Watene (1990)
6. *Evening Post* (14 June 1967), 'Obituary', p 6
7. *Dominion* (17 June 1967), p 2
8. New Zealand Parliamentary Debates (1967), 1169. Retrieved from http://hdl.handle.net/2027/ucl.b2940057
9. *Dominion* (17 June 1967)
10. Watene (1990)
11. Retrieved from www.stupranchonline.com/SavageAncestry.htm
12. Retrieved from https://www.geni.com/people/BenjaminSavage/6000000010058106/9#/tab/overuer
13. Watene (1990)
14. Retrieved from https://www.geni.com/people/Ngatira-Savage/6000000008827980082
15. Parker, Rangi (2010), 'My Kia Ngawari Journey', Hamilton, Gregson Interview, p 79
16. Henare, Manuka (2000) 'Watene, Puti Tipene', Te Ara – The Encyclopedia of New Zealand. Retrieved from https://teara.govt.nz/en/biographies/5w12/watene-puti-tipene
17. *Ibid*.
18. Watene (1990)
19. *Te Karere*. Retrieved from https://archive.org/stream/tekarere3900chur/tekarere3900chur_djvu.txt
20. Watene (1990)
21. *Ibid*.
22. *Ibid*.
23. Henare (2000)
24. *Auckland Star* (16 September 1942) Vol. LXXIII, Issue 219
25. Matai Whetu Marae or Study of the Stars (1979). Retrieved from https://www.aucklandmuseum.com/collection/object/am_library-catalogq40-61757
26. Watene (1990)
27. *Ibid*.
28. Retrieved from https://www.mormonnewsroom.org.nz/article/mormon-and-maori. MAC was dedicated on 6 April 1913, in Hastings, Hawke's Bay. The 1931 earthquake rendered the building unsafe and the Church closed the College
29. Graduated from Brigham Young University, Provo, Utah, in 1934. Retrieved from https://archive.org/stream/commencementexer1934big/commencementexer1934brig_djvu
30. Graduated from Brigham Young University, Provo, Utah, with a Masters in Art in 1951. Retrieved from https://www.myheritage.com/research/recod90100-70045036/brigham-young-uni.commencement.exercise-prog-provoutah
31. Newton, Marjorie (2012) *Tiki and Temple: The Mormon Mission in New Zealand, 1854–1958*, Greg Kofford Books, Utah, p 179

32. *Auckland Star* (8 August 1928), Vol. LIX, Issue 186
33. *Ibid.*
34. Watene (1990)
35. *Ibid.*
36. Watene (1990)
37. New Zealand Parliamentary Debates (1967)
38. *Ibid.*, 1166. Retrieved from http://hdl.handle.net/2027/ucl.b2940057
39. Puihipi, James Rukutai (1877–1940) was a New Zealand rugby league player and coach who both represented and coached New Zealand. The Auckland Rugby League's minor premiership, the Rukutai Shield, is named after him. As a memorial of his contribution he is immortalised in bronze in a statue on One Tree Hill, Auckland. Retrieved from http://en.wikipedia.org/wiki/Jim_Rukutai
40. Watene (1990)
41. Anderson, Atholl, Binney, Judith, and Harris, Aroha (2014) *Tangata Whenua: An Illustrated History*, Bridget Williams Books, Wellington, p 328
42. Coffey, John, and Wood, Bernie (2008) *A Hundred Years of Māori Rugby League (1908–2008)*, Huia Publishers, Wellington, p 92
43. New Zealand Parliamentary Debates (1967), 1169
44. Watene (1990)
45. New Zealand Parliamentary Debates (1967), 1165. Retrieved from http://hdl.handle.net/2027/ucl.b2940057
46. Coffey and Wood, p 92
47. Watene (1990)
48. Henare (2000)
49. Millar, Grace (2013) 'Families and the 1951 New Zealand Waterfront Lockout.' Doctoral Thesis submitted to Victoria University of Wellington, Wellington.
50. Henare (2000)
51. Watene (1990)
52. Millar, p 54
53. *Ibid.*
54. Henare (2000)
55. New Zealand Parliamentary Debates (1967), 1171. Retrieved from http://hdl.handle.net/2027/ucl.b2940057
56. Henare (2000)
57. Henare (2000)
58. New Zealand Parliamentary Debates (1967), 1171
59. The Maori Affairs Amendment Act 1967. Retrieved from http://nzetc.victoria.ac.nz/tm/scholarly/tei-HilMaor-t1-body-d7-d4.html
60. Taylor, M. J. (1967). Retrieved from http://teaohou.natlib.govt.nz/journals/teaohou/issue/Mao60TeA/c2.html
61. New Zealand Parliamentary Debates (1967), 1165
62. New Zealand Parliamentary Debates (1967), 1166
63. New Zealand Parliamentary Debates (1967), 1170
64. *Te Ao Hou* (September 1968), issue 64
65. Karina Elkington (née Watene) (2020). I have treasured memories of Grandpa (Steve Watene). The whole whānau lived on Te Puni Street in Petone. I lived next door

to Grandpa, my backyard was the paddock where all the stock to be slaughtered at the Gear Meat Company grazed. I would sit on the back fence to wait for my Dad (James Rukutai Watene) to come back from work, and/or Grandpa from the hostel

66. New Zealand Parliamentary Debates (1967), 1167

REFERENCES

Amaru, Wi Pere. Retrieved from https://archive.org/stream/commencementexer1934big/commencementexer1934brig_djvu

Auckland Star (8 August 1928) Vol. LIX, issue 186

Auckland Star (16 September 1942) Vol. LXXIII, issue 219

Anderson, Atholl, Binney, Judith, and Harris, Aroha (2014) *Tāngata Whenua: An Illustrated History*, Bridget Williams Books, Wellington

Coffey, John, and Wood, Bernie (2008) *A Hundred Years of Māori Rugby League (1908–2008)*, Huia Publishers, Wellington

Dominion (17 June 1967)

Evening Post (14 June 1967) 'Obituary'

Grellet, Stephen (1869) Retrieved from https://en.wikiquote.org/wiki/Stephen_Grellet

Hapi, Joe. Retrieved from https://www.myheritage.com/research/recod90100-70045036/brigham-young-uni.commencement.exercise-prog-provoutah

Henare, Manuka (2000) 'Watene, Puti Tipene', Te Ara – The Encyclopedia of New Zealand. Retrieved from https://teara.govt.nz/en/biographies/5w12/watene-puti-tipene

Maori Affairs Amendment Act 1967. Retrieved from http://nzetc.victoria.ac.nz/tm/scholarly/tei-HilMaor t1 body-d7-d4.html

Matai Whetu Marae or Study of the Stars (1979) Retrieved from https://www.aucklandmuseum.com/collection/object/am_library-catalogq40-61757

Millar, Grace (2013) 'Families and the 1951 New Zealand Waterfront Lockout.' Doctoral Thesis submitted to Victoria University of Wellington, Wellington

Mormon and Māori (2014) Retrieved from https://www.mormonnewsroom.org.nz/article/mormon-and-maori

Newton, Marjorie (2012) *Tiki and Temple: The Mormon Mission in New Zealand, 1854–1958*, Greg Kofford Books, Utah

New Zealand Parliamentary Debates (Hansard) 351: 1164–1171

Parker, Rangi (2010) *My Kia Ngawari Journey*, Hamilton, Copyright (2010) Gregson Interview

Puihipi, James Rukutai. Retrieved from http://en.wikipedia.org/wiki/Jim_Rukutai

Savage, Benjamin. Retrieved from https://www.geni.com/people/BenjaminSavage/6000000010058106/9#/tab/overuer

Savage, Ngatira. Retrieved from https://www.geni.com/people/Ngatira-Savage/6000000008827980082

Taylor, M. J. (1967) Retrieved from http://teaohou.natlib.govt.nz/journals/teaohou/issue/Mao60TeA/c2.html

Te Ao Hou (September 1968), issue 64. Retrieved from http://teaohou.natlib.govt.nz/journals/teaohou/issue/Mao60TeA/c2.html

Te Karere. Retrieved from https://archive.org/stream/tekarere3900chur/tekarere3900chur_djvu.txt

Watene, James Rukutai (1990) *He Kaimahi o te Tāngata (1980–1990)*, unpublished, Hamilton

V

Ahorangi

Pateriki Te Rei (1912–95)

Maric Waaka (née Te Rei)[1]

E hika e[2]	My esteemed one
Mōteatea nei te ngākau	I lament thee
Mōhou rā kua haere i te tai o te ahiahi	For you have perished on the evening tide
Taku ariaritanga, taku purutanga mauri	My champion, protector of vitality

Whakapapa (Genealogy)

Pateriki Te Rei was born on 7 October 1912 at Matauri Bay in the Bay of Islands, Northland, among his mother's people. His mother, Miriama Te Wainokenoke Thoms, was born in 1884 at Matauri Bay. Her tribal affiliations were Ngāti Kura, Te Āti Awa and Ngāti Toa Rangatira. Pateriki's father was Ihaka Te Rei, born 1863, in Manaia, Taranaki, and was of Ngā Ruahine, Ngāti Toa Rangatira and Ngāti Koata descent.

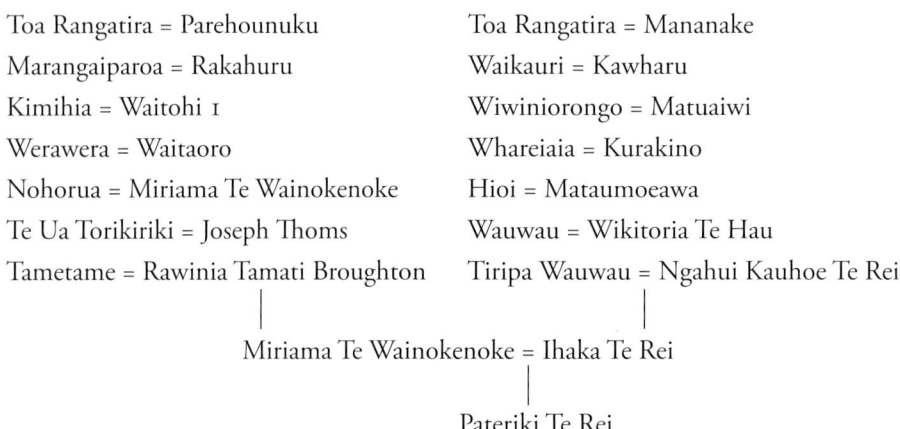

Pateriki had an older brother, Ritimana Tatana, by his mother and her first husband, Te Peeti Tatana of Ngāti Huia. His full siblings were Ariana and Charlie, who were born in Nelson; Erama and Tiripa, who were born on D'Urville Island and who died as little girls and were buried there; Rawinia and Wauwau, who were born in Taranaki; and three little girls, Tiripa, Ngawhakaahua and Titi, who were also born in Taranaki but died and were buried there. There was also Ti Paea, who was born in Manaia, Hamiora, who was adopted by Taeti and Hamiora Kamau, and the youngest, Wikitoria.[3] Pateriki was his father's first child and, according to Ariana, was given parental authority over his younger brothers and sisters.[4]

Pateriki's father, Ihaka, was married to Hinganga Kapua, but there were no children from their union. Then, while at a hui at Porirua, Ihaka met Miriama. He was told that she had been widowed and had a young son. He was encouraged to consider her as a wife who could provide him with children. He returned to Taranaki and shared with Hinganga how he had met Miriama and that she could give him children, and he wanted this. He also shared this with his brothers and Hinganga's whānau. While Hinganga was supportive of him marrying Miriama, his brothers were not. They strongly objected to this plan; however, Hinganga helped Ihaka to leave Taranaki and return to Porirua so that he could marry Miriama.

When Pateriki was only two weeks old he and his parents left Matauri Bay and travelled to South Taranaki where they made their home for a while in Manaia. They initially lived with Ihaka's first wife, Hinganga. From Pateriki and his sister Ariana Rene's perspective, they all lived together quite happily. Pateriki and Ariana talked about Hinganga with much affection. Ariana spoke about Pateriki being Hinganga's favourite. The home was one room with two beds. One bed for their parents, and one for Hinganga and all the children. While living there, the children were fed by Hinganga from one bowl, the children sitting around her as she fed them. Ariana reflected that the image was like a bird feeding its nestlings. His parents milked cows and worked for Hinganga on her land. They moved to his father's land to farm when they were able to purchase their own cows. Their father made a living by farming his land and by hiring himself out to other farmers, building fences, shearing, haymaking and clearing land.

Ihaka was a convert to the Church of Jesus Christ of Latter-day Saints around the time his sister Ngatare was baptised in April 1912. His immediate family joined him in the Church, along with many of his relatives, including the Manuirirangi family. The Mormon faith became a big part of the Te Rei family's lives from then on.

The family moved about and made their homes in Manaia, Matauri Bay, Whareatea and Te Marua Bay on D'Urville Island, Nelson, Motueka and Whangarae. They also did a lot of visiting with their relatives in Te Tau Ihu (Northern South Island).

Mormon College, Mission and Marriage

Pateriki attended the Māori Agricultural College (MAC) in Hastings from 1928 to 1930.[5] This institution was established by the Church of Jesus Christ of Latter-day Saints in 1913 to educate Mormon boys in agriculture as well as to combine secular knowledge with spiritual teachings. It continued the church's focus on education. From 1886 primary schools were opened up by Mormon missionaries for Māori children in rural and scattered communities where basic subjects such as reading, writing and arithmetic were taught. Regrettably, MAC was badly damaged in the 1931 Napier Earthquake, which devastated the Hawke's Bay region. MAC never reopened. About a quarter of a century later, the Church was to replace MAC with a co-ed secondary school near Hamilton – the Church College of New Zealand.

In the 1930s Pateriki served a proselytising mission for the Church to spread the message of the restored gospel and to encourage people to convert to Mormonism. His missionary partner was Wi Karauria from Tolaga Bay and the region they worked was the Hawke's Bay. They mostly travelled by horse and cart.

At a Mormon Hui ā-Tau at Ngaruawāhia 13–17 April 1938, Pateriki met his wife Peti Maylia McRae, who was Ngāti Whakaue from Rotorua. The event was significant in that over 2500 people attended, along with two Mormon general authorities from America – George Albert Smith and Rufus K. Hardy. Hui ā-tau were annual church conferences eagerly anticipated every year by church members as a unifying force involving spiritual and sociocultural activities. The event attracted many visitors, with a format that generally included church meetings, and socialising with games, sports, dancing, oratory, drama, singing and Māori cultural activities. Paterikī and Peti enjoyed the wide variety of activities, including dancing where they danced almost every dance together.

(L–R) Alec Wishart holding George, Kelly Harris holding Lani, Paterikī holding Irlene, 1941.

Paterikī and Peti were married on 12 July 1940 at the Church mission home in Remuera, Auckland, by mission president, Matthew Cowley.⁶ Paterikī and Peti were one of three couples who were married that day; the others were Marie and Kelly Harris, and Lorna and Alec Wishart. Paterikī and Peti made their home in Rotorua among Peti's family. They had five children: Irlene Miriama, Otere Ihaka, Matiu Nohorua, Marie Waiata and the baby, Arta Kauhoe, who died not long after birth.

    Irlene's name was taken from both her grandmothers. Otere was named after Elder Sydney J. Ottley, a Mormon missionary (and mission president 1951–55), and also after Paterikī's father, Ihaka. Matiu was named after Matthew Cowley and Paterikī's ancestor Nohorua. Marie was named after Marie Harris and Paterikī's cousin Waiata Rei. Arta was named after Arta Ballif, mission president Ariel S. Ballif's wife, and Kauhoe Arthur, Paterikī's niece, who was raised as a sister.

Kauhoe was born in Manaia, Taranaki on 16 April 1905 to Te Akapikirangi Manuirirangi of Taranaki and Kaaro Katene of Wakapuaka, Nelson. Kauhoe's grandmother Ngatare Te Rei had welcomed the Mormon missionaries to Manaia in early 1912 when many joined the Church, including Kauhoe, who was baptised at the age of eight on Christmas Day 1913 by Elder W. L. Adams. At twenty-one years of age she married Karewa Moki Arthur of French Pass. They moved to Takapūwāhia, where they raised their fourteen children. It was there that Kauhoe, leading by example, served her family, community and Church in many capacities including as a devoted Relief Society president in the early Church branch in Porirua. Just like her grandmother, Ngatare, and her mother, Kaaro – who had converted earlier at Wakapuaka – Kauhoe provided strong matriarchal leadership, staying active in the Church all her life until she passed away in 1967 from cancer. Notwithstanding her large family's leadership and significant contributions to Ngāti Toa, support for local social and community services in Porirua and notable achievements in various sports and cultural pursuits, Kauhoe's legacy of which she would be most proud is her family's accomplishments in dedicating their lives in serving the Lord.[7]

Kauhoe Arthur

Air Force

During World War Two, Pateriki joined the Air Force, on 31 October 1942. Prior to that he had tried to join the Army but was rejected due to having had tuberculosis. However, the Air Force enlisted him and his time there was spent looking after the American flying boats and PT boats in Fiji and Tonga as a maintenance crew member. Following the war he remained in the Air Force. He was posted to Lake Rotorua, where he manned the Air Force launch and patrolled the shores of Lake Rotorua until the Air Force decided they no longer needed this service. He would have remained in the Air Force but felt that racism within the hierarchy excluded him from promotion.[8] His rank was Leading Aircraftman. He was discharged on 28 September 1946.[9]

Patereki joined the Rotorua Branch of the Royal New Zealand Returned Services Association (RSA) following the war but his only visits there were on ANZAC Day each year when he would enjoy a glass of lemonade and pay his subscription fee for the following year. He was unkindly referred to by one of his brothers-in-law as the wowser, a reference to his teetotalism. This was something his wife admired, having grown up with a father and brothers who at times drank to excess, which often led to brawling and other bad behaviour.

Following the Air Force, he completed his trade certificate in joinery and carpentry at the trade school on Whittaker Road, Rotorua, which had been set up by Tai Mitchell and Sir Apirana Ngata for returned servicemen following World War Two.

Community and Church Service

Patereki was an ardent sportsman. He was keen on rugby, rugby league, tennis, yachting, swimming, boxing, hockey, indoor basketball, wrestling and table tennis. He was a player, a coach, a committee member and supporter. He played representative rugby for Taranaki Māori, North Auckland and Whangaroa. He was an avid fan of 'Big Time Wrestling', with everything stopping so that he could watch it on television or live when the show travelled to Rotorua. He built a small yacht when his eldest daughter was four years old and named the yacht for her: *The Irlene*. He was the Commodore of the Rotorua Yacht and Powerboat Club for a year or so immediately following the end of the war.[10] At different times he was vice president of the Rotorua Indoor Basketball Association and a committee member of the Rotorua Boxing Club.

In the late 1940s the family lived in a humble four-roomed home with gaps in the walls and roof. Church families living in Rotorua would meet there for Sunday School and Sacrament meetings. A harmonica belonging to Lena Waerea was situated in one room and accompanied the singing of hymns. The families who attended the meetings at that time were Messines and Janet Rogers, Lily and Bill Winiata, Taeti and Joe Wharekura, Lena and Jim Waerea, the Hamons, Brother Earnest Scott and his brother Norman Scott, Elsie Chirney, who later married James Elkington, Di and John Josephs and their sons, Rangi and Tom Davis, and Cyril Clarke and Wati Chase. Church meetings were also held at the homes of Elsie Chirney and Rangi and Tom Davis. Services were later held at a room above Millers the Drapers, the Rotorua Concert Chambers, the Druids Hall, and at the Rotorua Professional Women's Club. Services then moved to the then newly built chapel on Rimu Street, Rotorua.

While the Rotorua chapel was being built, Patereki and Peti provided a home for labour missionaries, including Boy Harris, Grace Forbes and

Kahu Meha. Pateriki and other Rotorua church members regularly provided voluntary labour in helping build the chapel. Pateriki and Peti also provided a home for young Mormon missionaries serving in Rotorua. Those who made lasting impressions on the family were Elder Bill Gibbs, Elder Barney and Elder Vaughn Hughie. Work on the chapel was completed in 1961.

Family (L–R): Pateriki, Marie, Tere, Peti, Matiu, Irlene.

Pateriki built a home for his family at Koutu, Rotorua, on land gifted by his father-in-law, Nirai McRae. His father in-law and two of his brothers-in-law, Jimmy and Maka, helped initially with the build. He worked full time so it was after work and on Saturdays after rugby and other sporting activities that work on the house proceeded. Sundays were holy days of rest and for the family to attend Sunday school and sacrament meetings at Church. It took four years to complete the house. Work started in 1948 and the family moved into the house in 1952. A rehabilitation loan of £200 from the government paid for the build. Peti was very proud that they managed to repay the loan within two years. They kept a large vegetable garden with fruit trees on the property for the family. They were both keen gardeners.

Like many other Mormons and family at the time, Pateriki served a voluntary labour mission for the Church in 1956–7 and helped build the Temple and

Church College of New Zealand. Pateriki, Peti, Matiu and Marie moved to Tuhikaramea, near Hamilton, where the construction project was situated, and lived in accommodation provided by the Church. Matiu attended Frankton School while the two older children remained in Rotorua with family. Pateriki felt strongly that it was good for members to take part in the labour missionary programme and thereby strengthen their faith through their actions.

Arta was born at National Women's Hospital in Auckland in September 1957. Peti was at the hospital because she had been diagnosed with cancer and was receiving specialist treatment. The baby was delivered early and unfortunately only lived for a few days. On hearing of the baby's passing, Pateriki travelled from Rotorua to Auckland to uplift the baby but there were a number of undertakings he had to agree to first, one being that the baby had to be buried that day.

Peti had to remain in Auckland to receive continued treatment. She didn't get to see her baby. Pateriki returned to Rotorua where Arta was taken to her grandparents' home for an hour or so, and then onto Kauae Cemetery to be buried under her maternal grandfather's vault on a cold and windy night with the headlights of her uncle's Bedford truck shedding light on the graveside. At that time Kauae Cemetery was over-run with gorse and blackberry brambles.

Peti recalled that she was one of nineteen women with similar health issues in her ward, and that after five years she was the only surviving patient. Following the initial treatment, she travelled to Greenlane Hospital twice yearly for cobalt treatment and check-ups. While undergoing treatment Peti prayed that she would live long enough to raise her remaining children and fortunately these prayers were answered.

Pateriki held many positions within the Church including leadership roles. In 1964 he became the Bishop for the Rotorua Ward, in the Church of Jesus Christ of Latter-day Saints.[11] The bishop is an entrusted position of authority and oversight of several hundred local members of the Church.

Politics

Pateriki enjoyed politics, and was a staunch Labour Party man. He joined the party in the 1930s and remained a faithful member until his death in 1995. Pateriki fundraised for the Labour Party; he went door knocking to encourage people to vote for the Labour Party; he drove people to the voting booths, held official positions within the Party, was made a life member and attended Party Conferences.

Pateriki supported Sir Peter Tapsell in his bid to be the Labour Party candidate for Rotorua in 1975 and 1978. Peter lost those elections, but from

1981 to 1993 he was elected into Parliament as the Labour Party candidate for the Eastern Māori electorate. Pateriki travelled around New Zealand as Peter Tapsell's kaumātua (respected elder), when he was Minister for the Arts (1984–1987) and Minister of Defence (1990).

Pateriki also supported the Māori Women's Welfare League and was made an honorary member.

Te Ao Māori (The Māori World)

Ties to whānau and iwi saw Pateriki travel often to North Auckland, Taranaki, Porirua, D'Urville Island and Nelson for tangihanga (funerals), celebrations, including the Waitangi Day celebrations at Waitangi and iwi hui (tribal meetings). He was a regular at the Koroneihana (annual gatherings commemorating the ascension of the Māori King) and at gatherings at his wife's marae (community centre) of Tunohopu, Te Papaiouru, Te Kuirau and Tumahourangi. He was at different times the marae secretary, treasurer and fundraiser. He was sought after by many to assist because of his karakia and oratory abilities.

While Pateriki was a native speaker of te reo Māori, his skills and knowledge in oratory, whakapapa, tikanga and kawa were greatly improved through his association with Kepa Ehau, a Te Arawa leader of note. From the 1940s through to 1970, Pateriki accompanied Kepa Ehau to many gatherings. Kepa had lost his legs through war injuries and Pateriki's car could accommodate Kepa and his wheelchair, so Pateriki was regularly called on to take him wherever there was a hui. Pateriki was particularly interested in listening to the speeches and ideas of the many orators when attending hui. Lessons were learned.

Pei Te Hurinui Jones was another who shared his knowledge with Pateriki.[12] Kepa and Pei were his role models. Pei especially was a great influence on Pateriki. A Ngāti Maniapoto tribal leader, Pei had no formal education but his knowledge of Māori and prowess as an orator in the English and Māori languages made him a 'torch-bearer, a good man, with plenty of vision, a first-rate Māori scholar, steeped in West Coast folklore, and a very competent master of English ... and he has the fire that kindles hearts.'[13]

In June 1983 Pei Te Hurinui Jones was awarded an OBE for his services to Māori.

Pateriki was heavily involved in Te Māori exhibition of traditional Māori art, which toured the US cities of New York, St Louis (where Pateriki was especially involved), Chicago and San Francisco in 1984. It was a hugely important display of 'the Māori cultural renaissance' that had taken place since the 1970s and the first occasion on which Māori art was shown internationally. Te Māori exhibition 'was a great success and returned to tour New Zealand, again to applause, and a swelling of Māori pride'.[14]

Pateriki became involved with Te Wānanga o Raukawa, an indigenous tertiary institution situated in Ōtaki on tribal land belonging to a confederation of three iwi: Te Āti Awa, Ngāti Raukawa and Ngāti Toa Rangatira. It was established by these three iwi in 1981 to promote higher learning opportunities for Māori, offering undergraduate and postgraduate programmes incorporating Māori knowledge into the core curriculum. His initial contact was through his connections with Whatarangi Winiata, the architect of Whakatupuranga Rua Mano (Generation 2000). This twenty-five-year tribal experiment or vision was designed to assist the three local tribes to achieve their educational aspirations. Pateriki's involvement with the Wānanga was crucial as one of only four Ngā Purutanga Mauri in 1990 who were appointed guardians of tikanga (correct customs) and kawa (protocol) at Te Wānanga o Raukawa and acted as senior scholars and advisers on a range of issues important to its ongoing development. He soon became the first Ahorangi (senior person of high esteem and standing) of Te Wānanga o Raukawa.

Pateriki also supported other wānanga (forum for teaching, research and dissemination of knowledge), noho marae (overnight stays on a marae) and hui rumaki reo (Māori language courses) organised by Te Wānanga o Raukawa as a kaiāwhina (assistant, helper).

Pateriki celebrating his eightieth birthday at Takapūwāhia Marae, October 1992.

Pateriki performed the official karakia (prayers) at the openings of the wharekai (dining hall) Te Puawaitanga at Te Tāpui Marae, Matauri Bay,[15] the wharenui (communal meeting house) Tama Ariki at Pukearuhe Marae at Taranaki, the wharenui Ngātokowaru at Hokio Beach, Levin, the wharenui Hekemai Raro at Hongoeka, the wharekai Parehounuku at Takapūwāhia, and for many art exhibition openings and book launches.

In 1991, Pateriki and Canon Hone Kaa led a pilgrimage of Māori to Raiātea in the Society Islands. The purpose was to retrace the journey of the ancestors from Tahiti to Aotearoa

New Zealand.[16] While there he collected soil, water and rock samples from the tūāhu (sacred places) and brought them back home to Aotearoa.

After a short illness Pateriki passed away at Rotorua Hospital on 23 May 1995. He lay at the home he built for his family for a night and then was taken to Te Papaiouru Marae, Ōhinemutu, Rotorua where he lay in the wharenui Tamatekapua. His service was held at the Latter-day Saints Chapel, followed by interment at Kauae Cemetery among his wife's family. Four years later, in May 1999, Pateriki's wife, Peti, died, aged eighty.

Recently, the multi-purpose educational facility Te Ara a Tāwhaki was opened at the Ōtaki campus of Te Wānanga o Raukawa. On the front pou (post) just above the carved image of his nephew Iwikatea Nicholson, a carved image of Pateriki stands looking out across the campus. This was a thoughtful and generous tribute by Te Wānanga o Raukawa.

Legacy

Pateriki's legacy is as a revered elder Māori statesman of his immediate and extended whānau (family), hapu (sub-tribe) and iwi (tribe). His kaumātua (Māori elder) status was recognised throughout the country. His elevated status as Ahorangi was an acknowledgement of his special role as a distinguished teacher of high standing equal to that of a professor within the confines of a Māori university. It was also recognition of his skills and expert knowledge of Māori cultural traditions. It was his belief that being a faithful Māori member of the Church of Jesus Christ of Latter-day Saints is also being able to live as Māori: being proud of one's heritage, respectful of one's traditions and practising one's culture.

Ever proud of his family, Pateriki would have been pleased that his son Matiu was appointed a Knight Companion of the New Zealand Order of Merit for services to Māori in the 2016 Queen's Birthday Honours.

Pateriki held important leadership roles as a Mormon bishop and patriarch of his extended family. His influence and commanding presence, especially at Takapūwāhia marae as the rangatira (chief) and torch-bearer among his Ngāti Toa people was unrivalled, and he left a huge gap at his passing.

NOTES

1. Marie Waaka (née Te Rei) is the daughter of Pateriki Te Rei
2. Waiata composed by Ruihapounamu Rūwhiu about Pateriki Te Rei entitled 'Taku Rau Kōtuku'
3. Rene, Ariana (n.d.) 'Witness Brief', The Northern South Island Inquiry (WAI785). Retrieved from http://www.ngatitoa.iwi.nz/sitecontent/images/Folders/General/Ariana-Rene.pdf, p10
4. Rene, Ariana (7 May 1994) personal communication
5. NZDF, Military Service Personnel File for Pateriki Te Rei
6. NZDF, Military Service Personnel File for Pateriki Te Rei
7. Arthur, Adele, personal communication
8. Interview with Pateriki Te Rei
9. NZDF, Military Service Personnel File for Pateriki Te Rei
10. Searancke, I. M. (5 September 2018) personal communication
11. A ward is a district under the pastoral care of the bishop in the Church of Jesus Christ of Latter-day Saints
12. Williams, Haare (1992) Transcript of Audio Recordings of Pateriki Te Rei, Item 7
13. MANU AO Motivational (2013) Massey University, Wellington
14. Royal, Te Ahukaramū Charles (2005) 'Māori – People and culture today', Te Ara – The Encyclopedia of New Zealand. Retrieved from http://www.TeAra.govt.nz/en/photograph/3831/te-maori-exhibition
15. Pomare, Anahera (2004) *A Biography of Pateriki Te Rei*, Selected Private Studies, Te Wānanga o Raukawa, Otaki
16. Walker, Ranginui (1991) *The Voyage Home*, Geonews, Wellington, nzgeo.com

REFERENCES

Arthur, Adele, personal communication

MANU AO Motivational (2013) Massey University, Wellington

NZDF, Military Service Personnel File for Pateriki Te Rei

Pomare, Anahera, (2004) *A Biography of Pateriki Te Rei*, Selected Private Studies, Te Wānanga o Raukawa, Otaki

Rene, Ariana Eileen, 'Witness Brief', The Northern South Island Inquiry (WAI785). Retrieved from http://www.ngatitoa.iwi.nz/sitecontent/images/Folders/General/Ariana-Rene.pdf

Rene, Ariana (7 May 1994) personal communication

Searancke, I. M. (5 September 2018) personal communication

Royal, Te Ahukaramū Charles (2005) 'Māori - People and culture today', Te Ara – The Encyclopedia of New Zealand. Retrieved from http://www.TeAra.govt.nz/en/photograph/3831/te-maori-exhibition

Walker, Ranginui (1991) *The Voyage Home*, Geonews, Wellington, nzgeo.com

Williams, Haare (1992) Transcript of Audio Recordings of Pateriki Te Rei

VI

Humble Converts

IAN GARRY (1915–97)

Peter Garry[1]

Helensville, New Zealand, was Alfred Ronald Ian Garry's (commonly known as Ian) birth place on 18 July 1915. The midwife who took care of Ian at birth persisted in calling him Peter (a name that has stayed with him all his life) in spite of being christened otherwise the day after his birth. His parents were Alfred James Garry and Clara Elizabeth Carroll, both born in New Zealand, as were their parents. Ian was their third and last son and had no sisters, although after his mother died in 1926 his father married a second time and had a daughter, Patricia Helen.

Early Years

Ian's father was the manager of the Kaipara Dairy Company butter factory in Helensville. He was also a part-time soldier, a Lieutenant in the home forces. He had previously served as a private with the New Zealand troops in South Africa during the Boer War. In 1922 Ian's father joined the New Zealand Co-operative Dairy Company as manager of their butter factory at Paeroa. This company formed from an amalgamation of several other smaller companies, becoming probably one of the largest co-operative dairy companies in the world, and it was Ian's fate to have some connection with the firm throughout his life.

It was in Paeroa that young Ian unfortunately contracted pneumonia and spent some time in the Thames public hospital, where at one time his family despaired for his life. Ian attended school in Paeroa, as did his two brothers. Two young people he had contact with in Paeroa were Frank Gillman and Huhurere Tukukino. Both became associated with him as members of the Church of Jesus Christ of Latter-day Saints in later years.

In about 1923 the family relocated to Ngaruawāhia, where Ian's father managed the New Zealand Co-operative Dairy Company's butter factory. They lived near the factory in Princess Street in a large old house, which wasn't particularly comfortable. While living at Ngaruawāhia, Ian's mother was in and out of the Waikato hospital in nearby Hamilton. She had tuberculosis and eventually succumbed to the illness on 25 March 1925. Ian was then under ten years old.

Ian wrote in his diary of a typical boyhood growing up in Ngaruawāhia in the 1920s:

> There was much open space around, the adjacent Hakarimata hills, the two rivers (the Waipā and the Waikato) so I became a reasonably proficient swimmer. Rugby football was my favourite sport although because of circumstances I did play rugby league for a brief period. Cricket I never did like and played only under duress. Apart from a few trips to the beach at Raglan and the odd trip to Auckland I seldom left Ngaruawāhia. School holidays in the summer were generally spent on the river banks or in the hills. There was a period, very brief no doubt, when I was in Mrs. Gerring's boys' choir in the Anglican Church! I enjoyed the singing but I don't know that anyone else did!
>
> Boy Scouts started up one time too, I became a patrol leader and had lots of fun. We raised money for our Easter camps by selling official programmes at the annual Ngaruawahia regatta held on St. Patrick's Day. We camped at the Raglan County depot at the foot of the hills. It was here that we dammed the stream to make a swimming pool and built a corrugated iron cookhouse.[2]

In May 1926, some thirteen months after his mother's death, Ian's father married Alice O'Conner.

Education

It was at Ngaruawāhia that Ian spent the balance of his primary school years, completing standard six in 1928 and attaining his Proficiency Certificate. This entitled him to two years of free secondary schooling. Also, in 1928 the

Ngaruawāhia butter factory his father managed burned to the ground in a spectacular fire, which required the family to move to a new, enlarged factory at Taupiri, just north of Ngaruawāhia.

The secondary school of Ian's choice was the Hamilton Technical College, now known as Fraser High School. Here he embarked on a builder's course, hoping to become a cabinetmaker, but other things were in store for him. The headmaster, 'Womp' Fraser, had Ian transfer to an academic course with a view to taking the university entrance examination and eventually going on to study architecture.

Ian wrote:

> With hard work and application, I accomplished some degree of eminence to finally becoming head boy and 'dux'. In 1933 I applied for, and received, an architectural bursary which enabled me to attend the School of Architecture at Auckland University.[3]

Ian's time at secondary school was well spent and he enjoyed himself. The only sport in which Ian took any real interest was Rugby football in which he excelled to some degree and became captain of the first fifteen rugby team and represented Hamilton in the junior grade competition.

One of the interesting aspects of attending secondary school in Hamilton was that it was necessary to travel to and from Hamilton by train. 'One of my travel mates was Jack Murphy who I was later associated with when he and his family joined the Church. Hugh Piper who also joined the Church was also on those trains.'[4]

The bursary of fifty pounds plus fees enabled Ian to attend the School of Architecture at the University of Auckland. However, it meant leaving home in Taupiri and boarding in Auckland. 'My father put a five-pound note in my hand, took me to the railway station and put me on the train to Auckland.'[5]

The early 1930s were Depression times in New Zealand and regrettably only a very small proportion of the population had the chance or the means of attending university, even with the help of bursaries. Money was tight in those days.

> My bursary paid my university fees and allowed 50 pounds per year as a boarding allowance. I found that with care I was able to live on 50 pounds through the school year of 9 months. Together with two other architecture students I shared a large room in a small boarding house on Eden Terrace. This cost me seventeen shillings and six pence (17/6) per week, including laundry.[6]

His favourite sports included rugby, boxing and rowing. He represented the university at a 1938 inter-university boxing tournament in Christchurch. Ian never qualified for the university's top 'eights' rowing team but he did row in other university crews.

In March 1938 when the university rowing team participated in the annual Ngaruawāhia Regatta Ian became reacquainted with his girlfriend from his school days, Theo Rene Clark.

Theo Rene Clark

Theo also went to primary school at Ngaruawāhia and then Hamilton Technical College for high school, where she took the homemaking course. She wrote, 'in 1935 I was intending to do training as a nurse but my father wanted me to stay home. He bought me a 1934 Austin 10 car and paid me to stay home.'[7]

Both Ian and Theo would travel on the school train together and as senior pupils were on very friendly terms. However, as Ian went off to university, they lost touch with each other. Once reacquainted, they saw a lot of each other, becoming engaged in September 1939 and marrying in Ngaruawāhia on 9 December 1939.

Theo's mother, Bernice Agnes Bregman, was thirty-nine when she married James Arthur Clark. He had waited ten years for her. She had previously married Edmond Burke in 1898 but divorced him in 1903, before their second child Beulah was born.

Theo wrote:

> I was never told much about him except that he drank too much alcohol and was Catholic, and in those days, they were two very bad things. So, mother left Auckland with her two young children and went home to Churchill, on the west side of the Waikato river, north of Huntly. This is where her parents Edward and Agnes Bregman lived, Mama and Papa. She lived there at home for some time and there met my father, James Arthur Clark, who fell in love with her. Eventually in 1913 she married him, just before the First World War. My father had built a nice new house and furnished it grandly for her. This place was on the west side of the Waikato river at Rangiriri. My mother's two younger brothers Theodore and George Bregman went off to the war and as they owned land my father decided to work the land and develop it for them as he had not been accepted into the army. So, my parents sold their home and built another one on the brothers' Rotongaro land. This was a very nice home, on a rise over-looking lake Whangape. Father inherited £600 from his mother and with this money he bought a car and a steam tractor. And so, the land was worked, I was born and I can well remember that steam engine. It was used to saw timber and to run a milking machine for the cows. I can remember Dad walking over the swamp land with me on his back in a sugar sack taking a light step each time before he put his full weight down. When I saw wild flowers, I would have him put me down so I could gather them. When we got home with the flowers my mother would help me to put them in water to give them a drink. The war ended and after a while my mother's brothers,

Theodore and George, came home. They said 'Thank you Arthur for developing our land and building a nice house for us.' You see Dad did not have title to the land and what he had put into it, including the house, legally belonged to my mother's two brothers. And so, Dad lost most of all he had. Even so he never argued with Theodore and George, but nonetheless, it was a blow to him.[8]

Theo's mother was a trained nurse, so the family up and moved from Rotongaro to Ngaruawāhia, where she opened a maternity nursing home. They bought a large home called 'Rathely', located opposite the Catholic Church. 'There was [a] large garden with shrubs, and a summer house covered with honeysuckle and red roses, also a lawn tennis court. I was just three years old at the time.'[9]

Dad took a job with J.B. MacEwan's as a salesman selling milking machines and pumps. He had a car, I don't remember the make of the first one but the second one was a blue Hupmobile then he also had a white Buick. He was a good salesman and made many friends around the Waikato. Mother made friends with the ladies in the town, she played croquet, joined the Church guild and also the Plunket Society. Beulah and Desmond played tennis and all was very happy in those years. There always seemed to be someone visiting, cousins or friends.[10]

Architect, Husband and Lieutenant

During his university studies Ian worked in various places but the Depression lingered on and work was not easily obtained or readily available. At the end of his first university year he returned home to Taupiri and worked in the butter factory. Other times during university vacations, 'I worked in various architectural offices, usually at 7/6 (75 cents) a week.'[11]

In 1936 Ian applied for and was accepted as an engineering assistant in the Engineers Office of the Pātea County Council in Taranaki. There, he was given the opportunity of doing unusual work, including the design of bridges.

It was in 1939 that Ian worked on his thesis for a Bachelor of Architecture degree at the University of Auckland and took for his thesis topic the design of the large butter factory at Taupiri. The thesis was accepted and he was capped Bachelor of Architecture in 1940. By then he was working as an architect for Lavington Architect, and then Edgecomb and White Architects in Hamilton.

On 9 December 1939 he and Theo were married and, in 1940, built a house in Marama Street, Hamilton, overlooking the Hamilton lake.

War had broken out in 1939 and in 1942 Ian volunteered for the Army and was sent for training in Trentham, Wellington, and posted with the 2nd New Zealand Expeditionary Force in the Pacific with the rank of Lieutenant. In April 1943, they were shipped to Noumea and then up to Guadalcanal and Green Island. By February 1944 he was sent back to Noumea where he

Ian and Theo on their wedding day, 1939.

Ian in the army, 1942.

contracted malaria and was subsequently shipped back to New Zealand and discharged from the army.

In 1945 Ian joined the New Zealand Co-operative Dairy Company as an assistant architect and later became the company architect. He remained in that position until 1955 when, with Rex Clapp, they formed their own private consultancy, Garry & Clapp Architects and Engineers.

Mormon Converts

Theo describes in some detail the family's introduction to the Church of Jesus Christ of Latter-day Saints:

In August 1952 two Elders were tracting (door to door proselytizing) Clarence Street in Hamilton and coming to the top end of the road walked through a small right-of-way to the top of Fowlers Avenue, a steep hill down to the Hamilton lake. It was raining – pouring rain, and the two elders knocked on all the doors and, eventually, number 4, our door. I was home with nothing special to do so answered the door and asked these young men in. I was pleased to have someone to talk to. I offered them some tea, which they declined, but they accepted an apple each. They gave me a Book of Mormon and told me that it was a history of people who at one time lived on the American continent. Well, I was interested in history so I read it. I had the idea that Mormons were a wicked people, and kept looking for something wicked, blasphemous or evil, but found nothing of the sort, nothing wrong, only interest. At that time, we were a happy enough family, but we had become discontented with the Church we attended, the First Presbyterian Church of Frankton. Our children, Peter and Caryl were bored with learning the same stories over and over. The elders visited us a few times but we lost contact with them for over a year. But then another set of elders started visiting. For several years they came to our home for dinner and spent the evening with us. They gave me a copy of 'Americas Before Columbus' and this book really fascinated me. About then, Caryl made friends with a Mormon girl, Farina McCarthy. She brought her home and we were greatly impressed with the way this girl behaved. Caryl joined the Beehive girls and wanted to attend the Mutual Improvement Association programme (MIA). Naturally we wanted to know what MIA was all about so we went to the meetings too. At MIA there was a Book of Mormon class taught by Sister Rosenvall. We found it all very interesting, Brother and Sister Whakahe Matenga were also in that class. About this time Ian had a malaria [r]elapse from his wartime infection. It was a 'notifiable' condition and usually meant a week or so in the hospital. But this time he did not notify the doctors and stayed home. He read the Book of Mormon from cover to cover and was convinced. Through all this we learned the gospel and got answers to all the mystery questions that were on our minds like 'where did we come from? Why are we here? And where are we going.' Then we learned about celestial marriage and families being sealed, we were nearly ready to join the Church, but we weren't asked. There were a few habits we had to break. When the elders eventually did ask us to be baptized, we broke those habits, and I mean broke them, completely destroyed them. We were all converted and in May of 1956 baptized in the baptismal font at the Auckland Queen Street chapel.[12]

When the Garry family had joined the Church of Jesus Christ of Latter-day Saints Theo approached her father with some excitement to tell him about the Church and the restored gospel of Jesus Christ. Theo states that his responses to the descriptions of the Godhead were, 'āe (yes) Theo āe, āe.' He had held these beliefs all his life. He died within the year.

The 1950s Period of Change

During the 1950s the Church of Jesus Christ of Latter-day Saints started a major building programme that included a secondary school, temple and meeting houses throughout the country, and around the Pacific. Ian wrote:

> As an architect I was very interested in the designs and construction methods employed by this American Church. My architectural practice gave some assistance by designing the health centre at CCNZ. Later, in May of 1960, when the labour missionaries decided to build the George R. Biesinger Hall we produced the design and construction drawings over a weekend.[13]

The 1950s saw a large number of families join the Mormon Church, many of whom later became leaders when the first stakes and wards were organised in New Zealand. Ian was ordained a high priest by Wendell B. Mendenhall on 18 May 1958 and assigned to sit on the stake high council.

The New Zealand Temple was dedicated in April 1958. Ian and Theo with their two children, Peter and Caryl, were sealed on 3 May that year. In 1960 the Church's Hamilton Stake was organised as the result of the reorganisation of the Auckland Stake – the first stake established outside of America. Theo was called as the Stake's first Relief Society president, in recognition of her considerable leadership qualities. Doug Martin was made the Bishop of the Hamilton ward and Ian was one of his two councillors. Two years later, in 1962, the Ngaruawāhia branch was organised and Ian became the branch president.

Theo's father had died in April 1957 and she inherited the farm across the Waipā river at Ngaruawāhia. They sold their Hamilton home and built a new house on the farm, with Ian commuting daily to his office in Hamilton.

On the business side, in 1965, Garry and Clapp joined with Frank Gillman and David Sayers to form Gillman Garry Clapp & Sayers Architects & Engineers. The office was located on Vialou Street in Hamilton. The practice flourished, designing the Te Rapa Dairy factory and the Clinical Services Block at Waikato Hospital. Later projects included designing hospitals in Tauranga, Palmerston North and the Pacific Islands, as well as dairy factories all over the Waikato.

Church Leadership

In 1958, once the Temple was dedicated, it became necessary to have available appropriate clothing for the Temple patrons. The New Zealand government at the time prohibited clothing imports. It was the Relief Society that handled this challenge by organising the making of the clothing. When Theo was made president of the Hamilton Stake Relief Society she was invited to the October 1961 Church General Conference in Salt Lake City, Utah.

Theo and Ian left for Salt Lake City in September 1961 and were met by Sister Spafford of the General Board of the Relief Society. As well as Theo receiving leadership training, both women figured out a way of ensuring that the appropriate temple clothing was successfully made and distributed to New Zealand temple patrons. Theo and Ian stayed with the Mendenhalls and the Evans families in Salt Lake City, and met up with some expatriot New Zealanders and friends, including the Wisharts, Oliphants, Clarkes, Ballifs, Bates and Browns. In addition, they had the opportunity to attend all conference sessions at the Mormon tabernacle.

By this time their two children, Peter and Caryl, had left home. Peter was called on his proselytising mission to Alaska and Caryl commenced nursing at Waikato Hospital in Hamilton. Ian's architectural practice kept him busy and Theo built her gardens and stone walls at home. Both Ian and Theo were active temple patrons and concentrated on their Church callings.

In March of 1969, Ian and Theo embarked on an overseas excursion. They took an Indiaman bus tour from Bombay to London, a three-month trip. They then toured Europe and Britain, returning through the United States, visiting friends and the early Church history sites.

Theo recalls their visits to Mormon sites of historical significance:

> We got to Palmyra and want to go to the hill Cumorah. There are no taxis. Ian asks the milkman and he gave us a phone number of a man who used to own a taxi. This man offered to come right away and take us there. We climbed the hill and looked at the statue of Moroni. The place is rather untidy after the pageant. There are fine trees planted on it and a sealed road up. It is not a very big hill, not much larger than ours. There are berry bushes growing but not good to eat. I tried the red ones, orange ones, white ones and black ones, but they were all horrid. Ian took a photo of Moroni and we had our morning prayers, then walked down to the Visitors Centre. There were Elders there, but they weren't any help except to wish us a good journey. We walked to the Joseph Smith Home and the Sacred Grove. It was hot and the road long and we were hungry and thirsty. The Lord provided, and we found a bush of ripe blackberries, different from our blackberries but looked like them and tasted better. We were truly thankful. There were two sisters at the Smith Home. They showed us through and told us about it. We were shown the place where Joseph was getting over the fence and had a vision by an apple tree which is a hollow stump now with just a few live limbs with little apples on it. The Sacred Grove is lovely. Some huge trees and lots of young ones. It is very still and quiet and the sunlight filters through the branches, just like the pictures. We stayed until the mosquitoes started biting then had a long walk back to Palmyra. Visited Nauvoo, Independence, then on to Salt Lake City. The $99 for 99 days Greyhound bus ticket is proving very useful.[14]

In 1973, Ian and Theo were called to serve an eighteen-month mission at the New Zealand Temple. Ian took a leave of absence from his architect's practice and they travelled each day from their home in Ngaruawāhia to Temple View, which involved a 44-kilometre round trip.

The following year, in February of 1974, Ian received a personal letter from Church President, Spencer W. Kimball, informing him that he was to be the next Temple president, with Theo as the matron. Interestingly, Fred Swendiman, who was currently serving as Temple President, had not yet been told of his release and Ian and Theo were instructed to keep it to themselves, which was not easy. President Kimball told the Garrys to set their affairs in order so they could serve for an indefinite period. So, with this in mind, Ian officially retired from Gillman Garry Clapp & Sayers, the first partner to do so, and set about subdividing their Ngaruawāhia farm. In time, they moved into the Temple president's house, and Ian became the first New Zealander to receive this calling. It was to last until 1978.

In 1974, Ian was called as President of the New Zealand Temple and Theo as Matron.

The Temple president's house became their home and they had a number of Church leaders visit and stay with them. Theo recalls:

> Perhaps the most memorable was President and Sister Kimball's visit for the 1976 area conference. They arrived at our home rather ill. Dr. Russell Nelson was travelling with them and advised them to immediately go to bed. Just before seven President Kimball woke up and announced that they were going to the cultural event that was to start at seven. The cultural session had already started as planned and during a long opening prayer by one of the youth, a direct request was made to the Lord for President Kimball to be well enough to attend. As soon as the prayer was finished President and Sister Kimball arrived. There was much rejoicing and shouting.[15]

Their release as Temple president and matron came at the end of June 1978. Bill and Norma Roberts from Auckland had taken their place. By that time, Ian and Theo had built a nice Lockwood home at the end of Fosters Road, Temple View. Their daughter Caryl's family had built there too. They named the properties Puke Kaari[16] and busied themselves with grandchildren and gardening.

In August of 1978 they went to Calgary, Canada, to visit their son Peter and his family before venturing to the Church October General conference in Salt Lake City, followed by a visit to Nauvoo, Illinois.

In 1980 Ian was approached by the Church Building Department to assist with some architectural work at the Church College of New Zealand and to supervise the construction of the new Sandwich Road Stake Centre in Hamilton. These projects ensured he continued to be busily engaged in the Lord's work.

In 1981 Ian and Theo were called on a temple mission to the Los Angeles Temple in California. They travelled to Salt Lake City, where Ian was given the sealing authority by President Spencer W. Kimball in a very moving visit in his office. Elder Robert L. Simpson, a former missionary to New Zealand and mission president, was the President of the Los Angeles temple at the time. Their call was for eighteen months. Returning home to New Zealand, they settled down to a normal but quiet time doing family research and temple work.

Ian and Theo's fiftieth anniversary, 1989. (L–R) Daughter Caryl Te Puke, son Peter, Ian and Theo.

Alfred Ronald Ian Garry died in Hamilton on 18 March 1997 aged 82. At his funeral service, general authority Elder Douglas J. Martin used the words 'he came down from the dress circle and sat with us in the penny seats'[17] to describe him. A year later, Theo Rene Nancy Garry died in Hamilton on 26 May 1998, also aged 82. A well-educated, professional businessman, Ian together with Theo made a significant contribution to the growth of the Church in Hamilton, and without doubt the Lord inspired and guided the right people, at the right time, towards the Church in recognition of their talents, experience and proven leadership qualities.

Ian and Theo's legacy is being the first generation of a family that has continued to honour that legacy with constant gospel service – to date, some thirty full-time missions and almost as many temple marriages. Their legacy will continue.

NOTES

1. Peter Garry is the son of Ian Garry
2. Garry, Alfred Ronald Ian Garry (1975) diary notes
3. *Ibid.*
4. *Ibid.*
5. *Ibid.*
6. *Ibid.*
7. Garry, Theo, diaries (unpublished), Hamilton
8. *Ibid.*
9. *Ibid.*
10. *Ibid.*
11. Garry (1975)
12. Garry, Theo
13. Garry (1975)
14. Garry, Theo
15. *Ibid.*
16. Puke being the name of Caryl's family and Kaari the Māori name for Garry
17. Martin, Douglas J. (1997) address at funeral service for Ian Garry, Hamilton

REFERENCES

Garry, Alfred Ronald Ian Garry (1975) diary notes

Garry, Theo, diaries (unpublished), Hamilton

Martin, Douglas J. (1997) address at funeral service for Ian Garry, Hamilton

VII

From Sheep Farmer to Shepherd of Souls
Kenneth Molony Palmer (1918–88)

Jennifer Beth Roberts (née Palmer)[1]

Genealogy

The following chart depicts the genealogical relationships (both biological and adoptive) for Kenneth Molony Palmer.

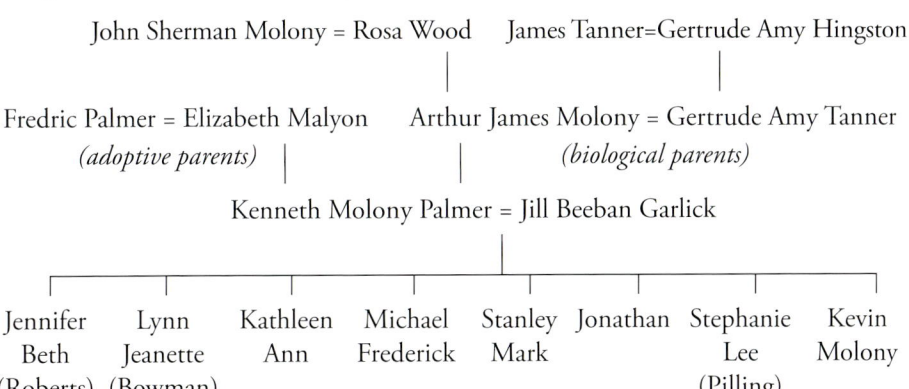

Kenneth Molony Palmer was born on 18 May 1918, the tenth child of Arthur James Molony and his wife, Gertrude Amy Molony (née Tanner). His mother gave birth at the old maternity home on No. 2 Road, Te Puke, Bay of Plenty. She was on bed rest in the home after the delivery for nearly a month. They were finally on the way home when Gertrude succumbed to a pulmonary embolism and died.

As a result of this tragedy the family was broken up. The two oldest boys had already left home. Truda (aged fifteen at the time) kept the household going and cared for some of the younger ones, but the three youngest were adopted. Kenneth went to live with Frederic and Elizabeth Palmer (née Malyon), a childless couple who lived in Te Puke. Elizabeth had actually been a nurse at the maternity home when Kenneth was born.

> Here I may pay tribute to these dear people because they became not only my foster parents, but as dear and loving to me as any flesh and blood parents could be … I was quite unaware of my true parentage, and indeed did not learn of this until I was 13 years old. However, the saying that 'blood is thicker than water', surely was borne out in my case because I always had a natural affection for my own kith and kin, even although unaware of our true relationship.[2]

At age eight Ken began to suffer from an undiagnosed heart condition, coupled with a bout of measles, and nearly lost his life.

> I well remember this particular time and the impression that I had of walking in a valley, the sides of which were dark but in front was light and peace. However, I did not complete the journey and for six long months I lay flat on my back while my erring heart slowly came back to normal. This experience taught me the value of patience, the companionship of books, and the experience of creating with my own hands, things made of wood …[3]

After all that time in bed, Ken needed to learn to walk again and for eighteen months was also part of a correspondence school. He was cautioned against strenuous sports activities and so compensated by fishing, boating, swimming and reading. After completing his schooling he became a clerk in the Public Trust Office, initially in Rotorua and later in Hamilton.

The War Years

Ken was now into his twenties and war clouds were gathering once again. Germany invaded Poland on 3 September 1939. He was with his adoptive father that day and they listened together to Britain's declaration of war on Germany.

KENNETH MOLONY PALMER (1918–88)

Spitfire pilot – Royal New Zealand Air Force, 1941.

New Zealand's Acting Prime Minister, Peter Fraser, issued a statement, 'Where Britain goes, we go, Where Britain stands, we stand. If Britain falls, we fall.'[4]

> I feel proud to say that New Zealand lived up to every word of that brave speech. The next day I returned to Hamilton and made my application to join the Air Force as a pilot. This was a period when there was a great deal of patriotic fervour. Most New Zealanders felt that the cause was just and the path taken was the only one open to us. We considered that we were with the right people and that this thing needed to be seen through until the world was rid of those who would tyrannize us and destroy freedom as we knew it ... We could not then perceive that the paths of the future on every side were to be fraught with danger from a relentless enemy whose cunning and treachery we scarcely could begin to realize.[5]

Freedom is not free and has come at great cost to many through the ages. In World War Two that cost for Ken was four years in a German prison camp. He rarely spoke of his experiences in captivity but the following is an excerpt from his autobiography:

> Over-riding it all was the boredom and tedium of seeing the barbed wire, guard-boxes and machine-gun towers. Then, too, was the close companionship of men all around you, all day and all night with little if any privacy. We learned that to 'live and let live' was a cardinal rule of life. One learned, too, that every man has strengths and weaknesses, and that it is better to seek out the strengths because by so doing you minimize your own weaknesses. You learned too, to keep a check on temper and to think before you hit. No one would or indeed could be the same in the years to come after the lessons of prison life ... A war on the scale of WWII was such a cataclysmic experience

> that only the generation that lived through it can realize the enormous impact that it made upon each of us. I hope that we will be the last generation to have such an experience.[6]

The war ended. Ken spent four months in England willing health to start creeping back into his body, both physically and mentally. Much of the time he travelled around the British Isles with fellow prisoners of war and grew to love the mellow countryside with the beauty of the small villages and country towns. It was the very depth and continuity of that life that helped with the healing process. One cold and chilly, raw September day in 1945, the ship *Orion*, laden with its 4000 troops, docked in Wellington. Ken had survived the war and went home to Te Puke to greet his parents.

> Te Puke seemed a very small town indeed, and five years of war had slipped by as though it had never been. My parents were older, but as I thought about it, I came to realize that I too was older; perhaps older even than they were in experience, and indeed it seemed a lifetime had been lived in those few short years.[7]

Marriage and Family

Ken's goal was to become a sheep farmer. The Government had set up low-cost financing to aid those returning from war to get on their feet but, even so, farms were difficult to obtain. His plan was to participate in a ballot for new farms being developed. That goal was realised in 1951 with the purchase of 378 acres in the Rotoehu Forest area in the Bay of Plenty.

His other goal, formulated in those prison camp years, was to find a wife and establish a family. Thus, he married Jill Beeban Garlick in 1948.

> I first saw Jill when visiting Massey College with a friend. I can see her as though it was yesterday. She was wearing khaki drill overalls; her hair was shoulder length and the sun was shining on her face. She was carrying a bucket, and as she walked, she limped a little … Even before I was introduced, I knew that I had met the girl who was to be my eternal companion … I believed then, and now know, that in the eternities before we came to this earth, we had been companions.[8]

The community in which the young couple lived was part rural and part forestry. Despite busy farm life, Ken became chairman of the local school committee and the social committee, as well as being involved with the National Party. During this time, three daughters were added to the family: Jennifer (1949), Lynn (1951) and Ann (1952).

(L–R) Lynn, Ken, Jennifer, Jill, Ann, 1953.

When Ann was eighteen months, she drowned in a tragic accident in December 1953. Ken and Jill were heartbroken. Where was their little girl? Was she gone forever? The minister was a good man but could only say that, 'She was somewhere on ahead and at least she had been spared the agony we were going through.' The years wore on with grief and sadness constant companions for them as they tried to come to terms with their loss.

> Certain events in one's life become like the lines seen on etchings or engravings. To this day, if I close my eyes, I can see the scenes of those days and hear the sounds as though it were yesterday. Children weeping and Jill's sobs when she knew our little one was gone; the kind words of friends; my own heart numbed with sorrow; the long journey back to the farm. How dear and strong were the good friends and family who came to lend of their strength. It was my duty to identify her as Ann. As I looked upon her face for the last time in this life, I gladly would have changed places if that were possible. I knew then what it was like to have a broken heart. As I attended to the business of seeing our little one laid to rest, it was only the thought of the sorrow Jill was enduring that gave me the strength to endure. The weeks and months that lay ahead were difficult. As time passed the healing process continued until the time came when we were able to smile again and every sound and memory did not bring a lump into our throat and tears to our eyes.[9]

Heavenly Father oversees our mortal journey and knows the end from the beginning. This experience, despite the apparent tragedy, was likely the catalyst for his joining the Church some time later, thereby paving the way for the blessings of the gospel to be bestowed on future generations. That posterity of children, grandchildren and great-grandchildren now numbers almost one hundred.

Conversion

In his autobiography, Ken wrote of his conversion to the Church:

> It was during the lambing season of 1954 that I developed blood poisoning for a second time. The first time in 1952 was nearly fatal because of a violent reaction to penicillin. On this second occasion, I was therefore treated with much milder drugs. Although they arrested the blood poisoning, they did not cure it. Several weeks passed. Jill was endeavouring to look after the lambing and I was in bed feeling like death and thoroughly depressed. As the weeks dragged on, and I did not seem to be recovering, she suggested we should get the Zion Elders to administer a blessing to me and thereby the Lord would do what the doctors had failed to achieve.
>
> Some years earlier, Jill's brother, Geoff Garlick and his wife, April, had joined the Church of Jesus Christ of Latter-day Saints. In their newfound interest, they endeavoured to convert everybody they knew, including us! We had received many of the Church tracts and a number of doctrinal books and were familiar with the basic tenets of the Church teachings. Jill had long been convinced that the teachings were true and would have joined but I made it plain that I was not agreeable to this proposition. Her mother had also joined and could never resist an opportunity to talk to me about the Church. I read a good deal of the material given to us and although I found much of it convincing, I really had no intention of getting closely involved. My pattern of life was well established and I was reasonably content with things as they were except that little Ann was gone. I felt her loss more deeply than I was prepared to admit.
>
> Then there were some bothersome worries whether this life was an end in itself. Perhaps, due to my childhood upbringing, there was a basic desire to believe in an afterlife. On the other hand, my religious experiences with the Churches that I had attended were empty and unsatisfying. Thus I had drifted, until I was really an agnostic. No one had succeeded to this point, in presenting any sort of belief in which I could genuinely believe or feel whole-hearted about. Much of what I had read about the Church carried with it the ring of truth. The Joseph Smith story, where it concerned the gold plates and the visit of the angel Moroni, seemed far-fetched, but the rest of the account did convey the stamp of truth.

I agreed for Jill to get the nearest Elders who were in Tauranga to give me a blessing. This involved a long trip in their little car. Eventually two pleasant young men, Elders Gary Sheffield and Boyd Green, arrived. When they came into our bedroom they brought with them a strange serenity, which seemed to whisper peace to my troubled heart. They blessed me by the authority which they bore and in the name of Jesus Christ commanded that I should get well. Then they taught us the first gospel lesson. Although the teaching was simple and direct, it bore the ring of truth even, 'unto the convincing of men'[10] I was impressed.

Because of the distance from their lodging, the missionaries stayed overnight. This became the pattern of their subsequent visits. Despite the blessing however, I was still ill. A few days later, Jill asked her brother, Geoff, to come from Auckland to help out on the farm, which he did. Then came a night when I felt so ill that I thought my time had come. I asked Geoff to come and pray for me. He and Jill knelt beside the bed and asked the Lord to ratify the blessing already given to me. As he prayed, a great feeling of peace came over me and it seemed almost as though liquid fire was surging through my body. This, indeed, was a witness to the power of prayer and priesthood blessings.

The realization came to me that now I had to investigate the Church with an open and prayerful heart devoid of criticism. Over the next few months the elders came regularly and I looked forward to their visits.

After about a year, the time came when the lessons were all given and yet I still had not made the commitment for us to join. The decision was not a light one for I realized that the consequences would be far-reaching. The Elders still continued to come but did not pressure me to join the Church. I knew that was their objective but was grateful that no pressure was brought to bear to influence me in my decision. (Jill had gained a testimony of the truth a year ago but in her own miracle, the spirit had told her to wait until I was ready so we could be baptized together.)

In March 1957, Elders Green and Sheffield were visiting with us again. I had a deep impression that the time had come and I told the Elders I would be baptized that day or never. The missionaries were not expecting my decision and had no white clothing. Taking me at my word, we went off to Ohope Beach and in a spirit filled occasion, Jill and I were baptized in our swim clothes. We were confirmed by the same missionaries that evening back at the farm and thus began our journey in the Church of Jesus Christ of Latter-day Saints.[11]

Early Church Experiences

Ken's autobiography also details his early years as a member of the Church:

After having made this major decision to join the Church, I realized that many changes would come into our lives. I belonged to the local club in Te Puke and was in the habit of spending time there on our visits to town drinking with the other members. Additionally I drank tea and coffee and had always smoked. Nevertheless, we had accepted these principles and it was therefore up to us to ensure that we did live by them.

Tithing was another principle that seemed particularly difficult. We were living on a tight budget, which left little over for anything but the necessities of life. Again we decided to observe the principle, albeit without a great deal of enthusiasm.

Other major changes were the observance of the Sabbath day, which, hitherto had been a day to do essential chores around the home. The Sabbath day was now about attending meetings in a Branch some 23 miles distant leaving early in the morning and staying at Church through the mid-afternoon until the meetings were done. For a time, because of the distance to the Branch, we held a Home Sunday School, which was a very enjoyable experience.

The everyday work of farming continued. As the years passed the improvements that had been planned were gradually implemented. During this period, three sons were also added to our family: Michael (1954), Mark (1956) and Brian (1958).

About a year after we joined the Church and had committed to live the law of tithing, we had an interesting experience that solidified our testimony of that law. Up until this time our hay barn had been more than adequate in size to take care of the hay crop. This particular year when the hay was harvested, I found that the hay barn was filled with several hundred bales stacked outside. As at the time it was difficult to cover baled hay successfully, I was determined that we would increase the size of the barn. During the winter months we doubled the size. The following season the extended barn was still too small to hold the bales. Once again we had to make a stack outside. I noted that my neighbours had not experienced such bountiful crops as we had. Once again I decided to increase the size of the barn. The enlargement was such that I felt it would be adequate for any crop that we were likely to produce – in excess of 3500 bales. Nevertheless when the hay was harvested the next season, the new barn was again filled to overflowing. We sold the excess to our neighbours who had not had such a great yield. We experienced a similar pattern with the stock on the property.

In 1958 after we had been members of the Church for a year, I received the Melchizedek Priesthood. Shortly after this we went to the newly dedicated New Zealand temple in Hamilton and were sealed as a family. April, Geoff's wife, was proxy for our precious Ann. What joy to know that we will yet have her with us to raise and to be part of our family through the eternities.[12]

Ken's tutoring in the Church continued. He was called to serve in an Elder's Quorum with not the remotest idea of what was involved. He learned quickly and in a year became the President followed by time serving as an alternate High Council member, having been ordained a High Priest by Elder Harold

B. Lee. All those responsibilities involved a great deal of travel over a wide geographic area. He estimated that his travelling on a monthly basis covered 1200 to 1500 miles.

> In 1962 after serving on the High Council for a couple of years, I was called as the Bishop of the Rotorua Ward. That necessitated the re-arranging of the ward boundaries to take in our farm, which was 40 miles distant, much of it over gravel roads. It was obvious that a major challenge was now presented to us. Both Jill and I had grown sufficiently to appreciate that a call from the Lord should be treated as just that, and if it was humanly possible, should be accepted.
>
> As far as possible we did as much of the bishopric work as possible on a Sunday. We would leave the farm early and go over together as a family, taking our meals with us. We stayed at the chapel until after the Sacrament Meeting in the evening, balancing up the tithing and arriving back at the farm somewhere around midnight.
>
> Leadership meetings were held in Hamilton twice monthly on a Saturday. I would go over in the morning, taking with me any ward members who wished to attend. When the meetings finished we drove back to Rotorua arriving about 1.00 am. The other Priesthood members would go to their homes while I went to the chapel and slept what was left of the night in the bishop's office. This arrangement at least had the merit that I was in the chapel before anybody else in the morning! Of course, on these occasions it was not possible for Jill and the children to attend so they would have the joy of a Home Sunday School.
>
> As my stewardship of the Rotorua Ward developed, it was becoming increasingly obvious that a decision concerning our future could not be long delayed. We loved the farm because it was really part of us and represented much effort and sacrifice. But we realized that the time was coming when in the interests of our family it would be necessary to sell and to take some other form of occupation. This decision was assuredly a major one and not lightly taken.
>
> Jill's brother Geoff, and his wife, April, approached us about joining them in a partnership to develop 10 acres of land in East Tamaki (South Auckland) in a joint glasshouse venture. The capital that they would gain from the sale of their current property added to the equity that we had in our farm would make it possible. We were indeed interested and told him so but emphasized that we could do nothing until the farm was sold … We made this a subject of much prayer and fasting. I received a very definite assurance that the farm would not be sold until the work I had been called to do in Rotorua was accomplished. This would not be until March 1963.[13]

The farm work coupled with my responsibilities as a bishop, left little time for recreation and although this year was rewarding, it was also most demanding. We had a number of prospective buyers who came and went, but none seemed to me as though they were really interested.

> In February 1963, the Stake President called and told me that I should prepare to go to April General Conference of the Church in Salt Lake City. I had told him on a number of occasions that I intended to sell the farm and did not altogether feel justified in making the trip because I might not be a bishop for very much longer. However, this did not seem to worry him unduly and so the necessary preparations were made. Jill came with me and the children went to various friends and family. Not too long before we left, an agent brought a Mr. Ward to the farm. As soon as I met him, I became convinced that he was the man who would purchase the property. This was unmistakably the prompting of the Spirit. I was so confident in that feeling that before leaving, I gave the necessary power-of-attorney to my solicitor in order that the sale might proceed in my absence … While in Salt Lake City, I received a cable from the solicitor to say the farm had been sold unconditionally to Mr. Ward.[14]

There was a tremendous amount of work involved in the transition of the property to the new owners as well as the packing up of fifteen years of the accumulation of married life. They were so busy with arrangements that they didn't have time to feel too melancholy.

> We left the farm with mixed feelings. It had been a happy and choice experience. For some of the best years of our lives, we had known happiness and sorrow. Responsible decisions had been made which were to affect our whole future. We had made many friends and left no enemies. The farm was in good heart and represented many years of hard toil and constructive thinking. It was like reading a book and coming to the end of the chapter. A new one was beginning for us.[15]

New Beginnings

Of their new life, Ken wrote:

> I do not believe that I had any real concept of the changes that we would find in our new home. For many years we had been 'masters of our own ship' and this was no longer the case. We were all particularly busy learning a new way of life and carrying out the property programmes together with the new development. The transition to city life as opposed to a rural one, was not particularly easy. We had also settled into a fairly populous ward and there was a great deal of Church growth in the area.
>
> After a few months, I was called to serve in the Auckland Sixth Ward Bishopric. In not too many more months there had been so many new move-ins, particularly from the Islands of the Pacific that the Ward was divided and I was called as Bishop of the Auckland Tenth Ward. The original membership was 450 but within 12 months it grew to more than 950 and a

further division took place. Fifteen months later the Stake was divided with Geoff now the new Stake President, Brian Snow the First Counsellor and myself as the Second Counsellor.[16]

(L–R) Kevin, Ken, Jill, Jennifer, Lynn, Michael, Mark, Brian, Stephanie, 1967.

During this period two more children were added to the family: Stephanie (1965) and Kevin (1967). There were the usual teenage challenges, more trips to Salt Lake for General Conference and training, children leaving for overseas and a wedding. With fewer children left to help on the property, a realistic review suggested that before long changes would need to be made. In 1968 Ken was offered a job at the Church Distribution Centre. Geoff started work in real estate and so thus began the liquidation of the property. When it was sold, Ken and Jill bought a home in Glenfield near the Distribution Centre where he was now the Manager. Not long afterwards he was made Area Manager for the Translation Department throughout the whole of the South Pacific. That added responsibility took him to the States twice a year and around the Pacific Islands and Australia on a regular basis. In 1973 the Auckland Harbour Stake was organised and Ken was called as Stake President.

> The children have always been our joy. Kevin and Stephanie were helping to compensate for the older ones leaving home … No man has been more blessed with his companion than I with Jill. Her loyalty is such that I have always had her sustaining strength. This coupled with her faith have made me richly blessed. Our love has had an eternal quality. As we have grown older, it has strengthened and deepened. I have depended on her so much and never has my trust been misplaced. What has been accomplished in our married life has come about as a partnership. This relationship has extended beyond the children, deep and abiding as that relationship may be. My responsibilities in the Kingdom have only been possible because of her qualities. No man could have had these assignments and carried them through without the loyalty of his companion. In this busy life, so much has been expected and many people have looked to me for guidance and strength that the responsibility has been awesome. The regular visits to Salt Lake have been an integral feature of my responsibilities.[17]

Missions

In his autobiography, Ken recounted the missions that took place over the following years:

> In January of 1975, I receive a long-distance call from President N. Eldon Tanner of the First Presidency of the Church calling me to preside over one of the missions of the Church. This was so unexpected that both of us could scarcely believe the news. On the other hand, we felt honoured and extremely excited. It was tantalizing to think where we might be required to go and of course, we had to keep the information to ourselves. In time we learned that Fiji was our assignment. We left New Zealand on June 14 for Salt Lake City to attend the Mission Presidents' Seminar. Kevin and Stephanie came with us but our third son, Brian, was to stay on at Church College of New Zealand [CCNZ] until the end of the year when it was planned that he should join us in Suva, Fiji. Our other two sons, Mike and Mark, were already serving in their respective missions.
>
> The seminar was a rich and spiritual experience although we had a very close and tight schedule. Each session was conducted by one of the General Authorities. The lunch and evening meals were opportunities to meet with and be instructed by the Brethren. Jill and I had the very rich experience of sitting

Fiji Mission President and Sister Palmer, 1975.

at President Kimball's table. This is an experience we will always cherish.

Mission life was not exactly what I had thought it would be. There was much, much more administration than I had anticipated and a lot of time spent in planning, interviewing and taking care of the immense amount of detail involved. The heat was oppressive and in honesty we could not say that living conditions were ideal. The mission home had no fly screens so we were forced to keep the windows closed at night. Kevin and Stephanie were enrolled at the Latter-day Saints primary school and it was a difficult adjustment for them. The mission covered a huge geographical area with often difficult and primitive travelling arrangements to be made.

By the time we had been in Fiji for some months we were adjusting to our new life and getting a handle on the administration when my health seemed to be deteriorating. I went to a specialist who prescribed pills for angina (chest pain symptomatic of coronary heart disease), which produced a frightful and alarming headache that almost seemed as though my head would burst asunder.

I took my troubles to the Lord, seeking an answer from him as to why a Mission President whose responsibilities were so far flung as mine and demanding much of one's physical resources, should suddenly be stricken with a disease, which very effectively and rapidly could completely incapacitate me. His reply came as a still small voice but so clearly that His words etched themselves upon my mind.

I was told that all through my life and especially since I had joined the Church, I had never really taken much time to listen to what he would have me do. To be sure in the various positions, which I had held from time-to-time, His guidance had been sought in prayer but essentially I had relied mainly on my own resources. He told me that now I had to realize that my life was completely in His hands and from this time on I would need to learn to listen and heed the guidance of the Spirit as I had not done in times past.

A testimony that this was the Lord speaking was to come to me later in the day when He promised me that I would then be visited by two of his choice messengers. After this experience, which was in the early hours of the morning, I fell asleep.

About 5 pm that day, the telephone rang and when I answered it, Bill Roberts [Regional Representative for the Quorum of the Twelve Apostles of the Church of Jesus Christ of Latter-day Saints] replied. He and Elder Robert L. Simpson [Pacific Area Supervisor and Assistant to the Quorum of the Twelve] were passing through Nandi on the way back from Samoa to New Zealand. I could hardly speak for the lump in my throat as this testimony from the Lord was made manifest to me. Of all the men in the Church, there are none for whom I have a greater personal regard than these two and they would be the ones whom I would choose to have help me in a time of crisis.

I briefly related the situation. They kindly offered to come over but I felt that this was not necessary. Arrangements were made that I visit Auckland early in January to get competent medical guidance from a specialist there, which I did. Unfortunately his diagnosis and treatment were faulty and I was in much worse condition than he indicated.

Elder Russell M. Nelson, a heart surgeon and General President of the Sunday School of the Church of Jesus Christ of Latter-day Saints at that time, was accompanying the General Authorities as they presided over the Area conferences scheduled for the South Pacific in February. Elder Simpson arranged for Elder Nelson to examine me at that time. Bill Roberts and Elder Simpson gave me a beautiful, special blessing. Elder Simpson pleaded with the Lord that as during past years I had been able to help other people, now in my hour of need, would the Lord be mindful of me. Bill was then voice and invoked the blessings of the Lord upon me even to that end that I would be completely healed and restored to normal health. How deeply grateful I am to these choice men for their faith. In the weeks that lay ahead as my condition rapidly deteriorated, I drew strength from the promises made by them on my behalf.

The Church Area Conference was scheduled for 23 February 1976. In late January I made a visit to the atoll Tarawa in Kiribati. This was a gruelling experience because of my extreme fatigue together with the knowledge that both Jill and I shared that a major heart attack was very possible. The final preparations for the Conference were very demanding with many details to be finalized. Our committee was valiant and I will always be grateful for their help.

Early February I got up one morning and felt the prompting of the Spirit and I knew that unless a miracle occurred my time was short. The Lord indicated that I had about two months left. As we neared Area conference it was becoming increasingly difficult to keep going. No one in the mission except Jill and the office couple knew that anything was amiss and I was determined to keep it that way in the interests of missionary morale.

On the evening of Area conference, Jill and I met with Elder Nelson. It was a choice experience. He is one of the Lord's special spirits and radiates serenity, spirituality and a large measure of everyday common sense combined with a tremendous vitality and inner power. His diagnosis took about 10 seconds and as he completed it, he matter-of-factly said that the heart was in crescendo and completely unstable. I needed to get to New Zealand immediately for heart surgery. I felt a deep sense of peace and knew that a choice and worthy servant of the Lord had exercised his Priesthood on my behalf.

I knew it would be very difficult to get immediate attention in Auckland, which proved to be the case. As a consequence, Elder Nelson performed double by-pass heart surgery on me, 17 March 1976 at the Latter-day Saint Hospital in Salt Lake City, Utah. Six days after the operation I was released from the hospital to begin convalescence at our daughters' homes who just happened to be living in Salt Lake at the time. Five weeks later I was back in Fiji on light duties in the Mission. We were greatly touched by the prayers and fasting of many on my behalf: members of our Stake, together with our missionaries and loved family members who all joined in their supplications to the Lord for my recovery.

This has been a testing period but one in which the power of the Priesthood has been made manifest and the unmistakable hand of the Lord in a very real way, has been evident in our personal affairs. I am truly grateful for the preservation of my life and the associated experiences.[18]

Not very long after arriving in Fiji, I had a very vivid dream. I found myself in a room, which was fairly large and in some way partitioned privately. There were some other men present. I do not know who they were and their presence was of no significance. In a very remarkable way, Church President Spencer W. Kimball was present and very close to me. I was also aware that close by was a lovely young woman whom I felt certain was Ann, our daughter whom we lost when she was 18 months of age.

I am not aware that any words were spoken but there was a feeling of almost indescribable joy and I felt as though the cares and troubles that are our normal lot, were quite alien to this occasion. Never have I been aware of such inner peace and serenity and so joyous was the experience that I felt a loss when the dream ended. It was as though for a brief moment I had tasted the blissful state of that world which lies beyond the veil.

Naturally I pondered the meaning of this vision but when I discussed it with Jill we could not at that time see its significance. The meaning of the dream became clearer to me as I went through the heart experience I have just described. Throughout his life, the prophet President Kimball has had many experiences that would have defeated a lesser man. Through his faith in the Lord and also because of his courage, he overcame them and prepared himself for the great calling the Lord had in mind for him. Through his example of courage

I gained great comfort and strength. On the corner of my desk I had a small photo of him and immediately on the wall opposite was his formal portrait together with those of his two counsellors. As I came to know increasing daily fatigue and distress his example gave me the courage to carry on.

President Kimball came to visit me in the hospital just before my surgery. There were two or three other men in the adjacent beds. Although I did not see her, I felt the presence of Ann and I knew that she was deeply concerned for me. President Kimball stayed with me for a few minutes and the same almost indescribable feeling of joy and serenity and peace with freedom from all earthly care came over me just as it had so many months earlier in the dream. Thus I have a very personal testimony that President Kimball is a prophet of the Lord.

Although I desired to live to fulfil the stewardships the Lord has for me, I knew that the veil for a brief time, had been very thin. With the joy and bliss of that other and eternal life made so real, why should I have any real fear of that experience which we call death.[19]

My health continued to improve as we continued to serve in the mission field. The average number of missionaries was 45 and yet we managed 463 baptisms in 1978, which was an impressive growth rate. I met with the Governor General, Ratu Sir George Cakobau, on a number of occasions in his official capacity. He came to the official opening of a beautiful bure constructed at the recently completed Church school. This was a memorable and important day in the history of the Church of Jesus Christ of Latter-day Saints in Fiji. It really marked the beginning of the Church's official recognition from the highest authority in the land. An immediate consequence of considerable importance was a request from Ratu Luke, the editor of the Fijian language newspaper, to contribute articles on the teachings of the Church – an assignment I decided to take. As this paper was read by at least 60,000 Fijians, the missionary impact was of great significance.

The last few months sped by rapidly. Each of us in our own way had grown. Our final visits to different parts of the mission were poignant occasions for us. As loved ones came and embraced us, our tears mingled with theirs and with the hauntingly lovely words of 'Isa Lei', we bade them farewell. On our final trip to the airport we were silent with our own thoughts as we drove through the small settlements and gazed upon the trees with their verdant foliage and bright flowers. The thin and slight Indians and especially the children, the languor of the heat, the slow-moving oxen, and the wide and sluggish Rewa River with its fine bridge that men were forever painting – all these images crowded memories in upon us.

In retrospect, there are certain things that one is able to do in an allotted period of time and to expand or extend becomes more than one is capable of doing. Always one is working with people and there is a danger of impatience when the programmes do not function or people do not conform to the standards we have set. Over all, I learned that people are so much more important than programmes.

Within 3 hours we were home in New Zealand. Home perhaps, but where is home? After a week or two I returned to the office to find a different world and organization to that which I had left. To come from the high tempo of the mission experience to the tedium of a job that was not really a job was an extremely difficult adjustment. A month later President N. Eldon Tanner [First Counsellor in the First Presidency of the Church] called me to serve as a Regional Representative, a Church position that included the preparation of a welfare master plan for New Zealand. This gave me new impetus and fresh challenges. When you have had great experiences and possess a fund of understanding, there is a need to be able to focus these into useful channels. For a time I was the temporary Regional Manager of the Temporal Administration of the Church in the South Pacific while the Department was being restructured. By 1982 the restructuring was completed and so I decided to try work in real estate, which I found satisfying and rewarding. I retired from professional life in 1983 but did not intend to stagnate. I was busy with long delayed and deferred projects around the house. We were also busy with family weddings and grandchildren, extended family reunions and travelling to visit overseas family.

Ken and Jill Palmer in Hawaii for a Distribution Center Conference circa 1980.

In 1985 we were called to preside over the Mission Training Centre at Temple View, Hamilton. This was another major upheaval in our lives. We had just one month to get our affairs in order and depart our comfortable home for a tiny apartment in the lee of Temple Hill. We settled into the routine of missionary life once again but found that we were working 70–80 hours a week. Understandably we felt tired. We were grateful to be able to receive most informative training at the Provo Mission Training Centre (MTC), in Utah at the end of the year when we had some downtime over the school holidays.

The MTC mission ended in January 1988. It was extremely demanding and physically taxing but we were grateful to be able to serve.[20]

On the morning of 12 November 1988 at the age of seventy, Kenneth Molony Palmer's heart finally failed him and he died of a heart attack at his home in Auckland. One of his big retirement projects was to finish his history and it is that record that is mostly drawn from for this chapter.

Legacy

For thirty years Ken, with Jill at his side, was focused on missionary work on both sides of the veil. Despite their busy lives, and without the benefit of modern technology, they submitted thousands of names to the temple in order that departed ancestors might also enjoy the blessings of the Gospel. The influence that ripples from their missions in New Zealand and to those living in other areas of the South Pacific is incalculable. That missionary legacy has been passed on to their descendants as well. They, along with their children and spouses, grandchildren and great-grandchildren have served, as of 2019, in forty missions all over the world.

When in her teens Jenny remembers going home from Church meetings one Sunday and in a misguided moment, announcing that she had just been to the most boring Sacrament meeting ever. Ken took her aside, looked her in the eye and said, 'Jenny you have a responsibility to contribute to the spirit of the meeting. You are only going to get out of something to the extent that you put in.' It's a lesson that has stayed with Jenny for over fifty years and reflects the way Ken lived his life. He gave 100 percent and more to whatever assignment was entrusted to him. He was known for his humility, patience and tremendous ability to get along with others. As a consequence, he was loved and respected by all who knew him. He also had an ability to analyse challenges and to make wise decisions for the good of those involved individually and for the Church as a whole.

Elder Glen L. Rudd (Counsellor in the Pacific Area Presidency) said of him:

> Ken was my friend. He was more than an ordinary friend. When I discovered we were born on exactly the same day and year, I had no problem in feeling

he was my own twin brother ... He was loved and honoured and respected by all the General Authorities and those of us who knew him well, knew that he was one who could be trusted and counted on under any circumstances. In all of the positions he held, particularly Bishop, Stake President, Regional Representative, Mission President, MTC President, Ken did outstanding work. He did not need to be checked on, he was given a job and he did it.[21]

Ken and Jill have worn out their lives in service to the God they came to know and trust. It is a story of challenges met and overcome, love of family, heartache and a desire for all to know the joy and the assurance of eternal life – until we meet again beyond that veil of tears.

From the foreword of his unpublished autobiography:[22]

To our children and grandchildren,

Dad had a great desire to complete his history. Many a night he sat writing this record until the early hours. I am grateful we are now able to refer to and learn from his experiences. How blessed we are to have the example of dedicated service, humility and the strength of character and fortitude he left for us. I thank the Lord for the privilege and blessing of 40 years together in mortality and the promise of life eternal with His choice servant, my beloved Ken.

His life was a life of preparation for his service to others. I love him with a love beyond this world. My prayer is that as family members we will strive to love one another and follow the guidance of our prophet and Church leaders. In this way, we will enjoy true happiness and peace of mind in our lifetime. And by righteously enduring to the end, we can be with him eternally. May we always keep the eternal perspective foremost in our lives.

Love, Jill Palmer (née Garlick) 1992

NOTES

1. Jennifer Beth Roberts (née Palmer) is the daughter of Kenneth Palmer
2. Palmer, Kenneth Molony (1992) *An Autobiography*, unpublished family record, p 2
3. *Ibid.*
4. Statement issued in place of Michael Savage, who was recovering from illness. Ministry for Culture and Heritage (n.d.) 'New Zealand Declares War on Germany'. Retrieved from https://nzhistory.govt.nz/new-zealand-declares-war-on-germany
5. Palmer, p 7
6. *Ibid.*, p 23
7. *Ibid.*
8. *Ibid.*, p 26
9. *Ibid.*, pp 30–31
10. *Doctrine & Covenants,* 11: 21, The Church of Jesus Christ of Latter-day Saints, Utah
11. Palmer, pp 32–33

12. *Ibid.*, p 35–36
13. *Ibid.*, p 44
14. *Ibid.*, p 47
15. *Ibid.*, p 48
16. *Ibid.*, p 53
17. *Ibid.*, p 58
18. Palmer, Kenneth and Jill (n.d.) *Faith Promoting Experiences*, Unpublished Family Record, p 4–6
19. *Ibid.*, p 8
20. Palmer, p 93
21. Rudd, Glen (1988), letter to Jill Palmer
22. Palmer, Foreword

REFERENCES

Doctrine & Covenants, 11: 21, The Church of Jesus Christ of Latter-day Saints, Utah

Ministry for Culture and Heritage (n.d.) 'New Zealand Declares War on Germany'. Retrieved from https://nzhistory.govt.nz/new-zealand-declares-war-on-germany

Palmer, Kenneth Molony (1992) *An Autobiography*, Unpublished Family Record

Palmer, Kenneth and Jill (n.d.) *Faith Promoting Experiences*, Unpublished Family Record

Rudd, Glen (1988) letter to Jill Palmer

VIII

A Record of Service

NITAMA PAEWAI (1920–90)

Api Te Rina Paewai[1]

Nitama Manahi Paewai, of Rangitāne o Tāmaki Nui a Rua and Ngāti Kahungunu, was christened Manahi after his paternal great-grandfather, a leader of Te Kotahitanga in Hawke's Bay, and Nitama after James Needham Lambert, mission president of the Church of Jesus Christ of Latter-day Saints (1916–20). To some he was known as 'Doc', to others as Nahi, while family called him Nitama.

> There are people in New Zealand whose records of service to the community at large and to the Maori race in particular equal that of Dr Manahi Nitama Paewai. There have been people in the past whose service exceeds that which he has up until now given. But of the first, there can be no more than a dozen or so. And of the second, even less – and they are looked at in the light of the accomplishments of lifetimes.[2]

Manahi Nitama Paewai was born 8 June 1920 before the Great Depression in 1929, which persisted through to 1941. In 1939, aged eighteen years,

Nitama entered the University of Otago in Dunedin. This was the year New Zealand, along with Canada, Australia and South Africa, rallied in support of France and Britain's decision to declare war on Germany, in response to Germany's invasion of Poland. Nitama's early years, framed by the economic and social disruption of the Great Depression and the global devastation of World War Two, provided a milieu of opposition that helped mould his resilient personality and a character forged by years of difficulty into one fixed and determined to achieve regardless of any desperate circumstances. With such resilience, Nitama would develop an uncanny ability to whistle through and smile at any challenge that beset him, treating the experience as if it were an opportunity to harness and hone his prowess – all undertaken with a very impressive grin.

Apikara Walker Paewai

Nitama was born on the ancestral lands of his father Nireaha (Niki) Paewai of Ngāti Rangiwhakaewa hapu, Rangitane Iwi, Makirikiri, Dannevirke. He was the fourth child born to Nireaha Paewai and Apikara Paewai (née Walker) and a loving, devoted half-brother to a further nine siblings born to Nireaha Paewai and his second wife Mavis Paewai (née Barclay).

Nitama's mother, Apikara (Api) daughter of William Walker and Kararaina Hineato Whaanga, was born 28 February 1895 in Nūhaka, northern Hawke's Bay. Apikara was of the Ngāti Rakaipaaka hapu of Ngāti Kahungunu. A member of the Church of Jesus Christ of Latter-day Saints (the Church), Apikara was baptised 21 March 1910, and confirmed a member of the Church the same day. Her father, William, was accidentally killed while playing football leaving Apikara a babe of just two years and five months old with no recollection of her father. She writes, 'I believed by instinct he lived within my heart always.'[3]

As was the custom, Apikara's tipuna (and her mother's relatives) Te Teira Te Oriki and his wife Here Waimanuka from Nuhaka helped raise Apikara and her twelve-month-old baby brother Jim to give their mother a chance to recuperate after their father's death. Te Teira was a horse breaker, besides having odd jobs on neighbouring farms, and a shearer. Being raised by her mother's relatives in Nūhaka, Apikara always maintained close ties with her mother, Kararaina, whose lessons were well remembered:

> When I am with my mother, it is not so happy for me. Too much indoors, washing dishes, making up the boys' beds before I go to school, scrubbing floors, cupboards at weekends, ironing the boys' shirts, oh so many small

things to do inside. Sometimes I ran out, jumped on Rainbow's back (one of the Shetland ponies) without saddle and bridle and chase the boys getting the milking cows from the hills. Although I am grateful to my mother, for she taught me a lesson and stayed with me all my life. For instance, our beds were kapok mattresses. I would straighten the blankets, sheets, quilts and pillows, but the hollow in the middle of the beds was still there. Mother would pull everything off the beds and quietly tell me to go and make the beds again. I dare not say, they are already made, for I knew the mattresses were not turned over. I learned the lesson then, do the job properly from the beginning. It saves time and unnecessary work. My dear mother had clean habits, good principles, the same every day. A wonderful cook, especially rhubarb pie, and apple pie, are my favourites. She cooks for weddings and bakes and decorates wedding cakes. Mother was marvellous to me, she had no education. We both rode horses in Nuhaka and Wairoa shows. On one occasion, out of the blue without any arrangement and practice, Tawa Maru of Mahia drove up with his flash gig and horse and said, 'Api, jump in and drive this gig in the Ladies Competition.' You had to knock the pegs by the wheel, the fastest time and most pegs knocked down won the prize. 'Sure,' I said. To my joy the horse and I won. A good eye, a good intelligent horse sensing the guidance of the reins, we could not go wrong. The pegs were placed zigzag on the track and the good horse and driver won.[4]

Nitama and his mother, Apikara.

Apikara met Nireaha (Niki) Paewai, a member of a well-known and widely respected Māori family of Dannevirke, when he was a student at the Māori Agricultural College, Korongota, in Hastings. Nireaha was of the Ngāti Rangiwhakaewa hapū of Rangitāne. They were engaged for twelve months, and married on 2 December 1916 at the Registry Office in Hastings. Moving to Dannevirke, Nireaha started working on his mother's farm, which became his life's work. Apikara and Nireaha had six children: Rachel, Pearl and Alice (twins), Manahi Nitama, and they lost two babies.

Whakapapa (Genealogy)

The Young Nitama

Nitama's early childhood was based around family, faith and farming in Dannevirke. In an interview with Dorothy Bowie,[5] Nitama expressed how he was very grateful that his parents were strong Church members who set high standards, as this had always been a large influence in his life.

In 1978, the Governor General Sir Keith Holyoake presented the Ahuwhenua Award to Nitama's brothers, Ringa, Punga and Hepa Paewai. He said they were known 'as good farmers, good shearers, good rugby players, in fact damn good Kiwis.'⁶ The Paewai brothers won the Ahuwhenua Trophy twice – the Māori farmer of the Year Award. Nitama's father, Nireaha, was an accomplished rugby player, and Nitama's uncle, Lui Paewai, represented New Zealand.

Nitama was only five years old when, in 1925, Apikara and Nireaha were called to Hawaii for three months to do work for the Church. In 1926 Nireaha received a government scholarship to study overseas. Nireaha chose to study at Utah State Agricultural College, in Logan, Utah. Nitama attended the Woodruff School in Logan City and was baptised in on 12 June 1928. In 1929 Nireaha completed his studies and received a Bachelor of Science degree in Agriculture. Few Māori had earned university degrees overseas at the time. They returned home to a royal welcome. Apikara recounted:

> We came home in June and brought the latest car (then, a Hudson Coach). It was good looking, rode smoothly and was comfortable. When we arrived in Dannevirke, all relatives of my husband welcomed us at the Marae, Aotea House, Tahoraiti. With tangi's (weeping) of joy at our return and tangi's (weeping) for those who passed on while we were away three years. My mother-in-law was one of them. She died just before we came home.⁷

Nitama continued his primary schooling at the Dannevirke South Primary School, and then from 1934 at Dannevirke High School, where he excelled at public speaking and sports (athletics, cricket, boxing, rugby), becoming head boy in 1938.

In 1934, when Nitama was fourteen his parents divorced. However, Nitama maintained a devoted relationship with his father and the second family that would ensue. Children of the first marriage remained in the custody of Apikara, who would go on to become a solo Māori mother throughout the Great Depression years, raising Nitama and his siblings in a very disciplined and dedicated Mormon home.

Concerned with Nitama's education, Apikara wrote:

> One day Mr Tait, the Principal sent for me. He counselled with me of Nitama's education. He said 'Nitama is a brilliant student, see that he gets to Varsity.' He asked if I had any means to keep him at school. I said, 'No. But I can work and earn the money.' He told me when Nitama is ready for Varsity, to apply for a Maori Scholarship. I thanked him and appreciated all that he had said, giving me thought and visions for the future to manage and plan for Nitama's education. Mr Tait left the following year for Oamaru High School. Again, I felt grateful to him for his interest in my boy. Mr Hogben replaced Mr Tait as Principal of Dannevirke High School. He treated Nitama the same as Mr Tait. He called me to his office. 'Mrs Paewai, I understand and know the story of why Nitama is not

playing football. I have already questioned him. The boy has to use his energy. Do you prefer him looking elsewhere to use it, say down the side streets with friends?' 'Mr Hogben, please, you won, but I hope he will not get killed like my father.' When Nitama passed his metric exams, Mr Hogben asked him what he would study at Varsity. He said 'My mother wants me to be a dentist.' Mr Hogben called me again to his office. 'Well, Mrs Paewai, why do you want Nitama to be a dentist?' 'Quick money,' I told him. 'It takes four years to be a dentist, six years to be a doctor, more if he fails in some of the subjects and I have to work more years to help finance him.' Mr Hogben explained his views that Nitama had plenty of reserve, when you push him he gives more so I suggested he take medicine, he can make it. Mr Hogben won again and no regrets.[8]

Apikara's mother Kararaina had worked hard to raise her children as best she could, and to ensure they received a good education. Apikara aspired to do the same. She supported Nitama at Otago University by working as a cook in hotels and for shearing gangs. She also catered for weddings and similar events. The people of Dannevirke were very supportive. Apikara said 'they would come and shake hands and ask how the boy was getting on at school. It's worth a million bucks to me for their interest in the boy.'[9]

The fiscal restraints Apikara experienced raising her children had an impact on Nitama later in life. His mother received a small allowance for herself from his father's estate. Raising a family on this amount was not an easy task, especially during the Depression. 'It was this stringent upbringing which enabled Nitama to survive on little or nothing at University and which convinced him that it is not important for children to receive a lot of clothes and money to be happy. Rather, it is more important for them to be able to survive on little when necessary and to be financially aware.'[10]

Medical School

Nitama would take with him to the University of Otago an imposing record of athletic, scholastic and extramural achievements attained during his years at Dannevirke High School.

> Head Prefect of Dannevirke High; Awarded Certificates of Merit in Physics, Mathematics, French and Woodwork; Awarded Higher Learning Certificate and Maori Boys Scholarship from NZ Education Department; Winner of Senior Essay Competitions; Winner of the Rotary Cadet Company for two years; Winner of the William Robert Friar Memorial Award given to the most efficient Non Commissioner Officer in the Central Command of New Zealand; four years member of Dannevirke High Rugby and Cricket Teams; Captain of 1st XV Rugby Team; Boxing Champion for two years and winner of MacMillan Award.[11]

In 1939 Nitama and his cousin Luxford Walker began their studies at Otago University in Dunedin, enrolling in intermediate science. Nitama was studying to be a medical doctor and Luxford a dentist. The prominent Māori medical doctor, Sir Peter Buck (Te Rangi Hiroa), was among the many exemplary individuals that Nitama would endeavour to emulate.

Home for the holidays, both Nitama and Luxford attended a conference in their home district at Dannevirke. Also present was Mission President Matthew Cowley. They mentioned to President Cowley that they 'don't get any encouragement from our people. They tell us we are only Maoris. We can't learn anything; they tell us to go out and cut scrub and make some money; so we are not going back.' President Cowley remembered that the principal of Dannevirke High School had earlier confided in him that Nitama wanted to go home for three days to fast and pray prior to sitting his matriculation examination for entrance into a university.[12]

> I knew they were not to leave, so I said, 'Well, if that's the way you feel about it, I am going to call you on a mission and advance you in the priesthood.' After the meeting I went out and put them into a room and ordained each an elder. I set them apart as missionaries in the New Zealand mission. They said, 'Where are we going on this mission?' I said, 'You are going down to the university. When you are not studying medicine and dentistry, you are to preach the gospel every opportunity you get.' They went back. They certainly preached the gospel, and they made a good job out of it because the first year I was invited by the dean of the medical school to come down there and talk to the graduates. It was the first time a Mormon had ever been permitted inside that university.[13]

Nitama recalled:

> Many of my fellow students came to me afterwards and said, they had learnt more from Tumuaki Cowley's talk on an 'Insight to the Maori Mind', in those few minutes than they would probably learn during the rest of their lives. In those few minutes that he was invited to take up, everyone present knew he was a man who knew and loved the Maori people with all of his heart. It made me feel elated and yet humble, for I would never fulfil even half of the qualities of character of the old Maori that he portrayed to his listeners.[14]

While attending the University of Otago in Dunedin, Nitama lived at Knox College, which posed multiple challenges for him as a Latter-day Saint. Regardless, he was determined to study the gospel to find out if the Church was true. By the end of his most challenging year at Varsity, his intermediate year, he had passed his exams and gained a testimony of the truthfulness of the gospel of Jesus Christ. He did have doubts, but without encouragement from Matthew Cowley to study, pray and to find out for himself, he would not have passed both tests.[15]

On one occasion when sacrament meeting in the Dunedin branch had just finished, Tumuaki and Sister Cowley were to catch the late-night train to Christchurch. Nitama was asked to walk with them to their hotel and to see them off at the station later. Just as they were in the middle of the Exchange, Dunedin's traffic centre, Tumuaki took something out of his pocket. 'Here you are, Sue. Not much for a wedding anniversary,' he said. Even though the Exchange was busy with streetcars and people coming out of churches, the feeling of this occasion spread out from this couple even to Nitama. Sister Cowley said she thought he had forgotten, but that she should have known better as he always remembered birthday greetings on the right days to all of his missionaries. She went on to tell Nitama as they walked along never to forget wife and family when the time comes. She related how Tumuaki, no matter how occupied with business matters, always practised having at least one night a week with his family.[16]

In 1944 Nitama moved from Dunedin to Auckland to complete his medical internship at Auckland Hospital, living with his mentor, Mission President Cowley. In 1945, he graduated from Otago University with his medical degree.

Sport

During Nitama's studies in Dunedin, he established himself as a gifted rugby player – tough, courageous and intelligent – attributes that were to distinguish him as a class player. It was in Dunedin that his first-class representative rugby career began. Many people claim him as being in the first half-dozen best half-backs New Zealand has ever produced; a few say he was the best of them all.[17]

Nitama played representative rugby for Otago and New Zealand Universities in 1941, the Army South Island team in 1942, the South Island team in 1943 and on several occasions played for Auckland 1944–45.

In 1946, after completing his internship, Nitama moved to Wellington, where he represented Wellington, played for the North Island, the New Zealand Māori side, the New Zealand Army and was named as a reserve in the New Zealand Rugby team (All Blacks) that played against Australia. All Black captain Fred Allen of the 1946 team said, 'it was a tragedy, if ever a fellow deserved to have represented New Zealand it was Doc Paewai, he was a wonderful player.'[18] In later years Nitama moved into rugby administration at both the local and national levels. In 1949 Nitama was ineligible for the All Black tour of South Africa, as South Africans would not accept Māori in the touring team.[19]

Church Service

From 1939 to 1943, while at Otago University, Nitama served as a counsellor in the Dunedin Branch Presidency. While in Auckland as an intern,

Nitama Paewai was awarded the Tom French Cup (right) for the best Māori player of the year 1946. The cup on the left is the Prince of Wales Cup.

Nitama recorded some of his experiences ministering with mission president Matthew Cowley.[20]

> February 13, 1944
> Tumuaki Cowley took me with him to administer to Sister Williams at Green Lane Hospital. She was in a wheelchair on a balcony with other patients. In order to have semi-privacy, we moved along to one end of the balcony. Even with the help of a screen, we could be partly observed by the other patients or by anyone who might be passing along the street out front and by people in other wards or adjoining buildings. I was very self-conscious of this. In performing the anointing, it seemed that I had a heavy burden and although short in words the prayer seemed a long one. But when Tumuaki sealed and confirmed the anointing, a different spirit came upon me. Still aware of our surroundings it no longer bothered me. I shall always remember how soothing was Tumuaki's voice. His words were simple and yet eloquent while his blessing was pronounced as sure promises with quiet confidence. It did not matter anymore how long this was to last. I wished I could go on listening to such a prayer. On our way home, he talked to me about human nature and how to get on with people. 'Do not judge or criticize harshly, be tolerant of other's faults, do not let their faults get you down,' he told me.

March 11, 1944

    Once again, I headed for another Hui Pariha [regional hui] with Tumuaki. On pulling up to the Marae in Utakura [Northland] I was surprised not to hear the usual mihi. Tumuaki said the custom in this village was different from most other parts of New Zealand. As we approached the Hui house, to take our seats, Tumuaki led the way with a stick in hand and his dark sunglasses and hat on. He took everyone by surprise when about forty paces from our seats he broke into an old Maori chant. His powerful voice must have carried to all parts of the Marae, for everyone came running out from their tents and the dining hall to see what was happening. He did not finish the chant by the time we had all four reached our seats of honour where we stood waiting for him to finish. It was a thrill to look down on that sea of faces as the people gathered to hear him. When he finished we sat down. Tumuaki turned to us with a grin on his face to say, 'You fellows didn't know I could do that, did you?' What a character! My heart, like so many other occasions, went out to this man who was indeed as an older brother to every one of us.

Matthew Cowley was also a mentor to Nitama's cousin, Luxford Walker, who wrote:

One of my greatest mentors was Matthew Cowley, president of the New Zealand Mission. He got me thinking about studying medicine, as he had already done in the case of my cousin Dr M. N. Paewai. So medicine loomed on the distant horizon. Later, Matthew Cowley said: 'You've already got one member of the family doing medicine, why don't you study dentistry.' Fortunately, in those days so few Maoris attended a university that I was able to get a Maori scholarship. In my first year at Otago University, there were about 120 students in one of our classes and only two of us were Maoris. I graduated as the first Maori Bachelor of Dental Surgery (BDS). Great credit, and a crown of achievement to Dannevirke High School that two of their relatively few Maori students at that time should go on to Otago university and graduate, Manahi Nitama Paewai in medicine, and I, Luxford Walker, in dentistry.[21]

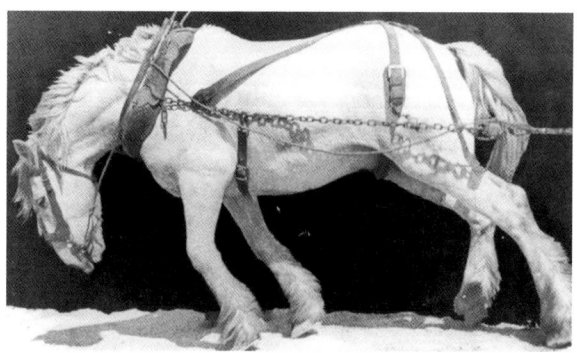

Tumuaki Cowley was like an older brother and one of the most influential characters in Nitama's life. The symbol that epitomised Nitama and Cowley's work ethic and philosophy on life is the picture of the workhorse.

The original photograph was taken in New Zealand when Matthew Cowley was a young missionary in the early 1900s. He displayed this photograph in his office when he was serving as an Apostle. It is a workhorse with its head down. The workhorse has received his instructions and he is pulling with all the strength that he can, as shown by the chain that connects him to whatever he is pulling. All four feet are off the ground. He is digging in and doing what he has been told to do. Whoever is behind him has let the reins drop a little because the horse no longer needs help from his owner. You can see that by the reins hanging just below the chain. This horse represents 'hard labour' and is doing exactly what he has been told to do.[22]

Doctor Paewai outside his surgery in Kaikohe.

In 1947 Nitama settled in Kaikohe. He contributed in many ways to the growth of the Church there. Taoko and Frances Wihongi recollect the following:

> One Sunday morning being told that Doc would be around to collect us for church. Sunday morning we remember hearing firm foot-steps drawing closer to the front door. Doc appears. I, Frances, greet him and return with him to his car. Taoko remains inside the house. Minutes later Doc bounds back up the stairs along the veranda and ka-boom! He kicks open the front door and

addressing Taoko says, 'don't you want to be with your family in the eternities!?' Taoko relents and joins them in the car.[23]

Taoko appreciated Doc and the impact he had on him and his family. The gospel is alive in their lives and they are thriving because of Doc. Their son-in-law is a stake president, their children have married in the temple and they have had grandchildren serve missions for the Church.

Nitama and Hineapa Paewai – church missionaries to Asia, 1985.

Nitama's service to the community was particularly evident in his commitment to the Church of Jesus Christ of Latter-day Saints. In his lifetime, Nitama held many local and regional Church leadership positions commensurate with his obvious expertise and knowledge of Church governance and administration. A highlight of Nitama and Hineapa's lives was serving an eighteen-month mission in Asia fellowshipping and supporting Church members in Singapore, Malaysia and India. At home, Nitama provided much-needed leadership advice and guidance during the watershed period of the development of the Church, as leadership shifted from American missionaries to Māori, then to European 'executive leaders' from the late 1950s. As a member of the Church College of New Zealand's Advisory Committee he was instrumental in ensuring the secondary school achieved high standards of scholastic excellence on a par with the best in the country.

Family Service

On 2 February 1949 Nitama married Hineapa Meha, from Waipawa, Hawke's Bay. Hineapa was born on 10 October 1925, and her parents were Stuart Meha and his third wife, Ivory Te Pora Morris. Stuart Meha was one of the great pioneers of the Church in New Zealand – 'leaving his family to serve missions without purse or scrip, preaching the Gospel and helping to establish Zion by gathering whakapapa and performing scared ordinances in the House of the Lord.'[24]

Top (L–R): William Walker; Kararaina Whaanga Walker.
Bottom (L–R): Wedding of Nitama and Hineapa, 2 February 1949; Apikara Paewai.

Nitama had known Hine's family for a long time before they married. Her second eldest brother was a neighbour at Makirikiri. When it came to making a choice, he considered among other things, her Church background as well as her capabilities. They considered that as both had come from large families they could enjoy and endure a large family.

Nitama and Hineapa had five daughters and three sons. Over the years Hineapa supported and encouraged her husband in his wide-ranging pursuits including his medical career, Church leadership positions and community service.

Nitama and Hineapa's family at Manahi and Martha's (née Fruean) wedding, 1993.
Front row (L–R): Nitama Cowley, Hineapa, Nahi Smith, Kareeve Witehira, Bree Hetariki, Niki Smith, Kurei Smith.
Back row (L–R): Brian Smith, Frank Witehira, Kamilla (baby), Manahi, Martha, Api Terina, Huiarangi, Ena, Noel, Alma, Kara Witehira.

Community Service

Nitama opened a medical practice in Kaikohe in 1947. His obvious interest in health brought him into close contact with the people with whom he lived and worked. From that point on he was known affectionately as 'Doc'.

> A number of Doc's patients were unable to pay him or could pay him only in food, but that didn't discourage him from treating them. Doc made it a policy never to accept payment from missionaries or others who served in the Church. He was a man 'whose pockets were light' but whose 'heart was full', a local newspaper once reported. A friend who served with Doc during his 18 years on the Kaikohe Borough Council remembered how Doc would stop to make sure his patients were alright if he noticed their lights on late at night.[25]

Nitama was the first Māori doctor who was a Mormon and he was committed to being as effective as he could. There were high expectations on him from others to be an expert with a Māori patient, and to be culturally and clinically competent with an emphasis on strong Christian values. In addition, it was expected that he would take on professional roles, serve on boards, take leading roles in health programmes and provide the latest information and health education initiatives. Building relationships was a strength of Nitama's. Giving back to the community and being a role model and leader to everyone was a high expectation, received with interest.

Having the interests of the community uppermost in his mind, Doc Paewai was loved by many. The Wihongi family are one such family appreciative of his service, reciprocated in the following way:

> He served as our family medical doctor to four generations in Awarua, 15 kilometres south of Kaikohe. He was always around home when I was growing up but a very busy person. Two things I remember was first his verbal appreciation for my mother's cooking. He always arrived whistling and hungry and my mother fed him well. Second was chopping wood in the bush at the back of our house to keep fit and provide firewood for his home and family in Kaikohe. This was a form of exercise he enjoyed.[26]

Nitama was a member of many organisations in the community. From 1947 to 1961 he was a divisional surgeon of the St John's Ambulance Brigade at Kaikohe. In 1966 he was awarded the Knight of Grace of the Order of St John for recognition of fourteen years of service as divisional surgeon for the St John's Ambulance Brigade. The case of the intellectually disabled child was always close to his heart. From 1960 to 1962 he was a member of the Northland special school committee for intellectually handicapped children. His service extended to membership of the influential New Zealand Māori Health Committee. Nitama was widely recognised as an important practitioner of public health policies by a doctor within the Māori community.[27]

In 1947, Nitama requested and was granted (in 1952) the import of a film projector to educate his local community on matters pertaining to social welfare and hygiene. By showing groups a film on the administration of local anaesthetic in operations he was able to demystify surgical operations and in so doing helped educate his patients on the importance of hygiene and preventative medicine.[28]

For eighteen years he served on the Kaikohe Borough Council. Nitama was also elected mayor of Kaikohe. Hineapa never shirked from her community responsibilities, particularly as the mayor's wife. 'During her time as Mayoress, she asked various women's groups in Kaikohe and beyond to contribute a signed square to a friendship quilt. Many of the groups responded, and the large quilt which has the Kaikohe Council Crest as its central square hangs in the Kaikohe Museum today.'[29]

Nitama played an active role in Rotary as a director, vice-president and president. He was also active in the Scouting Association and was presented with the Award of Merit for his work as a Scout Area Chaplain. In education he was on the Board of Governors of Northland College. In the 1967 New Year's honours he was appointed an Officer of the Order of the British Empire, for services to the Māori people in the Kaikohe district.

In his biography, first published in the *Dictionary of New Zealand Biography* in 2000, it was noted that Nitama was not afraid of controversy:

> Nitama Paewai once called for the phasing out of Māori rugby and he was a firm supporter of sporting contacts with South Africa. After a visit to the Philippines, he condemned psychic surgery and faith healing. He was critical of the welfare state and of 'handouts' which discouraged work and thrift.[30]

Work and Thrift Ethic

Nitama was a keen advocate for helping people break the cycle of debt. A significant contribution he made to Māori advancement was the Kaikohe Advice and Guidance Society. In 1960 he co-founded the Budget Counselling Scheme, which later spread throughout New Zealand. The Department of Māori Affairs drew upon many of the organisation's key principles for their own welfare policy. Nitama did not consider the scheme a 'handout'; rather it was enlightened self-help and 'a form of practical adult education. We are trying to curtail the expenses of the Maori people, trying to teach them the value of money and the need to stay out of debt.'[31] He ardently believed in work and thrift and that reward and success must be the result of honest effort and determination.

Nitama taught many people in his local community the principles of good budgeting. One such benefactor would record everything he purchased, even if it was a packet of Macintosh's lollies so that he knew fully where he had spent his money. This led to his making better decisions to manage finances and make savings.[32]

Self-reliance was something Nitama strongly encouraged. He had plans at one stage to 'open a small clothing factory in order to ease unemployment in the area', and 'ran a housing scheme.'[33] All were encouraged to buy their own homes, as opposed to renting. Through his scheme, when homes were being built, the prospective homeowners assisted the builders and tradesmen where permitted to help with the labour to reduce costs. He knew that the answer to people having ownership of their own homes was to get them financially stable and have good steady jobs as a source of income. People were prone to be content with their socioeconomic circumstances. Nitama had a vision of what could be if people raised their expectations. A lot of people didn't know where to go to capitalise on finance options from government agencies and Nitama was often called upon for advice and guidance.

Teaching self-reliance was something the wider Paewai family was also known for. In 2001 Nitama's brother Punga Paewai and his wife Josephine served as humanitarian missionaries for the Church of Jesus Christ of Latter-day Saints in Papua New Guinea, promoting self-reliance among that population, many of whom were suffering from high unemployment and 90 percent illiteracy.[34]

Close friend, and fellow local Church leader, William R. Gardner related:

> One of the things that I really appreciated about Doc Paewai was the fact that he was a great 'pointer,' – 'this is what you need to do; here is where you should go.' However, he was not given to carrying people or spoon feeding them, but he definitely showed them the right way to go about doing things, and then the choice was theirs to make. But he knew that if you propped things up for too long, they would collapse when the props were removed. In his twilight years as a GP in Kaikohe I had occasion to visit him for his professional services. In general conversation he related to me how many of the kaumātua and kuia with poor health came seeking his services. Subsequent to their check-up he said he would tell them what medication he was going to prescribe to help them be restored to good health again, only to be told, 'Waihongia te rongoā Pākehā. Homai ki ahau ngā manaakitanga nō te Atua i runga anō i ngā tikanga o tōu Tohungatanga Tapu,' 'Forget about the Pākehā medicine. Just give me a priesthood blessing.'[35]

In the practical field of help to, and vision for, the Māori people, Nitama's life's work pointed to families out of debt, to homes built, to children educated, to bodies healed, to sports administered, to a community served with energy, drive and selflessness. Nitama once said, 'Māori must be taught as the Pākehā has already learnt that he has to work for what he gets.'[36]

Nitama was concerned about young people's aspirations: what they were going to be, and do, in the future, and how they planned to get to where they wanted to go.

> He was a man that had a vision like no other person that I ever knew. I remember in the youth programme that he would bring people to mentor us. One such person was Flight Lieutenant Baden Pere. When Doc brought him to the chapel on the night that we had our scouting programme, our eyes were as 'round as saucers.' (Doc was an avid worker behind the scenes organising bottle collections etc. to raise funds). Baden Pere was flying in active duty on the fighter jets of the time which were the Vampires – but here was a real officer in the Royal NZ Airforce and on top of that, he was Māori. What Doc wanted

us to see was that with hard work, and high educational goals and aspirations that we could achieve anything we wanted to.[37]

An Authentic Leader

Well-known journalist Harry Dansey considered Nitama an authentic Māori leader with an abundance of energy and drive:[38]

> Many Maori professional men and women cannot be leaders of their people except by example. Their work removes them from close contact with the everyday problems and aspirations of the ordinary man. Not so Dr Manahi Nitama Paewai. He is the authentic Maori leader. A man of splendid physique, of bubbling good humour, of strong and compelling features, his work is ennobled by the honesty of his motives, the intensity of his convictions and the force of his moral courage. He is the Happy Warrior and there is no one else quite like him. Our Maori people could do with more cast from the same brave mould. Dedication to ideals lies at the heart of all he does. Astonishing, punishing, even frightening energy and drive is the secret of how he gets it done. An active, inquiring mind always open to suggestion, particularly when it stems from the United States which he knows well and admires, helps him to decide what to do. A morning I spent with him, caring for the sick, admonishing the wayward, encouraging the faint-hearted, arguing with the unconvinced, left me worn out. At one house it was pills and advice, at another, it was a tin of paint and a direct order to put it on the laundry, at a third it was medicine and gentle, even tender, words of comfort, at the next a pane of glass and finger shaken at a broken window. At another place, there was a discussion on educational policy in which his views were put forward with quite devastating bluntness. Then we climbed over a building project where men were working on a co-operative basis, 'you help me build my place and I'll help you with yours'. He left me to attend two meetings, four patients and a wedding. This is the pattern of all his days. He is the slave of his own high ideals and he is his own ruthless slave-driver. He charges at problems of economics, housing, education, health and equality with the same bounce and fire that drove him around a scrum in the good old days

In 1979 Nitama and Hineapa moved their family to Auckland. Nitama joined a medical partnership while commuting to Kaikohe to perform mayoral duties. From 1980 to 1983 he served on the Auckland City Council.

Confiding in a dear friend about life hereafter, he said:

> 'I can't wait to die,' and seeing the startled look on my face, explained, 'I will be able to do so much more in the next life than I can here.' Here he was again, looking far ahead. I have pondered on his words ever since. It still amazes me that he was always looking ahead and wanting to do more.[39]

Manahi Nitama Paewai died 10 October 1990 at Mt Eden, Auckland. His body was returned to Dannevirke and buried at the Kaitoki Māori Cemetery at the feet of his father. On the day of Nitama's unexpected death forty-one years after their marriage began, Doc paid Hineapa a moving tribute when he said, 'I could not have done anything in life without you.'[40] Hineapa lived for another nineteen years.

NOTES

1. Api Te Rina Paewai is the daughter of Nitama Paewai
2. Dansey, Harry (1965) 'Dr M. N. Paewai: A Leader with High Ideals and Astonishing Energy', Te Ao Hou, Wellington
3. Walker Paewai, Apikara (n.d.) Journal
4. *Ibid.*
5. Bowie, D. (n.d.) *Biography of Manahi Nitama Paewai*
6. Taylor, Kevin (22 March 2003) 'Prime Movers Sector Report: Maori Agriculture', *New Zealand Herald*
7. Walker Paewai (n.d.)
8. *Ibid.*
9. *Ibid.*
10. Bowie (n.d.)
11. Paewai, Walker (n.d.)
12. Cowley, Matthew (1954) *Matthew Cowley Speaks*, Deseret Books, Utah, p 281
13. *Ibid.*
14. Paewai, Manahi (2007) Note, Manahi is an uncle of the writer
15. Bowie (n.d.)
16. Paewai (2007)
17. Dansey (1965)
18. Paewai (2007)
19. *Ibid.*
20. *Ibid.*
21. Walker, Luxford, brief from an old pupil of Dannevirke High School
22. Courtesy of Elder Glen L. Rudd
23. Wihongi, Taoko and Frances, personal communication
24. Meha, Arapata (2014) 'Saviour on Mount Zion', in *Turning the Hearts of the Children: Early Māori Leaders in the Mormon Church*, (ed) Selwyn Katene, Steele Roberts Publishers, Wellington
25. *The Ensign* (January 1998) 'Doc's Legacy of Service', The Church of Jesus Christ of Latter-day Saints, Utah
26. Heperi, Patricia (née Wihongi), personal communication
27. *New Zealand Public Health Association Newsletter* (2010)
28. Sampson, Andrew (2017) 'What does it mean to be a Māori doctor? Historical and Contemporary Perspectives', submitted for the degree of Bachelor of Medical Science with Honours, University of Otago, Dunedin, p 38

29. *The Ensign* (January 1998)
30. Paewai, Manahi (2000) 'Paewai, Manahi Nitama', Te Ara – The Encyclopedia of New Zealand. Retrieved from https://teara.govt.nz/en/biographies/5p1/paewai-manahi-nitama
31. Dansey (1965)
32. Wihongi, Waikeri, personal communication
33. Paewai, Manahi (2000)
34. Retrieved from thechurchnews.com/archives/2003-01-18/self-reliance-a-plan-for-papua-new-guinea-104402
35. Gardner, William R., personal communication
36. Dansey (1965); MANU AO (2013) Tihei Mauriora Motivational
37. Gardner, William R., personal communication
38. Dansey (1965)
39. Gardner, William R., personal communication
40. *The Ensign* (January 1998)

REFERENCES

Bowie, Dorothy (n.d.) Biography of Manahi Nitama Paewai

Cowley, Matthew (1954) *Matthew Cowley Speaks*, Deseret Books, Utah

Dansey, Harry (September 1965) 'Dr M. N. Paewai: A Leader with High Ideals and Astonishing Energy', Te Ao Hou, Wellington

The Ensign (January 1998) 'Doc's Legacy of Service', The Church of Jesus Christ of Latter-day Saints, Utah

MANU AO (2013) Tihei Mauriora Motivational

Meha, Arapata, (2014) 'Saviour on Mount Zion', in *Turning the Hearts of the Children: Early Māori Leaders in the Mormon Church*, (ed) Selwyn Katene, Steele Roberts Publishers, Wellington

New Zealand Public Health Association Newsletter, 2010

Paewai, Manahi (2000) 'Paewai, Manahi Nitama', Te Ara – The Encyclopedia of New Zealand. Retrieved from https://teara.govt.nz/en/biographies/5p1/paewai-manahi-nitama

Paewai, Manahi (2007) Journal

Rudd, Glen L. (2005) 'Memories of Matthew Cowley: Man of Faith, Apostle to the Pacific', in Grant Underwood (ed.), *Pioneers in the Pacific*, BYU Provo, Utah

Sampson, Andrew (2017) 'What does it mean to be a Māori doctor? Historical and Contemporary Perspectives', submitted for the degree of Bachelor of Medical Science with Honours, University of Otago, Dunedin

Taylor, Kevin (22 March 2003) 'Prime Movers Sector Report: Maori Agriculture', *New Zealand Herald*

Walker Paewai, Apikara (n.d.) Journal

IX

One Called and Prepared

Geoffrey R. Garlick (1924–2010)

Barry Garlick[1]

The early 1950s was a time of conversion to the Church of Jesus Christ of Latter-day Saints for a few stalwart leaders who later formed the nucleus of Church leadership when the time came for stakes to be created in New Zealand. Among those the Lord led to his Church was Geoffrey R. Garlick. Geoff was born 14 December 1924 in Auckland, New Zealand, the third of four children born to Ada Jeannette Lundius and Stanley Clyde Garlick. The oldest of the children, Joan, died tragically in her infancy. The next oldest, Brian, died in World War Two, leaving Geoff and Jill (Palmer), who both lived to maturity.

Geoff's mother, Ada, was an important influence in his life.

Ada Garlick

Ada Jeannette Lundius was born in Wanganui, New Zealand, on 28 December 1897. She was the second child of Per Emil Henrik Lundius and Matilda Maud Lundon. She spent the first nineteen years of her life living in Wanganui. Her father was a surveyor and Crown Lands Ranger. She described her father as being incapable of small thought or mean actions and one who exuded kindness. Her mother was the daughter of David Lundon, who was the mayor of Tauranga for many years. She was a very intelligent woman who played the piano and sang beautifully. Ada described her as being very difficult and socially ambitious. Ada was more like her father.

Ada attended Wanganui Girls College and described her school days as happy and carefree. She said of her upbringing that she had all that she could wish for in love, security, friends and this world's goods. In 1914 war broke out. Ada spent two-and-a-half years working as a nurse, but contracted scarlet fever during a worldwide epidemic, which brought a stop to her nursing ambitions.

At age twenty Ada met Stanley Clyde Garlick and after twelve months of engagement, they were married on 15 October 1919. Stanley was from a well-to-do family and was raised in a thirty-room home on Khyber Pass Road in Auckland. However, much of the Garlick family wealth was later lost during the worldwide Depression of the 1930s.

Stanley and Ada were blessed with four lovely children. The first, Joan Ellen, and the second, Brian Lundius, were born while the Garlicks were living on their farm in Waipu. Geoff and Jill were both born after the family moved to Auckland in 1924.

Unfortunately, Joan died before her fourth birthday, having suffered with emphysema in both lungs. Ada said that Stanley was so affected by Joan's death that she did not hear him laugh for five years, and that he would not allow the family to celebrate Christmas or birthdays for many, many years. Brian also was taken from them prematurely when he was killed in action at age eighteen as a fighter pilot during World War Two.

While Ada was always religiously inclined, her spiritual life did not take on significant meaning until she had the following experience:

> When living in Rarere Rd, Takapuna, when Jill was a baby, I had the first startling spiritual experience. This was when Stan was indenting and used to be away six weeks at a time. With the three children and the inconvenience suffered as a result of an auto pedestrian accident I was finding things 'on top of me.' I was developing influenza. I had struggled through the day and had tucked the three children into bed, had filled a hot water bottle and crawled

into bed. The hot water bottle burst and soaked the bed. It was the last straw. All I could do was pray to my Heavenly Father to give me strength and the will to carry on. Clearly it came to me in illuminous thought 'Be still and know that I am God. I will never leave thee nor forsake thee.' He never has. Through the many years and many troubles, He has guided and upheld me. There are no words to express my gratitude.[2]

Later, Ada prayed to ask Heavenly Father to reveal to her if there was a work she could do, rather than 'rot out my life in idleness.' Within a short period of time a friend came to her and said, 'I have just been appointed Principal of the Whangarei Girls High School, will you come there with me as matron?' She said, 'I accepted this as answer to my prayers,' but when she asked Stan he protested strongly. However, Heavenly Father softened his heart. He then said, 'I suppose I am being selfish. The children are off our hands and it really does not matter what we do for the rest of our journey here. If I can have privacy I will consent.'[3]

Of the experience in Whangarei she said:

> I wondered why the Lord had guided me to Whangarei. I thought it must be something to do with the Maori people. I discovered that all the maids were Maoris and Mormons and not living by the principles of the gospel. I asked them where I could find their minister.[4]

This led Ada to Elder Christianson, president of the Whangarei district of the New Zealand Mission at that time. Ada told him that she would like to help these maids but that she was a member of the Anglican Church and was not likely to change so he arranged for a missionary couple, Elder and Sister Bigelow, to come once a week. Ada recognised that if she was going to be able to help these girls, she had to show them by attending their evening meetings with the missionaries herself. It only took a few meetings before Ada recognised that what the missionaries were teaching these girls was the truth. However, there were obstacles: her own pride and her husband. Coincidentally, Ada's interactions with the Latter-day Saint (LDS) missionaries were happening at the same time as her son Geoff and his wife April, who were living in Auckland, had also been meeting with the LDS missionaries and had decided to join the Church.

Ada's Conversion

Ada described the following:

> I decided that I must do likewise and approached Stan for permission for baptism. I can see him now with a back like a ramrod as he sat to sign for me saying, 'I do this under the greatest protestation. I think you are crazy.'

Ada Jeanette and Stanley Garlick.

This truly was a time of my being born again: coming to my Saviour, contritely, humbly, anxiously trying to find the way back to Him.[5]

During this time of conversion, Ada recognised that her experience at Whangarei High School was a training time for her future assignment at the Church College of New Zealand (CCNZ) in Temple View. She said:

> When I told Stan, he declared that if I went there it would break our marriage and asked 'if after 40 happy years together, was I prepared to do this?' I knew that if I had this work to do the Lord would not let it come between us.[6]

Time passed and by 1957 Ada decided that she was too old for the responsibility. Later that year she received a letter from Dr Owen J. Cook of the Church's Pacific Board of Education, asking if she was prepared to serve the Lord? And her thought was 'that I could not very well say no to that.' Stan, however, said that if she went there, she would go alone.

> Oh, what heartfelt prayer I offered to the Lord. Then I received a letter asking me to attend CCNZ for an interview. I asked Stan to please get my bus ticket and he said that he had to go to Auckland so he would take me that far, then he took me the whole way.[7]

During the interview Ada advised Dr Cook and Dr Clifton D. Boyack, the school's first principal, that she would be willing to join them at CCNZ. She said:

> Stan and I drove for many miles and he said, 'Well are you going to that place?' 'Yes dear.' 'Then what is your position to be?' answer 'I don't know.' 'Great scot girl, they might make you one of the maids. What are they going to pay you?' Answer 'I don't know, we did not discuss money.' He stopped the car and looking at me said, 'You are crazier than I thought.' To me it was the work I had prayed for, and I did not wish to bring money into it, though I supposed they would pay me something. To make a long story short, Stan did go with me

> and when we arrived, we were put into a caravan, a super one, but nonetheless I thought Stan would walk out then. Everyone was so kind and understanding that he stayed. One day Stan came to my office with his suitcase packed saying he was going. The reason being that everyone was so kind to him he felt like a hypocrite. A little persuasion and all was well. Dr. Boyack persuaded him to take a course and he became the first postmaster of the Temple View Post Office. Stanley never did join the Church. His personal and family pride never would let him.[8]

Ada confessed that working at the college was very demanding. It required ten- to twelve-hour days, which was often difficult for a woman of sixty-nine years of age. Her first job was to recruit a manager for the cafeteria as well as hire a manager for the laundry. In addition, there was the sick bay, which needed a manager. She also trained and supervised the dorm parents. She made the travel arrangements for the students coming and going. Although demanding, she found the work very satisfying. She brought with her the experience from her prior employment at Whangarei High School. As a matron at the first New Zealand co-educational boarding high school, Ada tried to instil the ideals of proper deportment, social grace and responsibility in her young charges, many of whom were from rural areas and had never before been away from home.

Later in Ada's life as she reflected on her responsibilities at CCNZ she said:

> I was strict, and I think probably overly strict. I think that on many occasions I hurt feelings, which now I have great regret about, I wish I hadn't. But it was necessary that somebody found a way to understand that once children are in a boarding school, they don't run around the street in their night clothes.[9]

Feared, respected or loved, Ada left her imprint upon hundreds of students and faculty who passed through CCNZ.[10]

Geoff Garlick – The Early Years

> 'Geoff was a very naughty small boy and difficult to bring up,' his mother, Ada, admitted – before immediately clarifying: 'perfectly honest but exuberant and head strong. At 13 years of age we took him to Professor Thomas Hunter of Victoria University for psychological analysis. Instead of receiving my sympathy we received a severe scolding. Prof. Hunter said "Every once in a while, a personality is born and you have done your best to ruin this one by wrong handling".'[11]

That was all she and Stanley needed to hear. They took a new approach to parenting Geoff and it worked.

We changed his school and did not have much worry apart from the fact that he would not use the ability he had in class. He was a keen sportsman 1st fifteen rugby player and 1st eleven cricket player. He finished his education at Feilding Agricultural College and from there, spent several years with Stud sheep breeders.[12]

Geoff liked the sheep breeding work well enough. The trouble was, it wasn't the kind of work that allowed him much upward mobility. He soon learned that it was 'a costly business to become established in one's own place in that type of sheep farming in this country. Also, conditions are such, that a lad working for someone else could hardly ask the girl of his choice to share.' So, he cut ties with the business, moved to Motueka, and went into tobacco growing. It seemed like a good idea at the time until he realised that Social Security plus the New Zealand labour laws made it harder to earn the living he had imagined. The tobacco growers had trouble finding cheap labour, which meant wives often had to work alongside their husbands in the fields. At that point, Geoff's parents 'encouraged him to come North.'[13]

In February 1947, Geoff married a gifted and talented daughter of a barrister and solicitor from Greytown, Wairarapa. April Thompson was a trained schoolteacher, who was very bright and a fine athlete.

After moving from Motueka to the North Island, Geoff went into farming for himself. His mother said, 'They have a very nice place at Panmure, a few miles from Auckland.'[14] Geoff and April were earning their keep by growing tomatoes under glass, outdoor tomatoes, and Chinese gooseberries. Jeannette was impressed at the partnership Geoff and April had created for themselves so early in their marriage.

Geoffrey and April Garlick.

Near-Death Experience

At twenty-eight years of age, Geoff recorded the following near-death experience:[15]

> My father Stanley C. Garlick and my mother Ada Jeannette 'Bobbie' were employed as caretakers or rangers on the Auckland City's new 5000-acre watershed supply project in the Hunua Ranges about 30 miles south of Auckland.
>
> Their prime responsibility was to see that there were no unwelcome visitors on the project, lighting fires, or interfering with an impressive array of tunnelling and dam building machinery and equipment. Some 5 miles of tunnels and 25 miles of pipes would carry the water to the distant city.
>
> April (6 months pregnant) and I with our two children had gone to visit them one delightful sunny midsummer's day. After one of mother's scrumptious ample dinners and a good chat, dad and I went for a long walk to talk and look over the general progress on the main dam and the three tunnels that were being blasted through the heavily bush-clad hills north of the dam. On reaching the north portal of the second tunnel where we noticed a 20-foot, 2½ inch sapling had been uprooted and pushed over by a load of soil from the tunnel and had landed across two 'telephone' wires. 'I wondered why we have not been getting any phone calls this weekend,' said dad, 'that tree must be shorting out the transmission.'
>
> 'Oh, I'll take care of that,' said I with enthusiasm, 'that little tree should be easy enough to shift,' and with that jumped down the 6-foot face of the spoil gathering the sapling in my right hand and one of the wires with my left hand. What a shock, with unbelievable power my left hand locked onto the power line and my body vibrated violently as 240 volts of electricity coursed through every fibre of my being, for what seemed like an eternity. I lost consciousness for what must have been only minutes or even seconds I could not tell and was keenly aware of being totally enveloped in absolute blackness and in the distance, so very, very far away, the tiniest speck of the most brilliant white lights, which began to enlarge as without any apparent effort on my part was impelled with sheer ecstasy, and incredible speed toward it, the darkness disappearing behind with indescribable joy and a heart pounding with excitement and overflowing with love, I reached the end of blackness and burst out into glorious light. And there on a small green hill, clothed in a loose-fitting white robe was my brother, who had been killed in the war some five years earlier and pointing back over my shoulder said, 'You cannot come here Geoff, it isn't time, go back.'
>
> Without responding in any way, I turned and went back through the blackness and climbed back into my lifeless body. An experience, because

of the excruciating pain, like trying to climb into a glove full of needles all pointing the wrong way, I would never wish on anyone.

I lay on my back for several minutes with an anxious father looking over me, grateful that my eyes were open and my heart was beating. The whole experience left me bewildered and I shared it with few, keeping it to myself for many years.

The real significance of it did not dawn on us until we joined the Church of Jesus Christ of Latter-day Saints and learned the plan of salvation through the restored gospel and life after death took on its full meaning.

Conversion Story

Geoff described his conversion experience as follows:[16]

While working in our glasshouse one afternoon in early 1953 two Americans came down our drive on the pretext of buying tomatoes. We engaged them in conversation, only to find out they were Mormon Missionaries. They requested permission to come and tell us about their Church, the Church of Jesus Christ of Latter-day Saints, commonly known as 'Mormons'. To the best of my knowledge this was the first time I had ever heard the name Mormon. An appointment was made for 7 pm the following Monday evening. Elder LeRoy Morris (70 years old), well-spoken and somewhat dignified, was the son of a Methodist Minister and had trained as a young man to become a minister in the Church. His wife, Rachel (65 years old) was a Texan in every sense of the word, strong accent, outspoken, ready to challenge any and every statement with conviction at the slightest provocation. They arrived at the appointed hour and sat in our tiny eating alcove where they very quickly 'turned us off' by telling us that the Church that we belonged to, the Church of England, was one of the illegitimate offspring of the 'Great and Abominable Whore of all the earth' and if we did not change to their Church, which they claimed was 'the only true and living Church on the face of the earth today', we would not get to the highest degree in the kingdom of God. I spent the hour rolling cigarettes and blowing smoke across the table in hopes that they would get the message and leave. They did eventually, after about an hour of revealing conversation, using the scriptures to show us that following the death of the Lord Jesus Christ, the Church that he had organized on the earth had been destroyed by both external persecution and internal apostasy and that in keeping with Bible prophesy, the true Church, the Church of Jesus Christ of Latter-day Saints, had been restored to the earth in these latter days. We were relieved and happy that the appointment had come to an end and that they were leaving. But just as I was about to close the door firmly behind them as they left Sister Morris turned and said, 'See you same time next week.' I was too taken back to answer and closed the door behind them thinking that because we had not been very hospitable, and certainly not invited them that they would not come back. The following day in our mailbox was a typewritten list copied from our King James version of the Bible of all of the references to the prophesied 'Apostasy'. We were impressed with their obvious knowledge of the Bible and sat down to read through these references. Surprised we were to find that all of the quoted scriptures were there, and that they really did seem to say what they had said, namely that the original Church organized by the Saviour while with his apostles would indeed be lost to the earth. On Thursday there was another typewritten list in our mailbox of all the scriptures relating to the Prophesied 'Restoration'. Again, we were impressed by their apparent knowledge of the scriptures and sat down to read these new references. We learned that the 'Restoration' was truly prophesied in the Bible and that the Joseph Smith story pamphlet, that they had left with us was at least worth reading and investigating. The next Monday evening, right on the dot of 7 pm, the doorbell rang and sure enough there they were, large as life, not the least bit offended at our cool and casual attitude of the previous Monday's meeting. On this second meeting we reviewed all of the scriptural references that they had discussed previously. Before leaving they introduced us to the Book of Mormon saying that it was a new witness for Jesus Christ and it proved the Bible to be true.

We were however sceptical of their claim about their Church being the 'ONLY true and living Church on the earth today,' both of us having been brought up in Christian Churches, but we could not find any argument against their claim. For the next month or so they came to visit with us regularly on Monday evenings. We learned many wonderful scriptures and began to understand them as never before. Elder Morris decided that it was time for us to go to church.

We had been investigating the Mormon Church teachings for over three months now and felt good about what we were learning. But we still needed some outside opinion to help us in this important decision. My mother was at the time the Matron at the Whangarei Girls High School and who better to turn to but her. We asked the Mission President, Sydney J. Ottley, to send the missionaries to teach her and we would wait to see what her reaction was before making a final decision. To make a long story short – Mother joined the Church.

After attending their first sacrament meeting, Geoff reported:[17]

We said goodnight to Elder and Sister Morris at our bus stop and walked the half mile to our home in contemplative silence. April went into the house and I went down the garden to our half-acre tomato patch and knelt in fervent prayer.

The night was cold, there was a full moon and I was alone with my thoughts and hopefully the spirit of God. I knelt down in the middle of this field of tomato plants and began to pour out my heart to my Father in Heaven. Father if this really is the true Church on the earth today please tell me now, and if it is, will you forgive me for my past transgressions and have me as a member? I talked sincerely, long and hard seeking an answer. I was aware of the cold as I knelt there alone and pleaded with my God to please hurry as I really was very cold. My mind was racing through all of the experiences we had had with the missionaries, the scriptures, and now at this very different evening's meeting. It seemed that my mind was filled with all of these experiences and especially the many scriptures that we had been reading, pondering and discussing over the last three months.

Again, I pleaded with Heavenly Father to please hurry as it was cold out here. It was then that I realized that I was not cold at all, in fact I was gloriously warm and the warmth was not coming from outside but rather it was coming from inside me. I felt as if I had been lit up like a light bulb and that everyone in the houses across the road would be able to see me. The confusing mixture of scriptures that had been fogging up my mind, were now as clear as noon day, with all of the prophecies related to the apostasy and the restoration, lined up neatly in chronological order on one side of a page and the multitude of false accusations that we had been given by well-meaning friends were still in the fog on the other side of the page. I jumped up and in great joy began a hurried run to the house to tell April what I now knew. And then realizing that I had not said thank you to a loving Father in Heaven, I stopped and knelt again among our tomato crop, giving thanks from the very bottom of my heart for this wonderful revelation. I had never in my life known joy as it was manifest to me at that moment and I poured out my gratitude to God for this truly marvellous experience … Our baptism was arranged for the following Saturday afternoon. A simple service had been planned and as I came out of water, still standing in the baptismal font, I had the same glorious experience that I had had in the tomato field when I had asked my Father in Heaven for an answer to my prayer. I resolved to live the gospel from that day on and will be eternally grateful to a loving Father in Heaven for having me in His Church and giving me the opportunities to grow in the gospel.

After their baptism on 6 June 1953, Geoff and April developed a very close association with the mission presidents who served in New Zealand at the time, in particular with Ariel Ballif (1955–58) and Robert L. Simpson (1958–61). These associations lasted for many years.

Of their life after joining the Church in Panmure, Geoff's mother, Ada, wrote:

> The Church had brought them even closer together. They do everything together and are most interested in building the soil as God intended and not by constant use of artificial fertilizers only. They are living economically and paying off their mortgage. Their home is an attractive modern bungalow

Garlick family, 1958. Back row (L–R): Geoffrey, Jocelyn Garry, April. Front row (L–R): Barry, Beverley Rose.

and is a home and not a house. Great love is there and Geoff, April and the three children are one happy busy team.[18]

Early Church Leadership

Not only were the Garlicks united in their working life but they were also very supportive of the assignments they received to work to build a new branch of the Church in Panmure. Not long after he was baptised, Geoff was called as the first president of the Tāmaki Branch in Panmure. In 1957 construction on the Panmure chapel was started, and the building was dedicated in 1958 by David O. McKay, president of the Church of Jesus Christ of Latter-day Saints, one week after he dedicated the Hamilton, New Zealand, Temple. Within a few months of the dedication of the chapel, the Auckland Stake was created and the Tāmaki Branch became the Panmure Ward, with Geoff called as the first bishop.

The Panmure chapel was built by a crew of volunteer labour missionaries. During its construction, branch members were called upon to camp at the site to prevent any loss of the building materials. Geoff spent many nights sleeping on a cot at the construction site and learned to love the faithful branch members who gave so much to help build the chapel and the Lord's kingdom.

Two years after the creation of the Panmure Ward, the Auckland Stake was created, with William Roberts as president, Geoff Garlick as first counsellor and Matt Chote as second counsellor. This presidency was the first stake presidency created outside North America that was staffed entirely by local members and did not include any Americans. From their association in this presidency, these three men developed a powerful bond and enjoyed a feeling of love and unity that extended beyond their Church meetings to many social settings.

Every president of the Church who served during this period, as well as many apostles and general auxiliary leaders, travelled from Salt Lake City to New Zealand to train the local leadership, with instruction particularly focused on Church correlation. During their visits, many of these leaders stayed in the homes of stake presidency members, and these associations created bonds between members of the stake presidencies and the general Church leaders from Salt Lake City. Geoff recalled, while attending General Conference and walking down South Temple Street in Salt Lake City, hearing the familiar voice of Elder Thomas S. Monson call his name from the other side of the street.

Church Leadership and Work Balance

In 1963, Geoff and April Garlick moved from Panmure to a 10-acre property near Redoubt Road in Papatoetoe. There they established a sizeable glasshouse operation in conjunction with Geoff's sister Jill Palmer and her husband Ken, who sold their sheep farm in Te Puke and moved to Papatoetoe as well. The property allowed both families, along with Geoff and Jill's parents, Stanley and Jeannette Garlick, to each build new homes. They also built a packing shed to support the glasshouse business.

The glasshouse business took significant work to grow and then manage as it prospered, but the Garlicks and the Palmers also made time for Church service. In May 1968, the Auckland South Stake (later called the Manurewa Stake) was created, with Geoff Garlick as president and Ken Palmer as second counsellor. Both men put the Lord's work first and never neglected any request for counsel or help from Church members who needed them. During this period, the Church in New Zealand was growing. In an interview published in the *New Zealand Herald* on 27 September 1973, Geoff stated, 'We are growing so fast that we just cannot provide all the chapels we need. In South Auckland we have chapels in Pukekohe, Manurewa and Papatoetoe. But we also need chapels in Howick, Mangere and Papakura.'[19]

President Garlick had the ability to reach out to Saints from all the Pacific Islands and greet them in their native tongue. This, as much as anything, allowed him to connect with the people in his stake, whom he loved and served. Many stake members and former missionaries remember him with great fondness.

Elder Jack McDonald, an American who served a mission to New Zealand in the late 1960s, wrote:

> The first memory I have of [President Garlick] happened at a stake conference at the Pa Road Chapel. I was serving in Te Atatu. He started his talk by saying, 'Tena koe, tena koutou, tena koutou.' Many times. Oh, how the Maori loved the way he honoured them by beginning his remarks in Maori.[20]

A bishop who served under President Garlick told about the time one of his counsellors in the bishopric came to his office to resign from his calling. He had read some disturbing anti-Mormon literature and did not want to be a member any longer. The bishop immediately called President Garlick, who made an appointment with this person to review the material in question. The bishop commented that his counsellor showed up the next Sunday ready to continue in his calling, and he never looked back after his meeting with President Garlick.

Sister Kenyon (née Neale) stated that she was a teenager growing up in the Manukau Stake when President Garlick was the stake president. She said that she looked forward to and always enjoyed stake conference because there was an excitement in the meeting when President Garlick spoke to the members. She said that he always greeted her using her name, which made her feel like he cared about her and many members expressed the same sentiment.

Emigration to Canada and the USA

In 1976, after his release from the stake presidency, Geoff and April emigrated to Calgary, Alberta, Canada, to be closer to their three children, all of whom lived in North America. In 1978, they moved to Salt Lake City, where Geoff worked for the Doxey-Layton Corporation, managing the Foothill Village shopping centre. April became a full-time employee of the Church's Missionary Department, where she worked for twelve years. During this time of heavy career responsibilities, Geoff was called to serve as bishop of the Salt Lake Fourth Ward in the Liberty Stake, an assignment that put him in contact with many widows and struggling lower-income families in the downtown area of Salt Lake City. He loved the assignment and spent many hours ministering to families in need, helping them become more self-reliant and less dependent on Church welfare.

Retirement Years and Continued Church Service

After Geoff and April had both retired from active employment, they accepted a call in 1992 to serve as directors of the New Zealand Temple Visitors Centre in

Temple View, New Zealand. During their tenure there, they were instrumental in inaugurating a live nativity as part of the New Zealand Temple's Christmas lights display – something they had experienced while living in Calgary. The Garlicks loved their time serving 'back home', and it was difficult for them to leave New Zealand again and return to America.

Back in Utah, they served as ordinance workers in the Salt Lake Temple. In 1995, they built a new home in a retirement community in St George, Utah, which became 'paradise' for both of them. They became ordinance workers in the St George Temple, and also volunteered at the Dixie Regional Medical Centre. Both were very active in their family ward, where Geoff served for many years as the Gospel Doctrine teacher.

April passed away in St George on 19 May 2001. After missing his wife for two difficult years, Geoff met and married Gwen Stokes. Geoff and Gwen enjoyed seven happy years together, living in Ogden, Utah, during the summer months and spending their winters in Sun River, a St George retirement community. Never one to sit idle, Geoff enjoyed playing golf every morning and loved the community life at Sun River. During his later years, he taught himself to play the organ and enjoyed playing at home on a regular basis.

On 29 December 2010, Geoff passed away peacefully at his home in Ogden, surrounded by his family. He is buried next to April in the Saint George City Cemetery.

NOTES

1. Barry Garlick is the son of Geoffrey Garlick
2. Garlick, Jeannette (n.d.) *Life Story*, Brigham Young University Hawaii Oral History, NZ – 01 – 00004 B15 F1
3. Palmer, Jill (n.d.) memories of Ada Jeannette Lundius Garlick, NZ – 01-00004 B16 F4
4. Garlick, Jeannette (n.d.)
5. *Ibid.*
6. *Ibid.*
7. *Ibid.*
8. *Ibid.*
9. *Ibid.*
10. Palmer (n.d.)
11. Garlick, Ada Jeannette Lundius to J. Reuben Clark, 23 October 1953 and 29 March 1954, and Rowena J. Miller to Ada Jeannette Lundius Garlick, 27 January 1954, all in Joshua Reuben Clark Papers, MSS 303, b 388, f 9, L. Tom Perry Special Collections, Brigham Young University, Provo, Utah
12. *Ibid.*

13. *Ibid.*
14. The author
15. Garlick, Geoffrey (n.d.) Journal
16. *Ibid.*
17. *Ibid.*
18. Garlick, Jeanette (n.d.)
19. *New Zealand Herald* (27 September 1973) 'Mormon Membership Keeps on Growing', Auckland
20. McDonald, Jack, personal communication

REFERENCES

Garlick, Ada Jeannette Lundius to J. Reuben Clark, 23 October 1953 and 29 March 1954, and Rowena J. Miller to Ada Jeannette Lundius Garlick, 27 January 1954, all in Joshua Reuben Clark Papers, MSS 303, b 388, f 9, L. Tom Perry Special Collections, Brigham Young University, Provo, Utah

Garlick, Geoffrey (n.d.) Journal

Garlick, Jeanette (n.d.) *Life Story*, Brigham Young University Hawaii Oral History, NZ – 01 – 00004 B15 F1

New Zealand Herald (27 September 1973) 'Mormon Membership Keeps on Growing', Auckland

Palmer, Jill (n.d.) memories of Ada Jeannette Lundius Garlick, NZ – 01-00004 B16 F4

X

Honest Ben

BEN COUCH (1925–96)

Derek Couch[1]

Manuera Benjamin Riwai-Couch's Church patriarchal blessing stated that he 'would accomplish much good among the living; that he would comprehend the affairs of men; that he would have great influence with many not of the Church; that his life's experience would shine, and his life would be an example whereby people would be attracted to him sensing in him a great difference from other men.'[2] However, it stated that to have these attributes would require a lifetime of discipleship to learn the attributes of Jesus Christ and live them. He was counselled among other things to be humble and above all to be honest. This pathway would see him serve his Church faithfully in whatever he was asked to do and sit among the highest councils of Government (Cabinet), sport (New Zealand Rugby Football Union), Māoridom (New Zealand Māori Council) and other community services in New Zealand. All would know that Ben was a practising Mormon.

Beginnings

Manuera Benjamin Riwai-Couch was known throughout his life, by his own preference, as Ben Couch. He was born 27 June 1925, the first of eight children to George Manning Moke Couch, a farmer, whose father was English and whose mother was of Ngāi Tahu ancestry. George's wife, Hinerua Riwai, of Rapaki, had Ngāi Tahu affiliations by way of her father and Ngāti Mutunga affiliations through her mother. Until the age of eight years, Ben lived with his maternal grandmother, Mere Ngautanga Riwai, a redoubtable widow who reared ten children of her own after her husband was taken by the great Spanish influenza epidemic of 1918. Mere's simple Christian faith and strong, self-sufficient work ethic were to become lifelong influences on him.

At the age of eight, after some minor misbehaviours, Ben was sent to live with an uncle, Tahana Jack Riwai (Mere's son) and his wife, Heke Te Maari, at Kohunui, a rural Pā near Pirinoa in South Wairarapa. Kohunui was predominantly Mormon after Heke's grandfather, Piripi Te Maari, invited the Mormon missionaries to the Pā in the early 1880s. Not only was Piripi Te Maari one of the pioneer members of the Church, he was also a well-known tribal leader, farmer and prominent defender of the rights of his Ngāti Kahungunu people to their lands and lakes in the Wairarapa area. Jack and Heke were members of the Church but for some reason did not feel a need to have him introduced to the Gospel. Ben was to form a strong bond in the years ahead with this family and he grew to love the Riwai children as his own siblings. He attended Pirinoa School and later Ōtaki Māori Boys College, but was unhappy at the latter and returned to Mere to attend Christchurch Technical College from 1940 to 1942. He served an apprenticeship as a carpenter until August 1943, when he was allowed by Mere to join the Royal New Zealand Air Force learning to fly tiger moths on the Taieri Plains in Dunedin, and later at Woodburn in Blenheim. He did not complete his training as an advanced fighter pilot due to the conclusion of hostilities in 1945.

Family

In 1945, just before the rugby season got under way, Ben returned to Pirinoa and worked as a builder. He was reunited with his primary school sweetheart, Peti (Bessie) Tangihaere Carter of Ngāti Kahungunu, Ngāti Toa and Ngāti Raukawa descent. Her maternal grandfather, Paratene Matenga, was one of the first to accept baptism in the Pa in 1883. All of her whānau were members of the Mormon faith. They married in Masterton on 15 July 1947 and were to have seven children. Ben built their first home in Gladstone, Wairarapa, and then in Pirinoa, South Wairarapa. The strong attachment to wife and family was the first of several commitments, or guiding principles, which would direct the course of his life and his political decision making in the years ahead.

Rugby

One of Ben's great passions in life was rugby. He represented New Zealand as an All Black from 1947 to 1949 (three tests and four provincial games), and was a Māori All Black from 1946 to 1951 (six tests and fourteen provincial games). He said in later years that 'becoming an MP was a big thrill, but it was just as big a thrill becoming an All Black.'[3] Described as not tall at 1.73 metres he was sturdily built and a strong, physical player who was an excellent handler.[4] In playing for the Māori All Blacks he would play alongside Sanitorium (Tori) Reid, Nitama (Doc) Paewai and Gooch Parahi, who would all play significant Mormon leadership roles in future years,[5] and in their respective Māori communities.

Ben Couch, All Black 1947–49 and Māori All Black 1947–50.

One of Ben's highlights in his playing days was to lift the coveted Ranfurly Shield off Canterbury in 1951 while playing for Wairarapa Bush. It is the only time that the 'Bush' has ever held New Zealand's domestic rugby competition's coveted Shield. Regrettably, they lost it to their first challenger. In today's terms, his playing career was not long. He had a growing family of four children and any extra money was hard to come by to tour and play amateur rugby. A local Lebanese businessman, Joe Sabar, paid for Ben's playing boots and a couple of dress shirts to tour in 1948. What concerned him most was how he would provide for his growing family and, subconsciously, which Church would best suit their family.

Conversion

In the minds of many, playing for the All Blacks was sufficient achievement for one lifetime. However, happenings on the marriage/family front would have a deeper, more lasting effect on Ben. While living in Gladstone, just out of Masterton, Ben's wife Bessie with their three small children attended the Hiona branch of the Church of Jesus Christ of Latter-day

Saints. Sunday was rugby training for Ben and he thought nothing of playing rugby on a Sunday. The Saints met in an old house and Ben would arrive and sit on the doorstep waiting for his wife and children to finish Church. One thing of concern to Ben at that time was that his wife insisted they pay 10 percent of their income as tithing. He says, 'I wasn't impressed with the Church and I couldn't see how tithing would work, but we paid it and somehow we got by and we were never short of money, despite our very humble surroundings.'[6]

In those days the Mormon missionaries often visited the family but Ben never consented to being taught the formal missionary discussions, preferring to be with friends and at rugby training. In those days the missionaries played in the local rugby club team and were acquainted with Ben's friends. But gospel teachings and Mormon doctrine were never discussed openly.

One Sunday, while waiting for his family to finish Church, Ben's life was to take a different turn. That Sunday, President Te Weringa Naera, the Branch President, persuaded him to come inside and asked him to teach a Sunday School class.[7] This direct approach worked. Ben knew he would have to make some adjustments to his life, learn the gospel and get baptised. Along with his wife, his association with Te Weringa Naera was to be lifelong and have a major impact on his spiritual growth and wellbeing. He was taught the Saviour's great plan of salvation and exaltation and that he would have a role in his own deceased ancestors' redemption.

Ben was baptised on 27 February 1949 by Elder Carl Saunders and confirmed a member by President Gordon C. Young, New Zealand mission president at the time and great grandson of the Mormon prophet Brigham Young. He was also ordained a Priest that same day by President Young and confirmed a member of the Hiona branch, Wairarapa district, of the Church of Jesus Christ of Latter-day Saints. The following year in 1950 he received the Melchizedek Priesthood and was ordained an Elder by President Young at a gathering of missionaries in a small country hall, south of Levin. He did all of these things, laying the foundation for his spiritual growth, albeit continuing to play representative rugby at a national and provincial level. Ben was to end his playing career in 1951 somewhat early. One could say he took his eye off the ball and missed many more opportunities and accolades; however his eye was on bigger, long-lasting priorities, namely family, Church, career and public service.

Ben's wife, Bessie, was a third-generation member of the Church. She was of Ngāti Raukawa and Tainui descent on her paternal side and Ngāti Toa and Ngāti Kahungunu on her maternal side. Bessie's mother was a whāngai (adopted child) to a childless couple who were converts to Mormonism in the early 1880s.

Ben and Bessie started their family in Gladstone where he built their first home. Charmaine was their first child, later to be followed by another girl, Adelaide. The family then moved back to Kohunui, South Wairarapa, and lived with Bessie's parents. While living there Roy, Wayne and Kathleen were born. Sadly, Kathleen passed away at six months due to a birth defect. While living with his in-laws, Ben built their second home at Pirinoa into which they moved in 1955. It was to be their family home until 1973, during which time Derek and Zion were born. All the children attended Pirinoa Primary School, the same school both Ben and Bessie attended as children. In later years, Charmaine, Adelaide, Derek and Zion were to attend the Church College of New Zealand (CCNZ) in Hamilton, while Roy and Wayne attended Kuranui College in Greytown.

Church Service

On 13 January 1959 the family were sealed in the New Zealand Temple by Douglas Martin, who later rose to become a prominent leader and whose path Ben would cross many times in the future.

Couch whānau, 1982. (L–R) Charmaine, Derek, Ben, Roy, Adelaide, Zion, Wayne, Bessie (sitting).

Ben served in many leadership positions in the Church throughout his lifetime – Branch President on three occasions in Martinborough, Featherston and Hiona; District President for Wairarapa District; and Stake high councillor in the newly created Wellington New Zealand Stake in 1964. After his political career was over, he served as ordinance worker in the New Zealand Temple, ward mission leader and held a unique calling as Mini Mission President in the Auckland New Zealand Mission responsible for the Cook Islands (1985–86). He donated many free hours to the construction of the Masterton Ward chapel and the Wellington Stake Centre, utilising his building skills. A few weeks were spent on the building of CCNZ. Ben was also involved in fundraising activities, such as tree planting in rural south Wairarapa, as in those days local members of the Church had to contribute 20 percent towards building costs as a one-off special donation.

Living in Pirinoa, a rural village in south Wairarapa, was always going to be a challenge in terms of living the gospel. There were few members and great distances to be travelled to attend Church and fulfil Church callings. Ben, however, was steadfast in his commitment to live the gospel of Jesus Christ no matter what challenges lay ahead. He commented, 'I decided to be a good member rather than a Jack Mormon. If you believe something is true, you live it.'[8] Many miles on back-country roads were travelled over the years to get to and from Church activities.

The culmination of Ben and Bessie's Church service was to serve as full-time missionaries for the Church. Originally assigned to the Hawaiian Honolulu Mission, their service there was cut short when they were reassigned to the Auckland New Zealand Mission to serve in the Cook Islands.

Upon their release in September 1986, their Mission President, John R. Lasater, wrote of their service stating:

> Elder Couch has served in a very unique calling as Mini Mission President, having full responsibility in the Cook Islands for full time missionary work, training of the member district leadership and care of the Church facilities on the main Island of Rarotonga as well as three outer Islands – Aitutaki, Mangaia and Mauke. Under his direction and leadership a new momentum was established in building the kingdom of God among those people. Not only has the convert baptism rate dramatically increased but the image of the Church has been elevated significantly and the confidence and sense of belonging among the members has risen as well. We are now seeing a new resolve and greater determination to stand tall as Latter-day Saints among the members in the Islands. This has been a direct result of the loving influence, yet firm hand of Elder and Sister Couch.[9]

Mixing with the local Cook Island Māori came naturally to them both. They opened up the mission home at Black Rock to the membership and missionary work. Many family home evenings and firesides there brought investigators, members and missionaries together. Ben always believed that 'actions speak louder than words' and that Christ-like service free of charge will change people's perceptions of the Church in the future. Emori Waka, a non-member and maritime engineer living on the Island of Aitutaki was impressed that Ben would roll up his sleeves and help him put his new roof on his house. Emori would later join the Church and serve faithfully, notably on a full-time mission in the New Zealand Temple.[10] Ben and Bessie grew to cherish these South Sea Islanders and, as Māori themselves, had an immediate affinity with and love for them.

As a former New Zealand Cabinet Minister, Ben was to have some influence with the Cook Islands Government. On a number of occasions he was asked to say the opening prayer at parliament sessions. He agreed only if he could dispense with the set prayer and offer a prayer from the heart as directed by the spirit.[11] Numerous invitations from around the Island were extended from Government and embassies for Ben and Bessie to attend functions where there were visiting dignitaries. They always attended wearing their mission name tags, showing that they were Elder and Sister Couch from the Church of Jesus Christ of Latter-day Saints, and they were always ready and willing to promote the Church and strike up a gospel conversation where possible. To paraphrase the apostle Paul, they were not ashamed of the gospel of Jesus Christ.[12]

Ben's favourite scripture, which he was heard to quote many times throughout his life, was from the Doctrine and Covenants 82:10: 'I, The Lord am bound when ye do what I say; but when ye do not what I say, ye have no promise.' Keeping the commandments was just black and white to Ben. Keep them and be blessed, break them and suffer the consequences.

Ben had two favourite hymns – number 242, 'Praise God From Whom All Blessings Flow', by far the shortest hymn in our present day hymn book; and number 240, 'Know This That Every Soul is Free'.[13] His favourite lines from the latter hymn, which he quoted often, were:

Know this that every soul is free
To choose his life and what he'll be
For this eternal truth is given
That God will force no man to Heaven.

Ben believed no man or woman should be forced or coerced into something they did not want to do. This was to later influence his political thinking, especially when it came to institutions and governments.

Ben struggled with longwinded prayers and talks. He was never one for beating round the bush and liked to get to the core of things and move on. Patience was an attribute that did not come easily to him.

Upon their return to New Zealand in 1986, Ben would continue to serve in whatever capacity he was called to. His stroke in 1993 limited his capacity to serve but he always made sure he was worthy to attend the temple in Hamilton. Despite being in a wheelchair, he attended the Temple whenever he could. A poignant moment came when he chose to be sealed to his stepfather and birth mother in 1994. Douglas Martin coincidentally was the sealer again. Brother Martin observed, 'I was especially impressed with his extreme quietness on that occasion. I sensed his relief and joy that the link in the chain was now complete.'[14]

Community Service

Ben worked throughout the 1950s and 1960s in Pirinoa as a builder and, from the late 1950s, as a shearing contractor. Throughout this time his labour force consisted of many probationers referred to his custody by the law courts. Ben attempted, though not always successfully, to rehabilitate these people through contact with his own lifestyle of country living, hard work, sport and family. He became a probation officer, a Māori warden and a justice of the peace. Locally, he and his workers were affectionately known as 'Ali Baba and the forty thieves.' Ben gained further notoriety by delivering a baby in the back seat of his car while transporting one of his pregnant workers to Martinborough Hospital.

Community was very important to Ben and he committed significant time to the local community and Māori organisations including Pirinoa and Wairarapa Māori committees. For a time, he served on the New Zealand Māori Council. In 1973 he moved to Masterton, but retained strong links with Kohunui.

Political Service

From the early 1960s Ben took an interest in politics. He was influenced by prominent Mormon leaders in America who simultaneously served their country with distinction, such as Ezra Taft Benson, a former US Secretary of Agriculture in the Dwight D. Eisenhower administration. He had a strong belief that he could rise above his humble circumstances and by hard work and determination realise his political ambitions. His values and beliefs seemed to closely align with those of the National Party. It wasn't long before he rose in the ranks of the Wairarapa branch of the National Party and soon chaired the party's Southern Māori electorate. Twice he represented National in the southern Māori electorate. However, the Māori electorates had long been regarded as strongholds of the Labour Party, and it was no surprise when he was unsuccessful. In 1972 he tried again, this time for the general Wairarapa seat. Winning the nomination for this seat was a feat in itself as he stood against true blue farmers and businessmen. A strong swing against the National government dashed his chances and it seemed that he would never get into Parliament.

Then came a Church meeting in Porirua and a talk by visiting Apostle Neal A. Maxwell. Ben related, 'He told the members that they were going to have a member in government. I was standing at the time (the 1975 national elections were close) and so were a few other members.'[15] Barely three months later Ben was in Parliament as the member for Wairarapa. He was not to be the first Latter-day Saint elected to Parliament as Tipene (Steve) Watene (Eastern Māori) had that honour.[16] He was, however, along with Rex Austin, the first Māori to capture a general seat.[17] Ben held onto the seat at the next election in 1978 and after only three years in office was appointed Minister of Māori Affairs and Postmaster-General. In 1980 he relinquished the Post Office portfolio to become Minister of Police, retaining his Māori Affairs responsibilities.

A gospel principle that stood him in good stead in politics was his ability to support leaders. His unswerving loyalty to Prime Minister Robert Muldoon, a man quick to defend his friends, was well recognised. When Sir Robert passed away in 1993 Lady Muldoon allowed him to take the former Prime Minister's name to the temple. Loyalty to leaders and being a team player were traits he had learned by following the prophets and sustaining local leaders.

By its very nature, politics is stressful. The pressure was intense, yet in the hottest moments he appeared calm. Always he was resolute in his conviction that law and order must prevail. He stated:

> The Church has given me a sense of peace. When you pray before you go to bed and you get up with a clear head and a clear mind there is no need to fear and worry. You just do what is right and let the consequences follow. Whether it's church, home, or politics, the approach is the same. We've never hesitated to acknowledge the hand of the Lord in our lives. I have attempted to practise what I preach at home, in the community, and now in Parliament. We must remember who we are and act accordingly. We should not be afraid of the gospel of Christ. You have to be in or out. It is a black and white situation. There can be no grey. You can't afford that.[18]

Being a member of Cabinet, Ben was to witness and participate in some of the most important and perplexing social issues of the times. In his portfolio of Māori Affairs, he frequently referred to the family as a means of resolving pressing social issues. His speeches were peppered with 'no other success can compensate for failure in the home' and 'no family is a failure until they give up trying',[19] reflecting what he saw as one of the most important aspects of his job in politics, to emphasise the importance of the family as an important and basic unit of society. 'Wherever I speak, I try to get the message across. I am not what you would call an intellectual person in the sense that some of my colleagues are, but by trying to follow the teachings of the Church I have not come out so badly after all.'[20] He also commented, 'One thing I have been taught is to be honest with myself and with others. You could say that I am more noted for that than are some other politicians,' he chuckled, then became serious again. 'I am a Mormon and proud of it.'[21]

Regularly criticised by the national press, he often made blunt and politically embarrassing comments, but his electorate stood behind him nonetheless. His press secretary, Gordon Wills Johnson, said that Couch, 'never learned to lie, to quibble, or to evade an issue'. He was a man of clear beliefs, which he attempted to live by at all times.[22]

Tony Potter, a journalist for the *Evening Post* wrote, 'He probably summed up his philosophy best before his last foray in politics in 1986. "I never lied, always spoke the truth and that did upset some people".'[23]

When speaking informally Ben used colloquial language and humour, often directed at himself, appealing to a wide range of people. He presented direct views without pretension in a manner that left even hostile audiences convinced of his sincerity. On one occasion, touring a prison farm as Minister of Police, he stripped to the waist and sheared several sheep, to the surprise of the inmates. He was less comfortable with prepared speeches, rehearsing them diligently but not always enjoying the delivery. He spoke only a little Māori, but as Minister of Māori Affairs learned his speeches in Māori by heart.[24]

Despite his busy schedule Ben was always available to help and assist constituents. Equally, he was always ready to help the Church with visa issues for missionaries and was able to resolve high tariffs being applied to Temple clothing. The Church was grateful that Māori taonga returning from America would not be subject to tax or confiscation due to his intervention. When Ben was out of Parliament he used his influence in arranging various meetings with the right people. One such occasion led to some language in the Marriage Act being changed that eventually led to Temple marriage sealings becoming acceptable as lawful marriage in the New Zealand Temple.

A highlight for Ben was to host the first Presidency and some of the brethren from the Quorum of the Twelve Apostles who were in Wellington for an Area Conference in 1979. They met at the Beehive with Prime Minister Muldoon and other cabinet members, followed by a function. Regrettably President Spencer W. Kimball was ill and did not come. However, present were President N. Eldon Tanner (former State Energy Minister for the Alberta Government), Brother David Kennedy (longtime diplomat from the US State Department, and then roving ambassador for the Church) and President Ezra T. Benson (President of the Quorum of the Twelve Apostles and former Secretary of Agriculture in the Eisenhower Administration). They were to give Ben sage advice on remaining humble.

In a letter to him in 1979 President Benson said:

> I am very pleased to see a member of the Church in a high office in Government. It helps the church be recognised for what it is, and you will be able to influence legislation that will affect the freedom of your beautiful country. Don't waiver when the principle is right. I understand you have already taken a stand against your party on several occasions.[25]

President Spencer W. Kimball wrote to him, thanking him for sending a copy of Prime Minister Robert Muldoon's book, *My Way*. President Kimball was glad to see in the first part of the book a tribute to the Church.[26] Ben was to visit with President Kimball in 1983 as a Minister of the Crown, having government business to transact in the United States. Visiting him in his private residence was a humbling experience, to see him frail and ailing, worn out in his service for the Lord.

Ben's political career in office was to end in the snap election of 1984. The swing against the Muldoon protectionist government and the entry of a third party saw the Government swept out of office and Ben losing his seat, albeit by a few hundred votes. Disappointed, he picked himself up and felt it was time for him and Bessie to focus on serving their God.

Ben with President Spencer W. Kimball in Salt Lake City, Utah, 1983.

Let Their Light So Shine

Upper Hutt Stake President, Trevor A. Beatson, wrote to Ben and Bessie: 'On behalf of the Upper Hutt Stake members, I really do want to thank you both for the fine examples you have been to the whole of New Zealand. People nationally, now know the Church through your exposure while in high office and regard you brother Ben, as the honest politician.'[27]

In Ben's maiden speech made in the House of Representatives on 6 July 1976 he made this pledge to the constituents of the Wairarapa electorate:

> I hope when my time is done, that Wairarapa people will be able to say that they have, once again, been represented by a man who worked hard for his electorate, and said exactly what he thought, without bias or evasion, honest always. I promise them, and you, I shall try to earn that opinion. So help me God.[28]

Ben was not a person to seek his own gain and thought of other causes more worthy than himself. When he was defamed by the Post Office Workers Union, he was awarded damages in court but quickly gave all the proceeds to Tuhirangi Marae to replace all their ageing mattresses. Nor was he enamoured by the trappings of his position. Rather than use his ministerial car and driver, he would catch the workers' train from Masterton to Parliament in Wellington so he could talk to his constituents.

Apart from becoming a Justice of the Peace and honorary probation officer in the 1960s, Ben was given a rare honour usually accorded someone who has

Ben as Minister of Māori Affairs and Police, representing the New Zealand Government, presenting a handwoven Māori kete with kiwi feathers to Her Majesty Queen Elizabeth II at Government House Wellington, 1981.

passed away. A poupou bearing the Māori version of his name, Pene Kaute, was carved and erected outside the Tuhirangi wharenui. Ben was awarded the Queen's Silver Jubilee medal in 1977, the New Zealand 1990 Commemoration Medal and the Queen's Service Order in 1991 for public service.

He was a man of humble beginnings, and by his own admission he was not all that educated but he made up for it by reading and watching current events. His mokopuna knew that it was quiet time when Grandad was home and when the six o'clock news was on. Ben was not afraid to speak his mind in educated circles and leaned on his own version of 'common sense' combined with a reasonable judgement of human behaviour and character. He toyed with the idea, along with some others, of writing a book, which he would call 'Pa to Parliament', but the family laughed it off by asking, who would read it? If there was a task to be done, then it was all about doing it, be it in family, Church or the community.

In the early 1990s Ben was acting manager of the Iwi Transition Authority in Masterton, and from 1993 until his death he served as a Commissioner of the Treaty of Waitangi Fisheries Commission, attending meetings in a wheelchair after his stroke in 1993 and the loss of his legs through diabetes. Despite his stroke he continued to serve and used dry humour about the loss of his first leg by telling people he 'had one foot in the grave already.' He died at his home on 3 June 1996. His wife Bessie was to join him five years later to continue their service together.

Legacy

Among many accolades, spoken and written, of Ben at his funeral, the Mayor of Masterton at the time, Bob Francis, said this of him:

> I saw Ben as a person of integrity who treated all people as equal. His strong Christian beliefs and the influence he has had in his family and community is a legacy that will be with us for a long time.[29]

Perhaps a more touching tribute came from Douglas Martin, former Stake President and the then current New Zealand Temple President, who said:

> Over the years I have had great respect for Ben and his integrity in high office, honouring his Priesthood by letting his light shine before men. When passing through Hamilton he would join in class discussions and if it happened to be fast Sunday, he would bear his testimony. It was good for the saints to see a man in high public office remain a humble Saint.[30]

Ron Don, a fellow councillor on the New Zealand Rugby Football Union said, 'I always admired Ben. He was a good man in every sense of the word.

It is a sad reflection upon New Zealand and our present politicians when I say with knowledge and conviction that he was too good and too honest to be a politician.'[31]

Ben was not a perfect man. Like all of us he had his faults. He failed to heed good counsel about his health. He tended to be impatient and could come across abrupt and austere. He could be obstinate in his views in clashing with others. He worked too hard. He did, however, have the good sense to present his view with humour and self-deprecation. Above all, however, Ben was a worthy man, true to his wife, family and his God.

A letter from a Church leader, thanking Ben Couch for his diligent missionary service in the Masterton area, quotes Bryant S. Hinckley:

> Service is the virtue that has distinguished the great of all times and which they will be remembered by. It places a mark on its disciples. It is the dividing line which separates the two great groups of the world – those who help and those who hinder, those who lift and those who lean, those who contribute and those who consume. How much better it is to give than receive. Service in any form is comely and beautiful. To give encouragement, to show interest, to banish fear, to build self-confidence and awaken hope in the hearts of others.[32]

Ben tried his best to live by the creed of service to all. On his tombstone is a picture of the New Zealand Temple and the well-known slogan of Tumuaki Matthew Cowley, – former missionary to New Zealand, twice mission president to New Zealand and member of the Quorum of Twelve Apostles – 'Kia Ngāwari' – be humble, be patient.

Ahakoa ka ngau tēnei taniwha o te mokemoke, kua hoki koe ki raro i te parirau manahou o te Atua. Hei konā mai ōku Mātua. E moe kōrua i te kōpunipunitanga o te hunga wairua rā!
Even though the sadness bites, we know you reside in the close care of God. We will be with you someday our loving parents. Rest well!

NOTES

1. Derek Couch is the son of Ben Couch
2. Rosenvall, Eric Albert (28 February 1960), Patriarchal Blessing given by New Zealand Temple president
3. Potter, Tony (6 June 1996), 'Time and Tide, Politician Who Told it as it Was', *Evening Post*
4. 'Statistics, Ben Couch number #469'. Retrieved from All Blacks.com
5. Mulholland, Malcolm (2009), 'War interrupts Play', in *Beneath the Māori Moon: An Illustrated History of Māori Rugby*, Huia Publishers, Wellington
6. Dykes, Mervyn (April 1983), 'Ben Couch: Cabinet Minister in the New Zealand

Government', *The Ensign*, The Church of Jesus Christ of Latter-day Saints, Utah
7. *Ibid.*
8. *Ibid.*
9. Lasater, President John R. (15 September 1986) Honourable release letter from President of the Auckland New Zealand Mission to President Leslie Harris, of the Upper Hutt New Zealand Stake
10. Waka, Naomi (2017) personal communication. Daughter of Emori Waka
11. Couch, Bessie (n.d.) personal Missionary Journal
12. New Testament, Romans 1:16
13. Hymns of the Church of Jesus Christ of Latter-day Saints (1985) The Church of Jesus Christ of Latter-day Saints, Utah
14. Martin, Douglas J. (11 June 1986) condolence letter to Bessie Couch from New Zealand Temple President
15. Dykes (April 1983)
16. Henare, Manuka (2000) 'Watene, Puti Tipene', Te Ara – The Encyclopedia of New Zealand. Retrieved from https://teara.govt.nz/en/biographies/5w12/watene-puti-tipene
17. Gustafson, Barry (1986) *The First 50 Years: A History of the New Zealand National Party*, Reed Methuen, Auckland
18. Dykes (April 1983)
19. Direct quotes by Mormon Presidents David O. McKay and Harold B. Lee
20. *Ibid.*
21. *Ibid.*
22. Snow, S. G. (2000) 'Couch, Manuera Benjamin Riwai', Te Ara – The Encyclopaedia of New Zealand. Retrieved from https://teara.govt.nz/en/biographies/5c39/couch-manuera-benjamin-riwai
23. Potter (6 June 1996)
24. Snow (2000)
25. Benson, President Ezra Taft (4 December 1979) letter
26. Kimball, President Spencer W. (31 August 1981) letter
27. Beatson, President Trevor Beatson (8 August 1984) letter
28. Couch, Ben (6 July 1976) Address and Reply Debate, Ben Couch Maiden Speech, Hansard New Zealand
29. Francis, Bob (6 June 1996) letter from Mayor of Masterton
30. Martin (11 June 1996)
31. Don, Ron (9 June 1996) letter from former NZRFU colleague
32. Gardiner, Harvey (14 July 1993) Mission President for the Wellington New Zealand Mission quoting Elder Bryant S. Hinckley about service

REFERENCES

Beatson, President Trevor Beatson (8 August 1984) letter

Benson, President Ezra Taft (4 December 1979) letter

Couch, Ben (6 July 1976) Address and Reply Debate, Ben Couch Maiden Speech, Hansard New Zealand

Couch, Bessie (n.d.) personal Missionary Journal

Don, Ron (9 June 1996) letter from former NZRFU colleague

Dykes, Mervyn (April 1983) 'Ben Couch: Cabinet Minister in the New Zealand Government', *The Ensign*, The Church of Jesus Christ of Latter-day Saints, Utah

Francis, Bob (6 June 1996) letter from Mayor of Masterton

Gardiner, Harvey (14 July 1993) Mission President for the Wellington New Zealand Mission quoting Elder Bryant S. Hinckley about service

Gustafson, Barry (1986) *The First 50 Years: A History of the New Zealand National Party*, Reed Methuen, Auckland

Henare, Manuka (2000) 'Watene, Puti Tipene', Te Ara – The Encyclopedia of New Zealand. Retrieved from https://teara.govt.nz/en/biographies/5w12/watene-puti-tipene

Hymns of the Church of Jesus Christ of Latter-day Saints (1985) The Church of Jesus Christ of Latter-day Saints, Utah

Kimball, President Spencer W. (31 August 1981) letter

Lasater, President John R. (15 September 1986) Honourable release letter from President of the Auckland New Zealand Mission to President Leslie Harris, of the Upper Hutt New Zealand Stake

Martin, Douglas J. (11 June 1986) condolence letter to Bessie Couch from New Zealand Temple President

Mulholland, Malcolm (2009) 'War interrupts Play', in *Beneath the Māori Moon: An Illustrated History of Māori Rugby*, Huia Publishers, Wellington

Potter, Tony (6 June 1996) 'Time and Tide, Politician Who Told it as it Was', *Evening Post*

Rosenvall, Eric Albert (28 February 1960) Patriarchal Blessing given by New Zealand Temple president

Snow, S. G. (2000) 'Couch, Manuera Benjamin Riwai', Te Ara – The Encyclopaedia of New Zealand. Retrieved from https://teara.govt.nz/en/biographies/5c39/couch-manuera-benjamin-riwai

'Statistics, Ben Couch number #469'. Retrieved from All Blacks.com

XI

*E hoa mā (my friends) –
'In the service of the Lord …'*

DOUGLAS J. MARTIN (1927–2010)

Douglas J. Martin Jr[1]

Beginnings

On 20 April 1927 Elizabeth Stafford gave birth to a baby boy in Hastings, New Zealand, at the Salvation Army's Bethany home. Elizabeth was twenty-one years of age and unwed.[2] The boy's father, William Leslie Hart, was twenty-five years of age and would have little to do with the boy during his childhood. Named Eric Stafford at birth, the boy was later adopted by a Scottish couple, George and Jessie Martin, who lived a few doors down the road from Elizabeth, and had no children of their own. They welcomed the boy into their home and named him Douglas James Martin.

Douglas, or Doug, as he would come to be known, was blessed with two sets of parents – his natural parents and his adoptive parents.

Doug's Adoptive Parentage

John Martin = Isabella Marr	James Heddle Craigie = Jessie Birnie Carle
1867– 1866–	1875–1942 1880–1919

George Martin = Jessie Jamieson Craigie
1895–1979   1901–89

Doug's Natural Parentage

Charles William Hart = Margaret Elizabeth Laurenson	William Henry Stafford = Mary Thomas
1873–1941 1878–1941	1864–1950 ?

William Leslie Hart = Elizabeth Stafford
1902–79   1905–76

Douglas James Martin
1927–2010

Doug's natural grandfather, Charles Hart, was born in Canterbury and his family moved to Hastings, where he married Margaret. She was the daughter of a policeman, John Laurenson, who was originally from Unst in the Shetland Islands. Sadly, John died aged thirty, leaving his wife and five children behind. Charles had been successful in business, owning the coach service from Napier to Hastings, Tattersalls Stables, a farm and subsequently several hotels. Later in life, Elizabeth explained to Doug that his father William loved her but did not marry her on account of his family's wishes, so he had promptly left for Australia.

Doug with his adoptive parents, George and Jessie Martin.

Doug's adoptive parents, George and Jessie Martin, emigrated from Scotland in 1924 as assisted passengers to New Zealand.[3] George was a stone mason by trade. He was a mild and quiet-mannered man who had enlisted for World War One. Jessie was the daughter of a farmer. Both belonged to the Hastings and District Scots Society – the activities of which were of particular interest to Doug, including highland dancing, Hogmanay activities and singing Scottish songs. The Martins were excellent examples of Scottish folk – unemotional, honest, frugal and hardworking. But George arrived in New Zealand at the wrong time.

The 1931 Napier earthquake and the Great Depression of the 1930s left George struggling to find work, despite his skills. Jessie was often unable to work due to ill health and being bedridden while pregnant. She would have great difficulty carrying a baby to full-term. The doctor would ask her to lie down for weeks at a time. George and Jessie were childless until Doug was adopted. Doug was raised in poor circumstances. George finally obtained work at the Tourist Motor and Farming Co. as a mechanic, where he stayed until he retired at age sixty-five.

Jessie and George were strict disciplinarians. Doug would often be tempted by cookies in a jar in the kitchen. He would occasionally sneak a cookie – but if discovered, he would be beaten with a leather strap. Doug soon learned that telling the truth would not bring any rewards. As a boy, he learned to conceal or cover up things he did wrong out of fear of being punished. His adopted father George had little in common with him and did not attend any of his sporting activities. Doug grew up quickly, dropped out of high school and was keen to move out of home.

Who Are My Birth Parents?

Doug attended Mahora Primary School and wondered why his school records showed his name as Eric James Stafford. As he got older, and learned of his adoption, Doug began to wonder who his natural mother was. He developed a strong yearning to find that out. At the age of fourteen, Doug began delivering newspapers up and down the street he lived on. He was always interested when he would see Mrs Scott who lived only a few doors away and seemed to look kindly upon him. He began to wonder if she might be his natural mother.[4] He often asked Jessie who his natural mother was.

After pestering his mother with that question, Jessie finally relented and said she was going to tell Doug, when he interjected and asked if it was Mrs Scott. Elizabeth had married a man by the name of Scott. Jessie confirmed what he had come to suspect. Doug never contacted Elizabeth during his youth, preferring to observe her, along with her seven children who were his half-siblings, from a distance.

As an adult, Doug contacted Elizabeth and met with her on a few occasions, but normally in private. She would always cry when he left. When Elizabeth was near death, she phoned Doug to say goodbye. Shortly after that call, she passed away and Doug attended her funeral along with his seven surprised half-siblings.

It wasn't until Doug was twenty-one years of age that he learned who his natural father was. Again, he observed William from a distance and did not introduce himself. Doug always had a keen interest in people – no doubt born from days in his youth when wondering and observing who his relatives were. Being raised as an only child, with parents who had limited interest in his activities, Doug was a relatively lonely young man – although he never knew that growing up, as he had nothing to compare it with.

In later years, Doug did meet his natural father, William. When he introduced himself as the son of Elizabeth Stafford, William was visibly shocked. They continued to talk together, and Doug noticed that William could not look him in the eye. William said of himself, 'Well Doug, you'll hear a lot about me, but I don't think you will find anyone who'd say they don't like me.'[5]

Later, in conversation, William stated to Doug about his life: 'I've been a damn fool!' With that statement, any resentment Doug held against his natural father for being absent in his life was gone. Doug was a very understanding and forgiving person. William invited Doug to come inside and meet his family, but Doug declined to do so – something he regretted later in life when attending William's funeral, much to the surprise of William's family.

William married twice. His second wife was Alice Timu and they would have four children, many of whom would welcome Doug and become his close, immediate family, including half-brother Eric and half-sister Ella.[6] From an adopted lone child, Doug eventually came to know of twelve half-siblings from William and seven half-siblings from Elizabeth.

Dating Wati Crawford

Doug knew of Wati Crawford from a distance from a young age. He knew of her father, Syd Crawford, a well-known Māori about the town of Hastings. Standing 6 foot 4 inches, and with a successful trucking and shearing business, it was unusual in that day to see a Māori of such standing in the community. Generally, Māori mixed with Māori and Pākehā (Europeans) mixed with Pākehā.

Doug met and became interested in Wati in the latter part of 1950. They began going to the movies together. This would eventually lead to a significant change of course in his life. Doug soon found that Wati was a dedicated member of the Church of Jesus Christ of Latter-day Saints. After seeing a movie one night, they were walking home when Wati explained about paying tithes, a practice of paying one tenth of gross earnings to the Church. Doug remarked if he gave 10 percent of what he earned to the Church he would have nothing left. Wati quietly assured him he would still have nine tenths left. Doug did not reply.[7]

After two or three months, Doug began talking about marriage with Wati. She was quite certain that their marriage would be unsuccessful if Doug belonged to another church. Doug felt he was quite generous saying that Wati could take the children to her Church and that he would go to his Presbyterian church when he wanted. But Wati was adamant that would not work. Doug soon realised he had two options – to move on or to find out a little more about her Church.

Doug's life began to change. Doug no longer went to parties and was seeing less of his longtime friends. One young woman told him that going out with a Māori girl would ruin his life. Doug recalled seeing this young woman drunk at a party and violently ill – a stark contrast from Wati, who had never tasted alcohol in her life.[8] His parents were also mildly displeased with him dating a Māori girl and a Mormon. A respected co-worker said, 'I see you've gone to the blanket' – a reference to Māori who often carried and wore blankets. Doug was hurt by the comment but said nothing in reply. Sadly, many of his friends and acquaintances did not approve of his mixing with Wati and her family – yet Wati and her family were devout Latter-day Saints attending Church every Sunday. They did not smoke or drink and they paid a tenth of their income to their Church as tithing. Their example to Doug was commendable.

Attending Church with Wati

Doug decided to attend Church.[9] His first visit he recalled vividly, as he was the only non-Māori in the congregation. He recognised the person preaching from the pulpit as someone he had seen the night before intoxicated at the local pub. Doug never expected people to be perfect and always showed acceptance of people despite any shortcomings or weaknesses they had.

Doug would recall being in the Crawford home on a Sunday afternoon after Church services and having a meal with Wati's family. The interaction with family members, which included Wati's parents, grandparents, six siblings, and likely other close relatives, was a highlight of Doug's life. This was the first time he had experienced what a real family was like and the love and interaction that happens in a large family. Coming from a Scottish family of two parents and an adopted child, this experience was truly an eye-opener for Doug. Syd and Rebecca Crawford would each participate in leading the family, teaching the gospel and would exercise discipline over their children without any violence. Again, this was new for Doug.

By now, Doug had fewer close associates from his younger days – his friends and mentors were now predominantly Māori Latter-day Saints. In early January 1951, a large twenty-first birthday party was organised for Wati by her parents and held in the Cabaret Cabana at Awatoto on the beach close to Napier.[10] Doug and Wati had been dating only for a few months, so it was a significant step for Wati to invite Doug to be her partner at her twenty-first birthday celebration. It was a grand occasion – the ladies wore beautiful long ball gowns, and the men in darsuits, some in tuxedo and bow tie. Prominent farmers with whom the Kamau and Crawford families had generational shearing contracts were guests.

Doug with Wati at her twenty-first birthday in Hastings, 1951.

Later that year, Doug played rugby for Hastings High School Old Boys. They were the Hawke's Bay champions, winning the Madison Trophy, Hawke's Bay Challenge Shield and at the very end of the season tied in the finals of the Lane Cup against MAC Old Boys, the team filled with Māori Mormons. It was during this game that Doug's legs were taken out during a lineout.[11] He came crashing to the ground and broke his collarbone. Doug enjoyed playing rugby; after all, rugby was the man's game in New Zealand with no real alternatives.

Doug's nose was broken during another rugby game and he carried a slightly bent nose for the rest of his life.

Baptised during Hui Tau 1951

In late September 1951, a hui tau (annual conference of the New Zealand Mission of the Church of Jesus Christ of Latter-day Saints) was to be held in Bridge Pa, Hastings, with Church members from all over the country coming to attend. There were choir competitions and sports competitions (such as netball and athletics) in addition to Church meetings held in a marquee over the course of five days.

During the hui tau, Wati was presented with the first Golden Gleaner award in New Zealand – a rigorous programme that was both time consuming and demanding across a number of fields. Wati was required to give an acceptance speech, so she secreted herself away in her room to prepare her speech. Doug was impressed at Wati's speech and she was greatly relieved once it was all over. The hui tau was a new experience for Doug.

It was during the hui tau on Sunday 23 September 1951 that Doug was baptised as a member of the Church of Jesus Christ of Latter-day Saints by Elder Vaughan Milton Taylor from Canada, a direct descendant of John Taylor, former President of the Church.[12] Syd Crawford then confirmed Doug as a member of the Church. Doug's membership in the Church would be the beginning of a significantly new pathway in his life.

Six weeks later, Doug was ordained a deacon by Syd, then a teacher in June 1952 by James Archibald and finally a priest in March 1953 by Elder Glen J. Ellis, a missionary. Doug's first calling in the Church was as Assistant Master M. Man Leader – a fancy title for overseeing youth one night a week.

A Marriage Proposal

As the weeks and months passed, Doug was keen to marry Wati. He discussed it with her and decided to seek approval from Wati's father, Syd. When the three of them sat down to discuss the impending marriage, Syd got Rebecca to join them and, after some discussion in Māori, Rebecca told Doug that they had no land.[13] Doug was surprised and said he didn't care, only that he wanted to marry Wati. After further consideration and discussion in Māori, they said it would be fine for Doug to marry Wati.

A week later Doug and Wati visited Grieves Jewellers and bought a diamond ring for the sum of 27 pounds, about two–three weeks' wages. Doug worked at the Whakatū Freezing Works at the time and made good money. Wati worked at the Social Security Department as a shorthand typist. Things seemed stable and the future secure for them.

A Change of Plans

A short time later, Doug learned that Wati had been called to serve a Church mission at Temple View, near Hamilton. The Church had begun the construction of a temple, along with a co-ed secondary school and a number of meeting houses around the country. The project would last from 1951 to 1958 and involve significant sacrifice on the part of Church members both by way of donated goods and time.

Doug wasn't exactly happy about this turn of events and sought a meeting with Syd and Rebecca. Syd then proceeded to tell Doug 'in his kindliest voice' how they had always wanted Wati to serve a mission.[14] Despite Doug's reservations, Wati left Hastings to live full-time and serve a labour mission in Hamilton as secretary to the project supervisor, Elder George R. Biesinger.

Broken-hearted, Doug decided to move close to where Wati was. He succeeded in getting a job as a fitter and turner in Putaruru, not far from Hamilton. It was there that Doug first began trout fishing, a passion that continued through his life, albeit with limited success! Doug visited Wati on weekends and during one visit to Temple View he made it known that he would be willing to serve a labour mission. When Elder Biesinger learned of this, he most likely contacted president Sidney J. Ottley, the Mission President, who in short order called Doug to serve a proselytising mission instead.

Doug agreed and served in Auckland as a full-time missionary.[15] He was ordained an elder in the priesthood by president Ottley on 19 November 1953. In those days mission life was not as formal and structured as it is today. For example, the missionaries enjoyed going to the swimming pools on Saturday afternoons. However, the six-month mission experience allowed Doug to be influenced by American missionaries, some of whom were descendants of Church pioneers with strong gospel study habits and hard-working proselytisers.

Marriage, Finally

In time, Wati was nearing completion of her mission and Doug made an even better proposal than before. He wrote to Wati from Auckland as a missionary and proposed that he and Wati marry in the Temple in Laie, Hawaii.[16] He would sell his car to pay for the boat tickets. Wati agreed, so when both their missions ended they returned to Korongata, Hastings to begin preparations to travel to Hawaii.

Coincidentally, a group of eighteen people from Hastings were preparing to go to Hawaii at the same time. Wati's grandmother, Ani Tipare Stott, was part of the travel group. The Bridge Pa Relief Society was making temple clothing for the group and included Doug and Wati too. Passage for the group was arranged on the ship *Oronsay* and Wati's parents footed the bill for Doug since they said they didn't have to pay for a reception. Doug did not need to sell his car after all.

Wati and Doug were civilly married on 24 May 1954 by Elder Biesinger before travelling, due to a USA law requiring a period of residence in the country in order to be married there. The boat trip was about fourteen days in length with a stop in Fiji and Doug and Wati occupied separate quarters in the most economical rooms below deck. Doug was thrilled with the trip; however, Wati suffered with sea-sickness.

On 2 June 1954, Wati and Doug were married for time and all eternity in the Hawaiian temple by president Benjamin Bowring. A day later, Wati's grandmother, Ani Tipare Stott, was sealed in the temple to her deceased husband, Maraki Kamau. Wati and Doug assisted and witnessed this and other temple activities during this, their first-ever temple trip. Doug also mentioned a special experience he had in the temple, which is not recorded anywhere. Doug's first-time temple experience would be the beginning of many more such experiences.

Married Life

Doug and Wati returned as a married couple to Hastings. They lived in the front bedroom of the Crawford home. Wati found employment at Rainbow and Hobbs, an accounting firm that looked after Syd's business affairs. Doug gained employment at a start-up company called Harvey Can Company that had acquired the can-making operations of Wattie Canneries in Hastings.

Doug received a Church call to serve as district clerk. He loved his calling and was absorbed in record-keeping. He noted that many marriages and deaths had not been recorded. Being consumed with his calling he skipped Church one Sunday, assuming that working on his calling was of equal importance. Rebecca chastised him and Doug soon learned the importance of physically showing up for Sunday Church – something he did not understand up to this point in his Church membership. What he did observe at Church was individuals who read the scriptures, discussed them and made notes.

It was during this time that Syd Crawford was called to serve a labour mission at Temple View. Syd would leave his wife to supervise the store, post office, petrol pumps and shearing gangs, ably assisted by Wati's siblings – Buff in charge of shearing and Jewell in the store. Syd prevailed on Doug to leave Harvey Can and run the family trucking business.[17] Doug worked in the family business for a period of time but eventually grew restless.

A New Start in Hamilton

In February 1956, Doug and Wati left Hastings, much to the disappointment of Rebecca, and bought a newly built home in Melville, Hamilton. Regular bouts of homesickness ensued but they stayed put.

Doug tried a few different jobs and finally got a job at a plastics factory as assistant foreman after responding to an advertisement in the local *Waikato Times* newspaper. Doug interviewed with the founder of Plastic Products, Bill Foreman, and was called back to take the job. The factory was a twenty-four-hour-a-day operation, seven days a week, with three injection moulding machines.[18]

One afternoon a machine jammed and Doug came to help. Without thinking, he put his hand on the non-business end of the machine and it immediately opened and retracted, taking off the first joint of the index finger on his right hand. Immediate panic ensued and everyone was rushing around to get Doug wrapped up and off to hospital. The doctor examined his finger and asked if he played the piano. Doug replied no. He said he could try to save the black stump of his finger, but Doug replied 'no', realising that he would get compensated for the loss of limb. Proceeds were used to construct a garage at his home and Doug lived with a stumpy forefinger for the rest of his life.

Although frustrated at times in his career at Plastic Products (later Carter Holt Harvey Industries), Doug persevered for twenty-five years. On one occasion he was talked out of quitting by his boss, who asked him to stay and assist a consultant who was studying the business. When the consultant interviewed him, Doug told him his ideas on what needed to be done to fix things. Changes were made thanks to Doug's forthright input. Doug even benefitted from the changes with a better job and pay. Doug had an inborn ability to 'see things as they really are' and 'see what needs to change'. He always valued the input of others and frequently sought advice before reaching a decision.

Our Children

After some time, it became apparent that Doug and Wati were unsuccessful in having children. This was a great disappointment for them both. Wati's siblings had large families of their own. Wati's sister Gladys, her closest sister in age, would have eleven children. In a family meeting with Syd and Rebecca, it was agreed that James and Sydney, sons of Gladys and George, would be adopted by Doug and Wati. No greater love could be shown by a sister than to gift her childless sister two of her very own offspring.

In the second half of 1958, James, aged three, and Sydney, a baby, came to Hamilton with Wati and Doug. James was sad to leave behind his brothers and sisters, but, in time, they both realised the blessings of being in Doug and Wati's home.[19] Both served full-time Church missions – the only ones in their birth family of eleven.

James had already been sealed in the temple to George and Gladys and had the small challenge of being known as James Ferris when living in the Martin family. He would often be asked, 'why do you have a different name from Sydney and your family?' Doug always looked upon James as no less a son than any of his sons, both adopted and, later, by birth.

James was a talented athlete with natural speed and strength. He competed at an early age in gymnastics and won the local competition. He did not attend Church College of New Zealand (CCNZ), but instead went to Melville High School – a decision that Doug later regretted. James was a capable rugby player with speed, often playing winger and scoring tries.

Sydney attended CCNZ and was in the First XV rugby team. Doug was proud of Sydney and could be heard barking from the sidelines, encouraging his son in every rugby game. Sydney decided once to buy a motorbike against Doug's wishes. The motorbike was 500cc and in Doug's view too powerful for a young boy. After a discussion, the bike was returned at a loss, and Sydney learned one of many lessons from his adoptive father.

For ten years of marriage Doug and Wati were childless. Medical doctors examined both Wati and Doug and suggested if they were married to somebody else, they would most likely have children. They fasted and prayed much but eventually came to accept their lot in life, despite Wati's patriarchal blessing declaring she would have children. Doug learned never to make fun of childlessness.[20] Some years later, Wati returned from the doctor's office to announce she was pregnant.

After years of believing they would not bear children, Doug and Wati had been blessed. Shortly after the birth of Douglas Jonathan, Wati conceived again and Craig Tainui was born. For a short space of time, Doug and Wati enjoyed family life with four children. Doug purchased a section of land in Whangamatā, which was a popular holiday spot at the beach. The family and extended family would often spend Christmas in a tent at this beautiful scenic location.

Doug and Wati with James and Sydney and newborn Douglas Jr circa 1965.

Tragedy Strikes

Sadly, within twenty-two months, tragedy occurred. Doug was in Salt Lake City, when news arrived of the death of his youngest son, Craig, who had drowned in a shallow garden pool at a neighbour's house. Craig, a toddler, had slipped away down the road unknown to anyone. Doug travelled home with a heavy heart. It was the longest trip of his life. The tragedy would only be bearable with Doug's faith in Jesus Christ. Doug recounted he had never asked God why this had happened. He had accepted God's will in his life and looked forward to the day of a wonderful reunion, which occurred thirty-eight years later when he passed from this life on 23 January 2010.

Doug and Wati understandably became rather protective of their children after that incident. James and Sydney took their younger brother Douglas for a swim at a friend's pool which was over 6 feet in depth. When Doug and Wati learned of this, they rushed to the home in concern, only to find Douglas enjoying a swim doing dog paddle with the encouragement of his older brothers.

Douglas Jr saw his two brothers depart home and serve Church missions – James to the Philippines Cebu mission and Sydney to the Canada Calgary mission. Douglas spent his youth growing up alone at home with

Doug and Wati. Doug was often away on weekends with Church assignments and was unable to spend much time with his son, although he attended his basketball games when he was able. Douglas served a mission in the California Oakland mission, which was a very expensive mission in those days before equalised funding was introduced. Doug finally expressed complete faith that they would be able to afford to pay for Douglas's mission. He had not been convinced of this during James's and Sydney's missions. As Doug reflected, he was grateful that he never asked for Church assistance for his sons' missions, noting the Lord had blessed them to make ends meet.[21]

Employment at Plastic Products

Doug worked and qualified as a fitter and turner when he began at Plastic Products.[22] He worked there for twenty-five years and received a gold watch before retiring early at age sixty. He steadily worked his way from the factory floor into management, eventually becoming second in charge to the General Manager. He never considered himself gifted academically, having dropped out of high school, but he did earn a diploma in management, which allowed him to progress into a management role. He would always say mathematics was not his strength, but he was excellent at English. He was well read and he loved reading the newspaper every day and watching the six o'clock news on television every night. Douglas Jr would often seek his father's help on essay writing and English assignments. He was amazed how his father could take his writing and reduce the number of words significantly, yet increase the clarity of the message.

Doug's senior management role earned him the respect of his colleagues. He was always firm and direct in his approach at work and always put in his very best efforts. His association with senior management of the parent company, Carter Holt Harvey, allowed him the opportunity to travel the world and visit comparable manufacturing facilities in France, Europe and Asia. Wilson Whineray, former All Black captain and the Managing Director of Carter Holt Harvey asked Doug if he wanted to be General Manager of his own factory. Doug simply replied he preferred to be in Hamilton.

Doug's employer was very supportive of his Church service. He was able to use his work vehicle on weekends to travel all over the North Island attending stake conferences as a Regional Representative and not have to claim petrol. They also gave him time off to visit Salt Lake City once or twice a year as needed.

Other Interests and Hobbies

Doug always enjoyed the outdoors. In later years, he would wonder if he should have just been a farmer. He loved animals, he loved the bush, the hills and mountains. He had a particular interest in gardening.[23] Doug always had a large edible garden and he spent many hours outside tending to it, including a hothouse. He would harvest corn, carrots, potatoes, spinach, leeks and tomatoes, to name a few. He would have fruit trees, plums, apples and grapevines. Because he grew more than he needed, he was able to gift fruit and vegetables to other people, including his home teaching assigned widows and others.

Doug had a great love for the Māori people and bought and read many texts about Māori history. He was an avid genealogist in the days before computers. He maintained more than 3000 names on his PAF computer system and regularly provided names for family to do temple work. He and Wati were regular temple attenders, always setting aside Wednesday night to attend. He took pride in getting to know more about Wati's family than she or her family did.

Doug was given an assignment to oversee the Temple View farms for several years. He was Regional Representative for the Church and Operations Manager at Plastic Products at the time, but accepted the assignment from Church general authority Elder Loren C. Dunn. As Doug dropped his son Douglas Jr off at CCNZ each morning he would take the opportunity to look over the farm. This he did for many years without any remuneration. During his time, Doug engaged consultants to advise him on the farm, which eventually led to the farm converting to dairy.

Called to Church Leadership

Doug was called to be a Church leader soon after moving to Hamilton in early 1956. The Hamilton Branch met in a two-storey home in Te Aroha Street. Without a car, Doug and Wati simply walked everywhere, including from Melville across the Waikato River to Church. Doug was called to be branch president within two months of arriving – but he knew no-one in the ward. His counsellors were chosen by district president Dave Evans, an American serving a labour mission, and the mission president Ariel Ballif, both of whom interviewed Doug and extended the call with Lou Kingi and Horace Forbes as his two counsellors.

The next Sunday Doug conducted meetings for the first time as branch president. He noted an unsettled feeling in the branch and returned home to lunch with Wati and father-in-law, Syd, who was visiting and told them he felt a bad spirit in the branch and that no-one wanted him as branch president. Syd suggested Doug call a testimony meeting to gauge the feelings of the members. Doug did so and called a meeting for the next Sunday.[24]

The meeting started and there was a long pause, waiting for someone to be the first testimony bearer. Horace whispered to Doug, 'Perhaps you should call someone to speak first?' Doug replied, 'I'll sit here all day if necessary until someone gets up!' Finally, a woman stood and bore a sweet testimony. Next, a priesthood holder arose and said he had no confidence in Doug, that Doug had no experience and no idea how to run a branch and promptly asked for a release from all his callings. Next, an auxiliary leader arose and said he would be quite happy to be released if Doug so chose. Another auxiliary leader was next and said she would be OK if Doug wanted somebody else in her place. After several more expressed their feelings and testimonies, the branch presidency bore their testimonies.

Doug was the last speaker and he told everyone that he hadn't asked for the calling and agreed he knew little about Church administration and how to be a branch president, but since he had been called and had accepted the calling, he would simply do his best. He closed with the words 'E hoa mā' meaning 'my friends' – no doubt calling on all members to come together and be united.

The Golden Years of Church Growth

The late 1950s and 1960s was a marvellous time to be a Church member. Doug fondly recounts these times as the 'golden years' of the Church in New Zealand. With the building of the Temple and Church College, and the influx of American missionaries, there was a heightened interest in the Church and many new converts flocked to join. Their little branch grew quickly, with families joining who later became stalwarts in the Church – the Garrys, Manns, Murphys and Oliphants to name a few.[25]

The first purpose-built meetinghouse in Hamilton was constructed in O'Neill Street. In those days, leaders asked local members to contribute a third of the cost of chapels. The chapel had some marvellous functions for the predominantly young married families. With growing membership, the Hamilton Branch was elevated to a ward. Elder Marion G. Romney called Doug to serve as bishop of the new ward and set him apart in Auckland.

Elder Romney provided training to the group of bishops, but one statement stood out to Doug that he would never forget. Romney said, 'never let the cry of a widow ascend to heaven unheard.' Romney went on to teach them that the people that loved him the most were those to whom he had been a home teacher, then next were those whom he served as bishop. When he was a stake president, he no longer had the same personal relationships as an administrator and trainer. Now as an apostle he was just 'hit and run'. Doug never forgot Elder Romney's teaching.

The ward was assigned an American advisor named Collins Jones, the vice principal of CCNZ. He suggested to Doug that he organise Aaronic Priesthood quorums in the ward. Doug said they only had four or five deacons, one teacher and a couple of priests. Collins said, 'that's a beginning'. So, he did, and many wonderful young men participated and went on to become great leaders, including Robert Perriton (principal of CCNZ), Alan Perriton (CEO General Motors Asia), Peter Garry (Architect) and Malcolm Taylor (Woolworths Australia Executive).

Collins Jones also mentioned that a university had been announced, which was to be built in Hamilton. He told Doug, 'you have no idea what this will do for this city and the whole locality surrounding it!' The Church purchased 3 acres of land near the university and Doug visited the site with the Commissioner of Church Education, Jeffrey R. Holland, who told the group that 100 bona fide students were required to qualify for an Institute building to provide religious education to young adults aged eighteen to thirty years.[26] Silently, Doug thought he'd never live to see that day. He was wrong.

Hamilton Temple Recorder

As a new bishop, and as new production foreman at Plastic Products, Doug was asked by the new temple president Albert E. Rosenvall to accept the position of Hamilton temple recorder. Doug said he would only do it if it were a calling. Rosenvall responded, 'well I am calling you to be Temple Recorder', at which point Doug accepted.

Plastic Products multi-millionaire founder Bill Foreman said he was very disappointed Doug had resigned to take up the Church position, and would have prevailed on him to remain had he not been out of the country at the time. Doug went on to be trained by the recorder of the Manti Temple, Bengt Petersen. Doug and Rosenvall were the only two sealers in the Hamilton temple from 1958 to 1962.

Shortly after the dedication of the Hamilton Temple in 1958, Doug and Wati were asked to go to Auckland for unexplained reasons. Upon arrival at the Panmure chapel, Doug was told President David O. McKay wanted to see him. Stake president George Biesinger and Elder Wendell B. Mendenhall arrived with the Prophet and Doug was instructed to stand before him.

President McKay was much taller and had a magnificent appearance, broad-shouldered, a crown of wavy silver hair and said, 'Brother Martin, will you accept the sealing authority in the House of the Lord?' Doug was stunned and unable to speak. After being asked thrice, Doug finally said yes. President McKay then said, 'I don't usually ordain men to the priesthood, but you need to be a high priest to receive the sealing authority.'[27] So, they went into a room and the Prophet of the Lord ordained Doug and conferred the sealing authority. After that, Doug performed thousands of sealing ordinances in the temple for the deceased and hundreds for the living. Besides Elder Eldred G. Smith, no other person has served as temple sealer for more than fifty years.

Visiting Salt Lake City and General Conference

President George Biesinger called Doug a few months later to ask him if he would like to go to America. Doug thought he was joking, but he confirmed that Bishop Douglas Martin along with Bishop Selu Fruean from Auckland were to be invited to attend the October 1958 General Conference in Salt Lake City, the first bishops in the world to do so.[28]

Doug was met by Dave Evans, who hosted him during the visit. This was the first of many trips to Salt Lake City as Doug served as bishop, counsellor in the stake presidency and stake president. Whenever he returned home, it was a time of excitement for his children as he opened his bag with clothes and gifts from America.

Increasing Church Responsibility

Doug devoted significant amounts of time to Church service and leadership. He was initially called as second counsellor to Wendell Wiser, but Sister Wiser's illness necessitated their return to America. Harry Peckham was subsequently called to replace president Wiser, with Doug as his first counsellor.

Doug recalled learning so much from a small group of American Church leaders who served in New Zealand during this time – Ariel Ballif, Wendell Wiser, Robert L. Simpson, Loren C. Dunn and Jack Goaslind.

In November 1967 Elders Thomas S. Monson and Paul H. Dunn called Doug to serve as stake president of the Hamilton stake – a calling he would remain in for a decade. Doug oversaw the wards in Temple View (2), Hamilton (2), Huntly and branches in Ngaruawahia, Te Kuiti, Paeroa and Thames. The building of the Glenview chapel and Sandwich Road stake centre occurred during his tenure.

In 1977, Doug was released as stake president by Elder David B. Haight, who promptly called Doug to serve as stake patriarch.[29] Doug was a little fearful of this new calling. He did nothing until he was trained in Salt Lake City by Elder Boyd K. Packer with a group of thirty others. During the training, many questions were asked, but it soon became apparent that Elder Packer was not answering the questions. Instead, he counselled them all to return to their homes, learn and be guided by the spirit. A very successful American businessman who also attended the training session confided in Doug that he was terrified of this call until the meeting. Doug then felt it was not so wrong for him to be fearful. Nonetheless, he was determined to return home and get started.

A succession of young people began visiting the Martin home on Sunday afternoons, where Doug would conduct Patriarchal blessings. Wati would type them up before they were sent to Church Headquarters. This continued until Doug was invited to Salt Lake City again, where he was called as a Regional Representative and set apart by Marion D. Hanks of the First Quorum of Seventy.

As Regional Representative, Doug had leadership responsibility for the Lower North Island region. He would visit the stakes and support the presidents of eight stakes. After five years, Doug was reassigned to the Auckland region, supporting presidents of seven stakes.

Doug was widely known in Church circles. His namesake son Douglas Jr would be introduced to many people as Douglas Martin – and almost everyone would reply 'Are you Doug Martin's son?'

Retirement, Not Yet

Doug was looking forward to retirement from Plastic Products. When he was in his mid-fifties, Doug attended General Conference as a Regional Representative, where President Spencer W. Kimball urged older couples to devote a year or two in the mission field. Upon his return home, he discussed this with Wati and they agreed to prepare for missionary service. He informed his work colleagues three or four years ahead of his intended early retirement at age sixty.

As the time approached, all was falling into place. Doug was preparing to retire from work in April 1983 and looked forward to several months of relaxation around home and at the beach before their mission.

He was at the beach surfing the waves when he received a message that someone from Salt Lake City wanted to speak to him. He cut short his holiday and returned home to await a phone call. It was from president Gordon B. Hinckley, who called Doug to the First Quorum of Seventy and invited him to General Conference. Doug felt immensely humbled and moved by the call. A few weeks later president Hinckley set him apart and commented, 'that's the last time you'll be on the beach for a long time.'³⁰ Doug said of the calling, 'How grateful we are that we heeded the whisperings of the Spirit when listening to President Kimball several years ago!'

Elder Douglas J. Martin

Elder Martin, as he was now called, was the first native New Zealander called as a General Authority of the Church of Jesus Christ of Latter-day Saints. His first assignment was to the Philippines Area Presidency and he and Wati relocated to Manila. His first and only speech in General Conference was in October 1987, where he recounted his desire to serve the Lord full-time with Wati after hearing President Kimball speak some years earlier. He continued with experiences during his time in the Philippines. A year later he was called to the Pacific Area and served four more years living in Sydney, Australia, alongside longtime friends and fellow General Authorities, Elders Glenn L. Rudd and Rulon Craven, both of whom served proselytising missions in New Zealand.

Doug considered the men he served with in the First and Second Quorums of Seventy to be men of great accomplishment and education and considered himself the least of them. He said of his calling, 'maybe I feel a bit of the shy,

Hamilton New Zealand Temple President Douglas J. Martin and Temple Matron Wati Martin with all the temple workers.

insecure kid I used to be, but that doesn't stop me from having the confidence to go forth and do what the Lord requires of me now.' During his calling, he travelled all over the Philippines and the Pacific, including Australia, New Zealand, Samoa, Tonga, Fiji, Tahiti and Micronesia.

Doug was released in 1987 from the Second Quorum of Seventy and called as Temple President of the Hamilton Temple. Wati was called as Temple Matron. For three years they continued to serve the Lord, overseeing temple operations and living at the rear of the Temple. This was a wonderful time for Doug and Wati to see family and friends as they came to perform temple work.

Twilight Years

Finally, at age sixty-eight, Doug was able to retire from all work. He and Wati lived in a newly constructed home in Hamilton for many years, tending to his gardens, welcoming visitors to his home, doing his home teaching and attending the temple regularly.

Some years later, Doug and Wati moved to Sydney, Australia, to live with their son Douglas Jr and his family for two years. Douglas was offered a job with the Church in Sydney and asked his father for advice on whether he should accept. Doug offered no comment, leaving Douglas to make his own decision. He accepted Church employment, which only a few years later resulted in a transfer back home to Auckland. This meant Doug and Wati were also heading home to New Zealand, much to Doug's delight. They bought a house in Hamilton and moved back home. Doug died two years later, shortly after Wati celebrated her eightieth birthday with close friends and family. Wati continues to live in that house and celebrated her ninetieth birthday, surviving at least a decade longer than her eternal companion.

Legacy

Doug was an ordinary boy adopted out at young age by his unwed mother. As he grew older, he was keenly interested to find out about his birth family. His inborn curiosity to find his relatives incubated a lifelong talent to show personable and sincere interest in others. He made a significant change of course in his life when he met and married Wati Crawford and joined the Church of Jesus Christ of Latter-day Saints. Wati's influence on him was pronounced. He lived during the golden, transformative years of the Church's advancement in New Zealand when a temple and school were built near Hamilton, resulting in a membership boom.

Doug loved meeting and talking with people from all walks of life. He was gifted at writing and penned an autobiography for the benefit of his descendants. He was tutored by senior leaders of the Church throughout his life and given progressively increasing leadership responsibilities. He was devoted and steady in temple service and Church callings. Ultimately, he became the first New Zealander called as a General Authority in the Church. 'Douglas J. Martin, to me, was in a class all by himself,' said Elder Glen L. Rudd. 'In his positions he served faithfully and well in different assignments.'[31]

His lonely life as a youth was replaced with a very people-friendly life. He discovered much about his own family and was blessed with a large extended family through the Crawfords. Thinking he may never have offspring, he later was blessed with many descendants bearing his surname Martin. His life was well-rounded as he enjoyed many personal hobbies and pursuits in addition to his family and Church life. His years of Church leadership made him well-known and highly respected throughout New Zealand and the Pacific. He died aged eighty-two with Wati and his three surviving sons at his side.

NOTES

1. Douglas J. Martin Jr is the son of Douglas J. Martin
2. Martin, Douglas James (2000), *Hawkes Bay Born and Bred – My First 25 Years – An Autobiography*
3. *Ibid.* p 29
4. *Ibid.* p 10
5. *Ibid.* p 20
6. *Ibid.* p 23
7. Martin, Douglas James (2006) *A Change of Course For A More Excellent Way – My Next 35 Years – An Autobiography*
8. *Ibid.* p 2
9. *Ibid.* p 6
10. *Ibid.* p 18
11. *Ibid.* p 20
12. *Ibid.* p 21
13. *Ibid.* p 22
14. *Ibid.* p 25
15. *Ibid.* p 32
16. *Ibid.* p 40
17. *Ibid.* p 55
18. *Ibid.* p 73
19. *Ibid.* p 67
20. *Ibid.* p 153
21. *Ibid.* p 172

22. *Ibid.* p 73
23. *Ibid.* p 68
24. *Ibid.* p 82
25. *Ibid.* p 84
26. *Ibid.* p 93
27. *Ibid.* p 106
28. *Ibid.* p 96
29. *Ibid.* p 151
30. Rodriquez, Derin Head (1990) *From Every Nation – Faith-Promoting Stories of General Authorities from Around the World*, Deseret Book Company, Utah, pp 144-158
31. *Church News* (30 January 2010) 'Elder Douglas Martin, 82, dies', p 70

REFERENCES

Church News (30 January 2010) 'Elder Douglas Martin, 82, dies', p 70

Martin, Douglas James (2000) *Hawkes Bay Born and Bred – My First 25 Years – An Autobiography*

Martin, Douglas James (2006) *A Change of Course For A More Excellent Way – My Next 35 Years – An Autobiography*

Rodriguez, Derin Head (1990) *From Every Nation – Faith-Promoting Stories of General Authorities from Around the World*, Deseret Book Company, Utah

XII

A Product of His Environment

TE PUOHO KATENE (1927–2010)

Callum Katene[1]

Te Puoho spent virtually his entire life in Takapuwāhia, immersed in its history and cultural significance, contributing to the local community in many ways. He is particularly remembered for his artistic contributions in the fields of music and art, and also for his dedication to his faith and the years of service he gave. For such a person it would be remiss to attempt to describe him based on his personal attributes and achievements alone, many as they were, without an understanding of that to which his spirituality connected him: his Māori heritage and his faith. Of particular interest is how they became intertwined in his history and would eventually lead to the emergence of a person of his nature and abilities.

Te Puoho was born to a devout Mormon family. His father Te Oti had been raised in the Church of Jesus Christ of Latter-day Saints from a young age by his father's sister, Amiria, the twin daughter of Atanatiu Te Kairangi, a prominent chief of the Whanganui-based Ngāti Rangatahi tribe. Te Oti, whose family were of the Anglican faith, was the first of his line to be baptised (5 March 1990) into the Mormon Church.

Whakapapa (Genealogy)

WHANGATAAKI II = HINEWAIRORO

Te Puoho Ki Te Rangi = KAUHOE = TAAKU

Ngamianga (2) = PAREMATA TE WAHAPIRO = NGAHOPI (1)

Te Tapata = HEENI TE WAHAPIRO = GEORGE HOBY

Mary Hillman (2) = WI KATENE TIPO = HARETI TE KAIRANGI (1)

TE OTI (GEORGE) KEREI = Te Arohi (Rose) Maraea Poaneki Te Momo

TE PUOHO = Frances Anne Mackie

Te Puoho Katene was born on 21 October 1927 to Te Oti (George) Kerei and Te Arohi (Rose) Maraea Katene and grew up at the family homestead in Takapūwāhia, Porirua. He was named after his great-great-great-granduncle Te Puoho Ki Te Rangi,[2] a priest and fighting chief of the small but brave Ngāti Tama tribe that migrated from northern Taranaki to the Cook Strait district in the early 1820s.

Takapūwāhia

Te Puoho identified strongly with his Ngāti Toa Rangatira heritage, and also with his Ngāti Tama ancestry, and he lived most of his life at and around the Takapūwāhia marae in Porirua. In the 1820s the Ngāti Toa Rangatira people migrated from their homelands at Kāwhia harbour in Waikato. They had been battling their neighbouring tribes for many years and eventually made the decision that it was time to leave the area. Led by their warrior chief Te Rauparaha, Ngāti Toa Rangatira headed south[3] and would eventually settle throughout the lands surrounding the Cook Strait (Raukawa Moana), including Kāpiti, Waikanae, Plimmerton (Taupō) and Porirua harbour, and in the lands of the northern South Island (Te Waipounamu). The exploits of Te Rauparaha and Ngāti Toa Rangatira are well documented; suffice it to say, they made a significant impact on all they encountered, including numerous other tribes and, of course, the many European settlers. In addition, Te Rauparaha and his nephew Te Rangihaeata were particularly resistant to parting with their lands – lands coveted by the increasing numbers of new British settlers. So, in 1846 Governor George Grey visited Te Rauparaha at

Taupō Pā (village). Subsequently, British soldiers arrived and took Te Rauparaha captive. He was held without trial on the ship *Calliope* for ten months before being allowed to live in Auckland, although not permitted to return to his family until 1848.[4]

Grey's plan worked splendidly. With Te Rauparaha gone and Te Rangihaeata on the run,[5] the remaining Ngāti Toa Rangatira leaders were far more open to the advances of the Pākehā. Taupō Pā would eventually be abandoned and, by 1850, Ngāti Toa Rangatira had spread out around Porirua harbour in pockets of hapū (sub-tribes), which included the fortified Te Urukahika Pā and Takapūwāhia, both located near present-day Elsdon. Takapūwāhia remains to this day, along with Hongoeka, the heartland for the people of Ngāti Toa Rangatira in the lower North Island.

Like many tribes throughout the country at the time, Ngāti Toa Rangatira were in a period of rapid change, forced upon them by the arrival and encroachment of the European settlers. Queen Victoria was extending and strengthening her influence through the actions of her representatives in this part of the world, and many Māori were starting to think 'perhaps it is best to adopt the ways of the Pākehā.'

The Arrival of Christianity

Christianity had been introduced into the Kāpiti region more than a decade before. In 1839, Tāmihana Te Rauparaha[6] and Matene Te Whiwhi[7] travelled to the Bay of Islands, seeking a Christian missionary for their people. In response, Anglican Rev. Octavius Hadfield travelled from Paihia to Waikanae, arriving that December.[8] Under his influence, schools were established and many learned to read and write. Prominent members of Ngāti Toa Rangatira could see value in adopting the 'Pākehā way of life' and that conversion and education would be the primary mechanisms to achieve this goal. To this end, in 1848, the Whitireia lands (500 acres in Tītahi Bay, Porirua) were gifted to the Anglican Church[9] for the purposes of establishing a school to provide both secular and religious education. The school was never built and in 1850 that Church obtained a Crown grant for the land, with no consideration given to Ngāti Toa Rangatira or the purpose for which the land had been gifted.

Wi Parata Te Kākākura, a member of the Ngāti Toa Rangatira iwi and also a member of Parliament from 1871 to 1875, took the case to the Supreme Court in 1877 'over a breach of oral contract between the Anglican Church and the Ngāti Toa, and a breach of the principles of the Treaty of Waitangi',[10] seeking the return of the land. He was unsuccessful. Chief Justice James Prendergast ruled that:

'native' or 'aboriginal' customary title, not pursuant to a Crown grant, could not be recognised or enforced by the courts. He also claimed that the Treaty of Waitangi was a 'simple nullity' because the Maori were 'primitive barbarians' who were 'incapable of performing the duties, and therefore of assuming the rights, of a civilised community'.[11]

This ruling was devastating, not just to Ngāti Toa Rangatira, because it would be used to justify future alienation and confiscation of Māori lands and had a profound impact on many other Māori iwi around New Zealand.

In 1887, representatives of the Church of Jesus Christ of Latter-day Saints first arrived in Porirua. The New Zealand Mission of that Church had been established more than thirty years earlier, but it was not until 1881 that it began to include Māori in its proselytising efforts. They arrived while the memory of the betrayal by the Anglican Church still smouldered, with many negotiations and appeals for the return of the Whitireia lands having failed over the intervening years. The Mormons encountered a people with little loyalty to their existing faith and ripe for change.

The Porirua Branch of the Church of Jesus Christ of Latter-day Saints was established at Te Urukahika on 3 June 1887. In 1889 Te Urukahika was abandoned and the people, along with their Church, relocated the short distance to Takapūwāhia. In 1901 the meeting house, Toa Rangatira, was opened and in 1909 a schoolhouse was built on the marae, which would also serve the community for Church gatherings for another forty years.

Family Life and Upbringing

Te Oti Kerei Katene Snr.

Te Puoho's father Te Oti Kerei Katene was born on 28 March 1890 at Motueka to Wi Katene Hoby and Hareti Te Kairangi.[12] When Te Oti was only a few months old, his parents moved to Pukerua Bay, a small seaside settlement just north of Porirua. The journey would involve a ferry trip from the South Island to Wellington, and then a train ride the short distance north. Amiria, Hareti's twin sister who lived at Takapūwāhia at the time, wanted to meet her new nephew, so arrangements were made to view the baby at Porirua railway station, where the train would stop on its way to

Pukerua Bay. When the train arrived at Porirua, Te Oti's parents passed their child out the window for Amiria to hold. Eventually, it was time for the train to continue its journey, but as it pulled away from the station Amiria was still holding little Te Oti in her arms – something she had planned quietly to do all the time. Amiria had no children and planned to raise Te Oti as her own.

Te Oti was nine when his mother, Hareti, passed away in 1899 at thirty-five years of age, leaving most of her twelve children in the care of family with the three youngest children (Frederick, Manu and Ngaronga) placed in an Anglican orphanage in Motueka.

Te Oti was raised at the Solomon homestead on Nohorua Street in Takapūwāhia. Amiria was a member of the Church of Jesus Christ of Latter-day Saints and so Te Oti was raised in this faith. Te Oti married Te Arohi Maraea Poaneki Te Momo[13] on 6 May 1911. They lived at Pukerua Bay overlooking the ocean and Kāpiti Island.

With the advent of the World War One, Te Oti was recruited into the Home Guard. However, five of Te Oti's brothers – Hari, Rangi, Taku, Frederick and Manu – joined the army, becoming members of the Māori Pioneer Battalion and served in France during the Battle of the Somme. While they all returned home, the youngest, Manu, who changed his name to Joe Bird Cotton at fifteen years of age to join the army, died within two years of his return, diagnosed with 'war psychosis' commonly known as shell shock.

The Mormon missionaries have always been feted by the Katene whānau. But there was one memorable occasion when the situation was reversed. On 20 July 1920 Hanna Cootes Wineera wired the missionaries (Elders Harris and Clark) in Palmerston North, indicating that George (Te Oti) Katene 'was dying and to come at once.' After biking to Otaki and then catching the train to Porirua, the missionaries arrived the next day to find 'that George was about gone. We were admitted to the room and after some time administered to him. We stayed until after midnight.' On 22 July 'George began to improve.' The missionaries 'had to be with him almost continually.' On 25 July, and after four days of personal ministering, Elder Harris wrote, 'after an all-night with George, I left him for good, in the best of mind and improving in health. He acknowledged the hand of the Lord, and I hope he will be better for it.'[14]

Te Oti and Te Arohi would have fourteen children, some of whom would not reach adulthood. Te Puoho arrived in 1927. By this time the family had moved from Pukerua Bay to Takapūwāhia and established the Katene homestead on what would come to be known as 'Katene Corner'. Their home was always tidy but there weren't many luxuries. Missing wallpaper was sometimes replaced with newspaper. There was always food, usually cereals, or a flour and water combination brought to the boil and cooked, much like porridge. Te Oti had two cows and it was the children's daily routine to take them up the road in the morning to graze and bring them home at night for milking. They would separate the milk and cream; the cream was always thick, rich and delicious. The Katene family supplied many other families in Takapūwāhia with milk. Butter would be made from the cream but often there was not enough, as it would get eaten or be given to other families.

Te Oti worked several jobs to make ends meet. One was at the meat works, so he was able to occasionally bring meat home for the family. He owned a black pickup truck that would become an icon in the area. He would often return from work with offcuts that he got for free, piled in the back of his truck, and offer them for sale to the local families for tuppence each. Some of the families were a little irritated by this, knowing he got them for free but was selling them for a profit. On the other hand, quite often the verbal IOUs he received would never be honoured, so neither side had reason to be particularly aggrieved.

Te Oti Katene was a dedicated and faithful servant of his faith from his youth. Towards the end of the 1930s, Te Oti became the Church leader for their locality at a critical time. World War Two resulted in many foreign missionaries being recalled home and so it was up to local leaders to guide their faithful through this difficult period.[15] Te Oti would grow in his role as the Church's local leader and came to be known as 'the elder statesman' and local patriarch.

In 1940 many volunteers flocked to enlist in support of the Allied cause in World War Two. One of them was Te Oti's son George, following in the footsteps of his five uncles who served in World War One, and his father on the Home Front. Made a sergeant before the 28th Māori Battalion left New Zealand for Egypt, the twenty-five-year-old was soon promoted to the rank of lieutenant. In a letter on behalf of the Latter-day Saints in his battalion, to the Latter-day Saints in New Zealand published in the August 1940 edition of *Te Karere*, not intending to make it a letter of farewell, he wrote:

> To you dear fathers, mothers, brothers, sisters, and friends, we send greetings of good cheer to comfort and gladden you. Even though we are absent physically the cry for unity has never been so loudly proclaimed before. The whole Christian world calls for it. In the homes the bonds of love should bind together the members closer and closer. In the Churches the altars of love call to their members to come and share with them the warmth of spirituality. Somehow, I wish that I could walk up to each Latter-day Saint and make him realize that this is so; that it is time to grow out of our shells and expand our modes

of living so that we will be of more benefit to our neighbours. We must grow strong, because of troublesome times ahead. We must cultivate our physical beings so that we may withstand hardship. We must build up our mentalities so that we will have the determination to exist in righteousness.[16]

Sadly, on 7 December 1943, George Katene was killed in action as the Māori Battalion attacked enemy troops holding the town of Orsogna, Italy. Holder of the Military Medal, he became the first Māori to be decorated in World War Two. His sister Wikitoria continued as the only Māori nurse to volunteer for overseas service in World War Two. She later cared for veterans and was awarded the Queen's Service Medal in 1992.

Te Puoho Katene was raised and nurtured in this environment. He and his siblings loved the missionaries, they grew up heavily involved in the Church and their local community, under the guidance and direction of their parents. On occasion, Te Oti would arrange a trip to a Church hui tau (national Church conferences) and pack the tray of his truck with straw and boxes for the passengers. Te Puoho would be one of these huddled in the back, shoulder to shoulder with other faithful family members and relatives, cramped and uncomfortable for the duration of those long trips.

World War Two: brother and sister, Wikitoria and George Katene Jnr.

In preparation for the 1936 hui tau in Tahoraiti, Dannevirke, money was raised by Te Oti from the sale of a bull continually causing trouble by wandering onto the main road in Porirua.

> Once again, the bull wandered onto the Titahi Bay Road at Porirua and stopped traffic. And, once again, someone from the Katene family had to be called to drive the bull back to where it belonged. Enough, Te Oti thought; this bull was too much trouble. We will sell it, and use the money to take us to the hui tau. The Maori Latter-day Saints looked forward to these yearly gatherings, which lasted for days, filled with preaching and dancing and eating and sports and

other celebrations of both Maori and Latter-day Saint culture. It was expensive to provide transportation and supplies for this huge family, both immediate and extended, and selling the troublemaking bull would take care of everything quite nicely.[17]

Upon leaving high school, Te Puoho enrolled and attended the Canterbury School of Fine Art in Christchurch, which is where his love of piano and choral music first blossomed.[18] He left that school before graduating, returning to Wellington, where he enrolled to study music at Victoria University and had the opportunity to study under master composer Douglas Lilburn; this fortuitous circumstance would turn out to be a godsend for a person of his talents.

His growing skill and abilities in the field of music would overflow into his Church life. Te Puoho quickly became involved in performing, then arranging music for Church meetings, and soon became well-known as the pre-eminent choir master of the area.

On 30 May 1959, Te Puoho married Frances Anne Mackie, making their home in Porirua, and shortly thereafter were blessed with two children, Callum and Moira.

Te Puoho and Frances Katene.

In 1963, the Polynesian Cultural Centre at Laie, Hawaii, was to open its recently completed Māori village. The 150-strong Te Arohanui Māori Concert Party, comprised mainly of former Church labour missionaries involved in a major Church building programme,[19] would be travelling there for the December opening where they would perform and then go on to tour mainland USA. Te Puoho's reputation was already such that he was invited to travel as the cultural advisor for the group, which he declined. He was later invited to travel as the assistant cultural advisor and was eventually persuaded.

Te Puoho travelled with the group to Hawaii and then on to the USA, where they appeared on the Danny Kaye show[20] and then on to Utah where the group had the opportunity to sing in the Mormon Tabernacle, under

Te Puoho's baton. This was a source of great pride to Te Puoho; conducting a choir in the Tabernacle, from the same seats that the Mormon Tabernacle Choir sings from, was a highlight of his still young career. A majestic photograph of the event would hang from the walls of his home for the rest of his life.

By the mid 1960s, Te Puoho's musical and choral reputation was becoming established. His accomplishments were starting to be recognised within the wider community. So, when, in 1965, the New Zealand Opera Company needed a chorus of talented and capable choral singers with darker skin for an upcoming production, it was the perfect opportunity for Te Puoho and his contemporaries.

Porgy and Bess: New Zealand Opera Company's Production

New Zealand opera dates back to the New Zealand Opera Company, formed by baritone Donald Munro in 1958, following the creation of the National Opera of Australia and their subsequent tour in 1954. The early productions were small and modest. From 1963, however, the New Zealand Opera Company received funding from the QEII Arts Council, which allowed it to take productions on tour, when they would visit many localities throughout the country, with piano accompaniment in the smaller towns and full orchestras in the cities. One of their highlights was the 1965 production of *Porgy and Bess*[21] by George Gershwin.

Although that opera had grown to become very popular by the 1940s and 1950s, productions were rare, especially outside the USA, because the Gershwin estate insisted that the play could only be performed by a cast of black American opera singers.[22] The New Zealand Opera Company did, however, secure permission to perform the show by agreeing to use Māori cast members.

Cast auditions were held. About 300 Māori auditioned, from which the chorus of 30 were chosen.[23] Īnia Te Wīata was cast in the role of Porgy, as well as some other Māori in minor roles, including Mark Metekingi in the role of Jake and Toni Williams[24] as Sportin' Life. In addition to this, the cast included three professional African-American opera singers in the roles of Bess, Crown and Serena, due to the difficulty of these operatic parts.

Practice for the wider cast proved to be extremely challenging, particularly for those who had not been on the stage before. They would be required to perform six times per week at an extremely high standard, and the rigours of strenuous training and practice started to take its toll. Morale within the cast plummeted and they came close to abandoning the show. However, they were taken to task by Īnia Te Wīata and then addressed by Lieutenant Colonel Charles Bennett DSO, former commander of the Māori Battalion, who reminded them of the scale of this opportunity and encouraged them to do their people proud.

Porgy and Bess opened on 1 March 1965 in Christchurch and went on to perform in all the main centres before the final performances in Auckland in June of that year. The tour was a huge success and plans were formulated to take the show to Australia. While on the Australian tour, the Māori cast would be performing Māori items at the Asian Trade Festival, which was being held in Sydney while they would be there. Unfortunately, the Australian tour was a financial failure, but the seeds of Māori choral music had been sewn.

The New Zealand Māori Theatre Trust

The majority of the *Porgy and Bess* Māori chorus had little future in opera, not being professionally trained and mostly unable to read music. So, once the *Porgy and Bess* tour was over, they needed some avenue that would allow them to build on that experience. In August 1966 the New Zealand Māori Theatre Trust was formed,[25] with the goal being 'to encourage and develop the indigenous culture of New Zealand to a level of sophistication to enable it to be appreciated internationally.' The original members included Don Selwyn, Timoti Te Heu Heu, Tommy Taurima and Te Puoho. Their first production was to be a mythical folk opera called Uenuku, written by Pei Te Hurunui Jones, with music by Te Puoho and Tommy Taurima.

Over the next few years the New Zealand Māori Theatre Trust would put on more productions and also go on to make record albums, some with Viking Records. In 1970 they travelled to Japan to perform at Expo 70, then went on to tour in Russia.

During those years the New Zealand Māori Theatre Trust evolved from being primarily about Māori in theatre (both the people and the subject) to more of a concert party with a move to more authentic and traditional Māori performances.[26] Don Selwyn parted ways with the Trust around this time, preferring to focus on his acting career, and would go on to become a household name. It has been said that this change of direction by the New Zealand Māori Theatre Trust was at least partly influenced by the Māori renaissance,[27] which began around this time.

The Commonwealth Games – 'Join Together'

In 1973 Keith Southern[28] was working as a producer at Viking records. A television competition was to be held to find a modern theme song for the upcoming Commonwealth Games. Keith was working closely with Steve Allen at the time and encouraged him to write a song and enter the competition. Allen wrote 'Join Together' in about half an hour and it was recorded at the EMI studios in Wellington, with only a guitarist, bassist, drummer and Allen himself on the keyboards.[29] Keith had been quite keen to involve a Māori dimension and so a meeting was arranged between Keith, Steve Allen and Brian Hands, a composer, bandleader and arranger. A representative of the New Zealand Māori Theatre Trust had also been invited, having made recordings with Viking previously. This is where Keith Southern met Te Puoho Katene for the first time.

With the music and choral arrangements ready and the singers well-practised, the New Zealand Māori Theatre Trust travelled to the recording studio to record their parts, which would later be overdubbed onto Steve Allen's original recording of 'Join Together'. After the recordings of the vocal tracks were completed, Keith asked the singers to perform a rendition of Pōkarekare Ana, to wind up the session.

Keith and Viking were very impressed. They proposed making an album of Māori songs, with choral arrangements by Te Puoho and the music arranged and directed by Brian Hands and played by members of the New Zealand Symphony Orchestra.[30] The album would take a further two years to come together and in the process the New Zealand Māori Chorale would emerge.

The New Zealand Māori Chorale

In 1976 the album *Pōkarekare Ana* was released and was a huge success.[31] It featured fourteen mostly well-known Māori songs, but performed as choral arrangements, with the backing music of the New Zealand Symphony Orchestra. As can be expected, the singing was very reminiscent of the music of the New Zealand Māori Theatre Trust, but with more sophisticated and intricate choral arrangements and, of course, the quality of the musical accompaniment was of the highest national standard. The New Zealand Māori Chorale became internationally famous and would go on to perform on TV and give numerous live performances.

The New Zealand Māori Chorale went on to release several more albums, including *Songs of New Zealand* in 1978 and *New Zealand Sings* in 1979. They would eventually be awarded one platinum[32] and two gold records in recognition of their outstanding record sales.

The 1987 America's Cup: 'Sailing Away'

The 1983 success of *Australia II* in winning the America's Cup from Dennis Connor's *Liberty* of the New York Yacht Club caught the imagination of many in New Zealand and in 1984 New Zealand entered the America's Cup as the New Zealand Challenge.[33] Later in the challenge, Michael Fay[34] would be introduced to assist with organisation and funding.

It is a part of the New Zealand psyche to become overexcited at the prospect of any appearance on a world stage and the upcoming 1987 America's Cup would fit this perfectly. In an effort to further foment public excitement and involvement it was decided to release a pop song, featuring many well-known public figures, to help raise money for the challenge. The song 'Sailing Away'[35] was produced, using the melody of 'Pōkarekare Ana' but with re-written lyrics. Te Puoho arranged the backing vocals, which were performed by the New Zealand Māori Chorale. He was also credited as one of the lyricists.[36]

The song spent nine weeks at number one and went four times platinum. Not everyone was impressed, however. Sir Howard Morrison was quite vocal in his opposition to the use of 'Pōkarekare Ana' in this way.

Community Service

Te Puoho was heavily involved in many aspects of his local community. In October 1968 he was elected a member of the Porirua City Council at the age of forty, and would keep this position until 1977. During that period of time he was a member of the council's finance, cultural, welfare bylaws and town-planning committees, and also represented the council on the Free Ambulance Board and the Mana Arts Festival Trust.

In 1987, Te Puoho was awarded the Queen's Service Medal for community service.[37] The following year (1988), Te Puoho travelled to Canberra, Australia to deliver a paper on Māori music to the eighteenth International Society for Music Education conference. At that conference, he was elected a member of that society. That same year, Te Puoho was appointed Justice of the Peace, an acknowledgement of his standing in the wider community.

In 1990, Te Puoho returned to academic study, completing a BA in English, graduating in March of the following year.

In 2005, at the age of eighty-three, Te Puoho was awarded the Te Waka Toi Tā Kingi Ihaka Award and a life membership from the New Zealand Society for Music Therapy.[38]

Takapūwāhia Marae

By the 1970s, the wharenui (meeting house) of the Takapūwāhia marae, which had been standing for more than seventy years, was becoming run down and the people agreed it was time for it to be replaced. It had been built in 1901 under the influence of Christian missionaries and lacked many elements of the more traditional wharenui. Inspired again by the recent Māori renaissance, the new house would see a return to, or resurrection of, traditional Māori art and decorative techniques. However, this presented challenges. For example, there were no tukutuku (latticework) panels in the old meeting house; Ngāti Toa Rangatira had no tukutuku traditions to reference. While there was an understandable sadness due to this loss, it did create an opportunity and allowed for an amount of creative license to be expressed.

In August 1976, work began on the carvings (whakairo) that would adorn the new house, under the direction of Kohe Webster. As time progressed, Puhanga Tu Paea and Te Puoho Katene were brought in to take responsibility for the tukutuku panels and the kōwhaiwhai, respectively. All agreed that a single overriding philosophy was required to unify the three artistic disciplines and, since the whakairo was well underway, that would be the starting point. Te Puoho said:

> (the) decision to stain and oil the carvings was considered as being critically important. So too was the decision to use natural instead of manufactured materials for the tukutuku. Clearly the direction was toward nature. The philosophy was beginning to come into focus. It would be nature.[39]

To this end, the colours and layout of the interior of the house were chosen to reflect nature and to symbolise the circle of life, from the earth-coloured carpet to the tukutuku panels, whose slats were oiled green, evenly punctuated by the intricately carved pou. Standing there, one feels the familiarity of the New Zealand bush, with the productive brown soil beneath stockinged feet, the dense green of foliage between the trunk-like pou and the ceiling overhead oiled in yellow, the colour of dried kakaho. The combinations speak to the circle of life, growth potential from Papatuanuku below, the established flora of Tāne Mahuta all around and the colour of ageing above. With death, everything falls back to the embrace of Papatūānuku and the cycle starts again.

In addition to contributing to the overall design philosophy, Te Puoho was responsible for the creation of the kōwhaiwhai patterns that would adorn the house's tāhuhu (spine) and heke (rafters). His inspiration included 'Te Hau Ki Tūranga' (1842), the meeting house from Manutuke, Gisborne, that had been confiscated in 1867 by the New Zealand government and its carvings taken to Wellington. In the 1930s, the house was reassembled in the Dominion Museum under the direction of Sir Apirana Ngata, which is where Te Puoho would see it forty years later.[40]

A key component of Te Puoho's kōwhaiwhai design was the incorporation of the Te Ahi Kā symbol, a stylised representation of a cupped hand holding a flame. The inspiration for this came from the story of Māui obtaining fire for humankind, and by giving it the name Te Ahi Kā it was also a reference to the concept of traditional title to land through continuous occupation. In more colloquial terms, this is an acknowledgement to those that 'keep the home fires burning'. Toa Rangatira the meeting house was opened on 15 May 1982.

Te Puoho outside Takapūwāhia Marae, Porirua.

A Life of Faith

Te Puoho Katene was a person of considerable faith. He demonstrated a lifelong commitment to the Church principles and values that he was taught from a young age by his father, leveraging all his considerable talent to glorify and honour his God. His musical ability is well described above, and he continually used this ability to guide his fellow worshippers in creating a palpable spiritual ambiance. With every wave of his baton or stroke of his paintbrush he acknowledged his Saviour. It permeated his being and, for one such as he, it would be an error to consider his work or achievements outside of that context; it could be done, but the totality would be absent of detail.

He was also known as an articulate intellect with an uncommon ability to explore nuance and subtlety on a wide variety of religious subjects. He was highly regarded for his insight, the benefit of which was sought by many over the years.

Te Puoho followed in the footsteps of his father, Te Oti, in his role as a local leader in the Church of Jesus Christ of Latter-day Saints. The Church leadership position he will be most remembered for are the years he served as the Wellington Stake Patriarch. He was first called to this position on 30 October 1977 until being released on 6 February 1997, and was called to it again on 23 November 2009. Earlier, his first cousin Bill Katene had been called as one of the first Māori stake presidents in New Zealand, leading the Temple View Stake in Hamilton during the 1970s.

George Elkington, Wellington Stake President from 1989 to 1998, fondly remembers Te Puoho in this role, and even today recalls with affection the calmness and composure of his nature. George recounts an incident where Te Puoho's counsel was sought, and the simple, one-sentence response changed George's complete perspective on the issue at hand. George referred to Te Puoho as 'the third Stake Councillor'.[41]

Te Puoho Katene passed away on 27 June 2010 and is buried with his wife, Frances Anne Katene (née Mackie), and beside his parents at Takapūwāhia, Porirua. He is survived by two children, a daughter-in-law, four grandchildren and eleven great-grandchildren.

Legacy

Te Puoho Katene was a product of his environment, and it was this that gave him a platform from which to launch his considerable talents. His spirituality was innate, but was also fostered from a young age by his parents, extended family and his involvement with his Church and his Ngāti Toa people. They themselves were the products of their environment, which in turn emerged from the significant upheaval of the mid-nineteenth century colonial policies of the British Empire, with one particular incident leading to their widespread adoption of an American religion.

His legacy is not lost on his descendants, despite none of them having followed him in the field of music or art, certainly not to the level of expertise for which he was known. Although they continue his connection to their culture and heritage, none of them have retained his faith. But that isn't the point. The upbringing and guidance he gave his descendants was not supposed to make them copies of him; it was to give them a platform from which to launch whatever talents, whatever abilities they may have, in the pursuit of the things that they think are important. They may well be wrong in what they choose as being the important pursuits in life – but, right or wrong, it's their choice.

The best thing Te Puoho did for his children and grandchildren was to prepare and encourage them to grow their own abilities and talents so that one day they could be the best people they could be. He taught them how to think, not what to think; only they can decide what it actually means to be the best person they can be.

Te Puoho Katene was an example of this. This is what he did for his children and grandchildren; this is his legacy. The lesson is not lost.

'If I have seen further, it is by standing on the shoulders of giants.'
Isaac Newton, 1675

NOTES

1. Callum Katene is the son of Te Puoho Katene
2. Anderson, Atholl (1990) 'Te Puoho-o-te-rangi', Te Ara – The Encyclopedia of New Zealand. Retrieved from https://teara.govt.nz/en/biographies/1t59/te-puoho-o-te-rangi
3. Pōmare, Mīria (2005) 'Ngāti Toarangatira – Migration from the north', Te Ara – The Encyclopedia of New Zealand. Retrieved from https://teara.govt.nz/en/map/1350/ngati-toas-migration
4. Oliver, Steven (1990) 'Te Rauparaha', Te Ara – The Encyclopedia of New Zealand. Retrieved from https://teara.govt.nz/en/biographies/1t74/te-rauparaha
5. Ballara, Angela (1990) 'Te Rangihaeata', Te Ara – The Encyclopedia of New Zealand. Retrieved from https://teara.govt.nz/en/biographies/1t63/te-rangihaeata
6. Tāmihana Te Rauparaha was Te Rauparaha's son
7. Matene Te Whiwhi was Te Rauparaha's grand-nephew
8. Waikanae Anglican (n.d.) 'Our History'. Retrieved from http://www.anglican.co.nz/about/our-story
9. Solomon, Hōhepa (1987) *Hui Rau Tau: 100 Years Established in Porirua*
10. Wikipedia (n.d.) 'Wiremu Parata'. Retrieved from https://en.wikipedia.org/wiki/Wiremu_Parata#Wi_Parata_v_Bishop_of_Wellington_(1877)
11. Hannan, J. G. H. and Bassett, Judith (1990) 'James Prendergast'. Retrieved from https://teara.govt.nz/en/biographies/1p29/prendergast-james
12. Keriata Leavitt – as told by Te Puoho's sister Tiripa Katene, and other sources
13. Ngāti Raukawa
14. Harris, Edward Daniel (2006) *The Missionary Journals of Edward Daniel Harris (1917–1920)*, transcribed and edited by Mark F. Harris, Trafford Publishing, USA, p 141
15. Solomon (1987)
16. *Te Karere* (August 1940) Open letter to the Latter-day Saints in New Zealand from Sergeant George Katene on behalf of the Latter-day Saints of the 28th Māori Battalion
17. Keepapitchinin (1936) *A Bump in the Road to Hui Tau 1936*
18. Sounz (n.d.) 'Te Puoho Katene'. Retrieved from https://www.sounz.org.nz/contributors/1199
19. The Mormon Church building programme based in Tuhikaramea, west of Hamilton, included the construction of the first temple of the Church of Jesus Christ of Latter-day Saints in the southern hemisphere, the building of the Church College of New Zealand, a private secondary school and dozens of meeting houses for worship around the country. Over 500 labour missionaries participated in the construction project commencing in the early 1950s through to the 1960s.
20. YouTube (2013) 'Te Arohanui Maori Concert Party – 1963'. Retrieved from https://youtu.be/ko4zzlQVFVo
21. Carr, Malcolm (1965) 'Porgy and Bess – A Vibrant Theatricality'. Retrieved from http://nzetc.victoria.ac.nz/tm/scholarly/tei-Salient28061965-t1-body-d60.html

22. Radio New Zealand (n.d.) 'Porgy and Bess – 50 Years Since NZ Performance'. Retrieved from https://www.radionz.co.nz/audio/player?audio_id=201771047
23. Derby, Mark and Grace-Smith, Briar (2014) 'Māori theatre – te whare tapere hōu'. Te Ara – The Encyclopedia of New Zealand. Retrieved from https://teara.govt.nz/en/maori-theatre-te-whare-tapere-hou
24. Toni Williams was *Cook Island* Māori. Wikipedia (n.d.) 'Toni Williams'. Retrieved from https://en.wikipedia.org/wiki/Toni_Williams
25. Te Ao Hou (September 1966) 'Maori Theatre Trust Formed'. Retrieved from https://paperspast.natlib.govt.nz/periodicals/TAH196609.2.46.2
26. The Big Idea (2008) 'Matariki Forum: Where is Maori Theatre Now?' Retrieved from https://www.thebigidea.nz/news/industry-news/2008/nov/31395-matariki-forum-where-is-maori-theatre-now
27. The Māori renaissance reflected the revival of Māori culture, including the Māori language, pre-schooling for Māori children, broadcasting, the arts and business development
28. Keith Southern, personal communication
29. NZ History (n.d.) 'Join Together' Song, 1974 Commonwealth Games. Retrieved from https://nzhistory.govt.nz/media/photo/%26%23039%3Bjoin-together%26%23039%3B-song%2C-1974-commonwealth-games
30. Keith Southern, personal communication
31. Keith Southern, personal communication
32. Bourke, Chris (2014) 'Popular music – Origins of New Zealand popular music', Te Ara – The Encyclopedia of New Zealand. Retrieved from https://teara.govt.nz/en/interactive/42563/gold-and-platinum-new-zealand-albums-to-2013
33. Wikipedia (n.d.) 'New Zealand Challenge'. Retrieved from https://en.wikipedia.org/wiki/New_Zealand_Challenge
34. Wikipedia (n.d.) 'Michael Fay (Banker)'. Retrieved from https://en.wikipedia.org/wiki/Michael_Fay_(banker)
35. YouTube (2017) 'Sailing Away – All of Us'. Retrieved from https://youtu.be/K1Md20KNs98
36. Wikipedia (n.d.) 'Sailing Away (All of Us) Song'. Retrieved from https://en.wikipedia.org/wiki/Sailing_Away_(All_of_Us_song)
37. Citation: NZ 1990 Medal. Tribal affiliations: Takapūwāhia. Educated at Canterbury School of Fine Art; Victoria University. Career: Music composer, arranger and conductor; member, International Society of Music Education; Board member, New Zealand Drama School; Councillor, Porirua City Council, three terms; Chair, Māori Committee, Wellington City Council; Chairman, Kaumātua Council Takapūwāhia; President (Tumuaki), Rūnanga of Ngāti Toa. Cultural achievements: recordings of NZ Māori Chorale. Retrieved from: En.m.wikipedia.org/wiki/1987 Birthday Honours (New Zealand)
38. Sounz (n.d.)
39. Katene, Te Puoho, booklet written for the opening of Toa Rangatira
40. Graham, Brett (2014) 'Te Hau-ki-Tūranga Meeting House'. Retrieved from https://teara.govt.nz/en/interactive/43104/te-hau-ki-turanga-meeting-house
41. Elkington, George (2018) personal communication

REFERENCES

Anderson, Atholl (1990) 'Te Puoho-o-te-rangi', Te Ara – The Encyclopedia of New Zealand. Retrieved from https://teara.govt.nz/en/biographies/1t59/te-puoho-o-te-rangi

Ballara, Angela (1990) 'Te Rangihaeata', Te Ara – The Encyclopedia of New Zealand. Retrieved from https://teara.govt.nz/en/biographies/1t63/te-rangihaeata

The Big Idea (2008) 'Matariki Forum: Where is Maori Theatre Now?' Retrieved from https://www.thebigidea.nz/news/industry-news/2008/nov/31395-matariki-forum-where-is-maori-theatre-now

Bourke, Chris (2014) 'Popular music - Origins of New Zealand popular music', Te Ara – The Encyclopedia of New Zealand. Retrieved from https://teara.govt.nz/en/interactive/42563/gold-and-platinum-new-zealand-albums-to-2013

Carr, Malcolm (1965) 'Porgy and Bess – A Vibrant Theatricality'. Retrieved from http://nzetc.victoria.ac.nz/tm/scholarly/tei-Salient28061965-t1-body-d60.html

Derby, Mark and Grace-Smith, Briar (2014) 'Māori theatre – te whare tapere hōu'. Te Ara – The Encyclopedia of New Zealand. Retrieved from https://teara.govt.nz/en/maori-theatre-te-whare-tapere-hou

Graham, Brett (2014) 'Te Hau-ki-Tūranga Meeting House'. Retrieved from https://teara.govt.nz/en/interactive/43104/te-hau-ki-turanga-meeting-house

Hannan, J. G. H. and Bassett, Judith (1990) 'James Prendergast'. Retrieved from https://teara.govt.nz/en/biographies/1p29/prendergast-james

Harris, Edward Daniel (2006) *The Missionary Journals of Edward Daniel Harris (1917–1920)*, transcribed and edited by Mark F. Harris, Trafford Publishing, USA

Katene, Te Puoho, booklet written for the opening of Toa Rangatira

Keepapitchinin (1936) *A Bump in the Road to Hui Tau 1936*

NZ History (n.d.) 'Join Together' Song, 1974 Commonwealth Games. Retrieved from https://nzhistory.govt.nz/media/photo/%26%23039%3Bjoin-together%26%23039%3B-song%2C-1974-commonwealth-games

Oliver, Steven (1990) 'Te Rauparaha', Te Ara – The Encyclopedia of New Zealand. Retrieved from https://teara.govt.nz/en/biographies/1t74/te-rauparaha

Pōmare, Mīria (2005) 'Ngāti Toarangatira – Migration from the north', Te Ara – The Encyclopedia of New Zealand. Retrieved from https://teara.govt.nz/en/map/1350/ngati-toas-migration

Radio New Zealand (n.d.) 'Porgy and Bess – 50 Years Since NZ Performance'. Retrieved from https://www.radionz.co.nz/audio/player?audio_id=201771047

Solomon, Hōhepa (1987) *Hui Rau Tau: 100 Years Established in Porirua*

Sounz (n.d.) 'Te Puoho Katene'. Retrieved from https://www.sounz.org.nz/contributors/1199

Te Ao Hou (September 1966) 'Maori Theatre Trust Formed'. Retrieved from https://paperspast.natlib.govt.nz/periodicals/TAH196609.2.46.2

Te Karere (August 1940) Open letter to the Latter-day Saints in New Zealand from Sergeant George Katene on behalf of the Latter-day Saints of the 28th Maori Battalion

Waikanae Anglican (n.d.) 'Our History'. Retrieved from http://www.anglican.co.nz/about/our-story

Wikipedia (n.d.) 'Michael Fay (Banker)'. Retrieved from https://en.wikipedia.org/wiki/Michael_Fay_(banker)

—— (n.d.) 'New Zealand Challenge'. Retrieved from https://en.wikipedia.org/wiki/New_Zealand_Challenge

—— (n.d.) 'Sailing Away (All of Us) Song'. Retrieved from https://en.wikipedia.org/wiki/Sailing_Away_(All_of_Us_song)

—— (n.d.) 'Toni Williams'. Retrieved from https://en.wikipedia.org/wiki/Toni_Williams

—— (n.d.) 'Wiremu Parata'. Retrieved from https://en.wikipedia.org/wiki/Wiremu_Parata#Wi_Parata_v_Bishop_of_Wellington_(1877)

YouTube (2017) 'Sailing Away – All of Us'. Retrieved from https://youtu.be/K1Md20KNs98

—— (2013) 'Te Arohanui Maori Concert Party – 1963'. Retrieved from https://youtu.be/ko4zzlQVFVo

Contributors

Derek Couch

Derek Couch is of Ngāti Mutunga, Ngai Tahu, Ngāti Raukawa, Ngāti Toa Rangatira and Ngāti Kahungunu descent. He is married to Leah Broughton from Taranaki and is the father of two children. Derek is an avid reader and student of history, politics and religion, has a strong interest in genealogical research and enjoys jazz music. Derek and his wife live in Auckland and are members of the Glen Innes Ward of the Panmure, Auckland Stake.

Karina Elkington (née Watene)

Ko Moehau tōku maunga. Ko Tikapa te moana. Ko Ngāti Maru tōku iwi. Ko Ngāti Te Aute tōku hapū. Ko Mataiwhetu tōku marae. Ko Puti Tipene Watene tōku Koro, ko Phyllis Mei Rukutai tōku Kuia. Ko James Rukutai Watene tōku pāpā. Ko Emma Reynolds tōku māmā. Ko Raha Elkington tāku hoa tane. Tokowha āku tamariki. Tekau ma rua āku mokopuna. Ko Karina Watene Elkington tāku ingoa.

A sixth-generation Mormon, Karina currently is a Senior Manager at Oranga Tamariki (Government Child Welfare Agency) and has spent twenty-five years in contract management and strategic planning roles in the health sector. She has a Bachelor's degree in Social Work from Brigham Young University, Hawaii, and a Master's degree in Health Management from Massey University.

Barry Garlick

Barry Garlick and wife Eva are serving a mission as Directors of Matthew Cowley Pacific Church History Centre in Temple View, New Zealand. Barry graduated from CCNZ in 1969, served a mission in Melbourne, Australia, and attended BYU Provo, where he graduated with a degree in Business Management. His career has been in the textile industry, where he has had ownership in apparel companies until his recent retirement, as owner of a company that distributes fabric in the outdoor apparel industry. Barry and

Eva have five children and nineteen grandchildren and have lived most of their married life in Pacific Northwest and Highland, Utah, USA.

Peter Garry

Peter Garry joined the Church with his family when he was fourteen years old. Born and raised in Hamilton, Peter served a proselytising mission in the Alaskan Canadian Mission in 1962–63. A graduate from the School of Architecture at the University of Auckland, he practised architecture in Auckland and Canada for forty-eight years. Peter married Jocelyn Garlick and is the father of six children and twenty-four grandchildren. While retired and living in Canada, Peter and Jocelyn recently served a mission at the Matthew Cowley Church History Centre in Temple View, New Zealand. His interests are family history as well as New Zealand Pākehā and Māori church history.

Jeanette Grace

Jeanette Grace, of Ngāti Tūwharetoa, Ngāti Toa, Ngāti Koata, Ngāti Kahungunu, Rangitāne and Ngāti Rakaipaaka descent, is the daughter of Arthur and Terewai Grace (née Elkington). She is currently Dean of Te Wānanga Māori at Whitireia Community Polytechnic and previously worked in Mental Health and Addictions with Te Rūnanga o Toa Rangatira, and Indigenous Training and Education with Te Korowai Aroha o Aotearoa New Zealand. Jeanette is a member of Te Wānanga o Raukawa Foundation, Chair of Te Pūtahitanga o Te Waipounamu Independent Assessment Panel and Chair of the Toa Rangatira Education Achievement Team. She has been a past Chair of the Ngāti Koata Trust.

Callum Katene

Callum Katene lives in Wellington, New Zealand, where he was born. He grew up in a Māori community with strong Mormon traditions; both Callum's grandfather and father held numerous church leadership positions over the courses of their lives.

Professionally, Callum became involved in the information technology industry at a young age. In 1993, he was employed by Cisco Systems Inc., and so spent much time in the 1990s in Silicon Valley, California. Today, Callum is director and chief of technology at Atea Systems, a software development company he founded in 2002. Callum has many interests, including music, writing and history.

Selwyn Katene

Selwyn Katene, a fifth-generation Mormon, was Assistant Vice-Chancellor Māori, Director of Global Centre Indigenous Leadership and Director of MANU AO Leadership Academy at Massey University. Prior to that he was a senior manager in the public service and pharmaceutical industry. Selwyn's doctorate is from Massey University and he has two masters degrees from Victoria University. He has published seven books, including two on early Māori leaders in the Mormon Church. Of Ngāti Toa, Ngā Ruahine and Ngāti Tūwharetoa descent, Selwyn is married to Rahui, née Hippolite, and they have five children and ten grandchildren.

Douglas J. Martin Jr

Douglas J. Martin Jr is currently the Pacific Area Financial Controller for the Church of Jesus Christ of Latter-day Saints. He holds a Master of Business Administration degree from Brigham Young University Provo, Utah, and a Bachelor of Management Studies degree with Honours from Waikato University, Hamilton, and is a member of CPA Australia. Early in his career, he held senior financial positions in the logistics, travel and pharmaceutical industries. Douglas is of Ngāti Porou and Ngāti Kahungunu descent and is a fifth-generation Latter-day Saint.

Api Te Rina Paewai

Api Te Rina Paewai is of Rangitāne o Tāmaki Nui a Rua me Rongomai Wahine and Ngāti Kahungunu descent. She is a sixth-generation Mormon with over thirteen years' experience in career and economic provision throughout Te Tau Ihu o te Waka a Māui (top of the South Island). Api has double Bachelor Science degrees in Business Management and Travel and Tourism Management from the Brigham Young University, Hawaii, and a Master's Degree in Career Development from Auckland University of Technology. Api's interest in the field of economic/career development stems from a self-reliance culture forged in her formative years.

Jennifer Roberts (née Palmer)

Jennifer Roberts was born in Rotorua, New Zealand, to Ken and Jill Palmer. She was baptised in December 1958, six months after her parents' baptism. Jennifer married John Roberts in the New Zealand temple in 1970. They have lived most of their married life in New Jersey, USA, where they have raised their six children. John and Jennifer have since retired to Plymouth,

Massachusetts, USA, to be near children and grandchildren. They love serving together as ordinance workers in the Boston temple. They also enjoyed four years in Manhattan serving a Temple Mission and in the Temple Presidency under Stephen Bennion and his wife, Marjorie.

Michael Roberts

Michael Roberts retired as Academic Vice President of Auckland Institute of Studies, St Helens, in 2014. Prior to that he was a senior lecturer at University of Waikato, serving in various roles including Chair of Department (Japanese), Pro-Dean Academic Planning (Humanities), Pro-Dean International (Arts and Social Sciences) and Acting Manager of the University of Waikato Language Institute. He has a PhD in Japanese linguistics from the University of Hawaii at Manoa, MA (first-class Hons) and a BA in Japanese language and literature from the University of Auckland. He and wife Christine are blessed with three children and eleven grandchildren.

Marie Waaka (née Te Rei)

Marie Waaka, a third-generation Mormon, is of Ngāti Toa Rangatira, Ngāti Whakaue, Ngā Ruahinerangi and Ngāti Kura descent. She is a mother of two and lives in Ōtaki on the Kāpiti Coast with Reuben, her husband of forty-one years. Marie is currently the Director for Support and Residential Services at Te Wānanga o Raukawa and the author of two Māori language books for small children, *Te Whānau Moana* and *Te Whānau Pāmu*. In 1998 Marie graduated from the Wellington College of Education with a qualification in Library Studies.

Waana Watene

Waana Watene, a fifth-generation Mormon, currently works as a pouako/lecturer for Te Rito Maioha, Early Childhood New Zealand, and has worked in the tertiary sector specialising in early childhood education for the past seventeen years. Waana belongs to a large whānau, the Watenes on her father's side, and the Eketones on her mother's side. She first became interested in whakapapa while holidaying with her aunt in Waihau Bay in 1988 and it has since become one of her passions. She currently serves as ward Relief Society President in the Rotokauri Stake, Hamilton.

Glossary

MĀORI

Ahorangi	senior person of high esteem and standing
Aotearoa	New Zealand
aroha	compassion, love
Atua	god(s)
hāhi	church
haka	posture, dance
hapū	subtribe
hikoi	journey
hui	meeting — hui pariha: district conference; — hui tau: annual national conference
iwi	tribe
kai	food; kaimoana: seafood
kāinga	home
kaitiaki	guardian; kaitiakitanga: guardianship
karakia	chant, incantation, prayer
kaumātua	elder
kete	woven basket
korowai	cloak
mana	high esteem, influence, authority, prestige
manaakitanga	hospitality, care, support
Māoritanga	Māori culture, practices and beliefs.
marae	open area in front of a traditional house where formal greetings/discussions take place
matakite	vision, prophecy; prophet
mokopuna	grandchild(ren)
mōteatea	song of grief
ope	group of people moving together
pā	village

pūrākau	ancient legends, stories
rangatira	chief, chiefly
reo	language
rohe	district, territory
tamariki	children
tangata whenua	people of the land, local people
tangi	express grief, cry; tangihanga: funeral
tauā	war party
tikanga	customs
tipuna	ancestor(s)
tohunga	priest, expert
tupuna	ancestor(s)
waiata	song
wairua	spiritual dimension
waka	canoe; waka taua — war canoe
whakapapa	genealogy
whakatauakī	proverb
whānau	(extended) family; whanaunga: relation(s); whanaungatanga: kinship
whare	house
wharenui	meeting house
whare wananga	school of learning

MORMON TERMS

Aaronic Priesthood – the lesser priesthood that deals with the temporal and outward ordinances such as administering the sacrament and whose officers are bishop, priest, teacher and deacon

Bishop – the local spiritual leader and common judge of a ward (diocese) who holds a position of responsibility in the Aaronic Priesthood

BYU – Brigham Young University, a private university owned by the Church of Jesus Christ of Latter-day Saints with campuses in Utah, Idaho and Hawaii

Councillor – a member of a committee such as a bishopric (leadership of a local diocese) who provides support and counsel to the bishop (local church leader)

Elder – the title given to all holders of the Melchizedek Priesthood, for example, male missionaries are addressed as elders

First Presidency – the President of the Church of Jesus Christ of Latter-day Saints and his councillors who preside over the whole Church

Gather/gathering – the assembling in Zion (Utah) of members of the Church in the last days before the coming of Jesus Christ

General Authority – a member of the highest levels of leadership within the Church of Jesus Christ of Latter-day Saints who has administrative and ecclesiastical authority over the church

Labour mission – members of the Church called to serve a voluntary mission usually to build meeting houses, schools and temples

MAC – Māori Agricultural College – a secondary boarding school for boys in Hastings built by the Church of Jesus Christ of Latter-day Saints in 1913 but closed in 1931 due to an earthquake that rendered the buildings unsafe

Melchizedek Priesthood – the greater priesthood that deals with the rights to administer all spiritual blessings, such as blessing the sick, and whose officers are elder, high priest, patriarch, Seventy, and Apostle

Relief Society – a world-wide women's organisation of the Church of Jesus Christ of Latter-day Saints established in 1842 to advance the spiritual welfare of all its members, including the poor and needy, widows and orphans, and for other benevolent purposes

Saint – a faithful or active member of the Church of Jesus Christ of Latter-day Saints

Set apart – to be selected to a specific service within the Church such as a proselytising mission

Seventy – an office to which men are ordained in the Melchizedek Priesthood to preach the gospel and be a witness of Jesus Christ

Stake – an organisational and administrative unit of the Church that is composed of a number of wards or branches (local dioceses)

Temple – literally the house of the Lord, a holy place of worship where worthy members of the Church perform sacred ceremonies and ordinances of the gospel for themselves and the dead

Temple recommend – a permit given to a worthy member of the Church to enter a temple and perform sacred ceremonies and ordinances of the gospel for themselves and the dead

Temple sealing – to make valid in heaven the sacred ordinances performed on earth in temples

Zion – a place where the 'pure in heart' or righteous members of the Church live

Index

Entries in *italics* refer to figures. Entries of the form 'XnY' refer to footnote Y on page X. Alphabetisation ignores the Māori word *te*.

A

Aaronic Priesthood 48, 188
Adams, W. K. 81
Te Ahi Kā 207–8
Ahuwhenua Trophy 125
Aitutaki 162–3
All Blacks 65, 128, 159
Allen, Fred 128
Allen, Steve 204–5
Amaru, Wi Pere 63
America's Cup 205–6
Anderson Plan 40
Anglican Church 5, 13, 37, 90, 143, 148, 196–9
Apikera 6
Te Ara a Tāwhaki 87
Te Arawa 60
Archibald, James 179
Te Arohanui Māori Concert Party 202
Arthur, Karewa Moki 81
Arthur, Kauhoe 80–1
Asper, A. E. 14
Te Atairangikaahu 71
Te Āti Awa 20, 77, 86
Auckland City Council 138
Auckland Grammar School 36
Auckland Harbour Stake 112
Auckland Stake 44–7, 152; presidency of *46*; priesthood training in 48
Austin, Rex 165

B

Ballif, Ariel S. 80, 150, 186, 189
baptism 3; of Ada Garlick 143; of Apikara Paewai 122; of Ben Couch 160; for the dead 22; of Doug Martin 179; of Garry family 95; of Geoff and April Garlick 150; of Kenneth Palmer 107; on Kenneth Palmer's missions 116; of Matene Rutatenga 5, 13–14; of Mita and Kataraina Watene 8; of Steve Watene 62; of William Roberts 41
Bean, Merena Hall 3
Beehive girls 95
Bennett, Charles 204
Benson, Ezra Taft 164, 167
Boer War 36, 90
Book of Mormon 95, 149
Bowie, Dorothy 124
Bowring, Benjamin 181
boxing 82, 91, 125
Boyack, Clifton D. 144–5
Bradley, Amelia 63
Bregman, Agnes 92
Bregman, Bernice Agnes (Clark) 92–3
Bregman, Edward 92
Bregman, George 92–3
Bregman, Theodore 92–3
Brigham Young University, Hawaii 30
Broederlow, Oscar 41
Brown, Victor L. 49
Buck, Sir Peter 71, 127
Budget Counselling Scheme 136
Burgess, Joseph 8
Burke, Beulah 92–3
Burke, Desmond 93
Burke, Edmond 92

C

Cakobau, George 116
Canada 47, 99, 122, 153, 179, 184, 216
Carroll, Clara Elizabeth (Garry) 89
Carroll, James 71

Carroll, Patricia Helen 89
Carter, Peti Tangihaere (Bessie) 158–63, *161*, 167–9
Carter Holt Harvey 182, 185
CCNZ (Church College of New Zealand) 28, 79; Ada Garlick at 144–5; Advisory Committee 132; building of 42; Couch family and 161–2; Elkington at 29; Ian Garry's architecture at 96, 99; Pateriki Te Rei and 84
Chase, George 28
Chase, Ngahuia 2
Chase, Wati 82
Chirney, Elsie (Elkington) *27*, 28–30, 82
Chote, Matthew T. 41, 45, *46*, 152
Christy, Sidney 3
Church Construction Programme 27, 42–5, 95–6, 180, 210n19
Church of England *see* Anglican Church
Clapp, Rex 94, 96
Clark, James Arthur 92–3
Clark, Theo Rene (Garry) 92–100, *94*, *99*
Clarke, Cyril 82
Commonwealth Games, Christchurch 1974 204
Cook Islands 162–3
Cottle, Archie 27
Couch, Adelaide *161*
Couch, Ben 2, 157, *161*, *167*, *168*; beginnings and family 158–61; church leadership 161–4; conversion 159–60; legacy 169–70; political and community service 164–9; *see also* Carter, Peti Tangihaere
Couch, Charmaine *161*
Couch, Derek, biography 215
Couch, George Manning Moke 158
Couch, Kathleen *161*
Couch, Roy *161*
Couch, Wayne *161*
Couch, Zion *161*
Cowley, Matthew viii, *30*; adopted son of 61; and conversion of Watene family 8–11; and Elkington family 24–6, 29; marrying Pateriki and Peti 80; and Nitama Paewai 127–31; slogan of 170
Cowley, Tony 61
Craven, Rulon 191
Crawford, Gladys 183
Crawford, Rebecca 177, 179–83
Crawford, Sydney 3, 176–7, 179–83, 186–7
Crawford, Wati 176–86, *178*, 188, 190–3, *191*

D

Dannevirke High School 125–7, 130
Dansey, Harry 138
Davies, Rangi 27
Davis, Rangi and Tom 82
Dennis, Tom 63–4
Don, Ron 169–70
Duncan, Polly 3
Dunn, Emile 27
D'Urville Island 19–20, 23–4, 30, 78–9, 85

E

Eastern Māori electorate 58, 69, 85, 165
Ehau, Kepa 85
Eketone, Pepene 3
El Alamein, battles of 38
Elkington, Arthur *30*
Elkington, David 24
Elkington, Emily 24–5
Elkington, Emron 24, 26
Elkington, George 208–9
Elkington, Herbert 23, 25
Elkington, Huiarotu 24
Elkington, James Rongotoa vii, 2, 19, 82; church leadership 29–31; as labour missionary 27–9; life on D'Urville Island 23–5; at MAC 21–2; in Porirua 25–6; whakapapa of 20–1; *see also* Chirney, Elsie; Meha, Huitau Mere
Elkington, Jamesina 24–5, 30
Elkington, John 25–8, 30–1
Elkington, Karina 74–5n65, biography 215
Elkington, Kay 25
Elkington, Madsen 25–7
Elkington, Olive 23, 25–6, 30
Elkington, Patricia 24
Elkington, Rangikauia *see* Liahona Moleni, Rangi
Elkington, Ratapu (John) 19, 23
Elkington, Sam 23, 25–6
Elkington, Son (Turi) 23, *30*
Elkington, Terewai 23–4
Elkington, Wetekia (Ruruku) 3, 19–21, 23
Ellis, Glen J. 179

F

Ferris, James 183, *184*
Fiji 81, 112–13, 115–16, 181, 192
First Quorum of Seventy 2, 190

Forbes, Grace 82
Forbes, Horace 186–7
Foreman, Bill 182, 188
Francis, Bob 169
Fraser: 'Womp' 91; Peter 103
Freyberg, Bernard C. 38
Fruean, Martha *134*
Fruean, Selu 189
Fyans, Tom 49

G

Gardner, William 1, 8–9, *10*, 12–14, 137
Garlick, Barry *151*; biography 215–16
Garlick, Beverley Rose *151*
Garlick, Brian Lundius 141–2
Garlick, Geoffrey R. 2, *46*, *151*; church leadership 151–4; conversion of 143, 148–50; early years 145–6; family of 141–3; in Hamilton Stake 45, 111; and Kenneth Palmer 106–7; near-death experience 147–8
Garlick, Geoffrey R. *see also* Stokes, Gwen; Thompson, April
Garlick, Jill Beeban (Palmer) 104–7, *105*, 109–15, *111*, 117, 118–19, 141–2, 152
Garlick, Joan 141–2
Garlick, Stanley Clyde 141–5, 147, 152
Garry, Alfred James 89–90
Garry, Caryl (Te Puke) 95–7, *99*
Garry, Ian (A. R. I.) 2, *94*, *99*; and Church Construction Programme 95–6; church leadership 96–7; conversion 94–5; death of 100; early years 89–90; education 90–3; war service 93–4; *see also* Clark, Theo Rene
Garry, Jocelyn *151*
Garry, Peter 95–7, *99*, 188; biography 216
Gear Meat Company 58, 69
George R. Biesinger Hall 96
Gershwin, George 203
Gibbs, Bill 83
Gillman, Frank 90, 96
Going, Lionel 27
Going, Percy 3
Grace, Jeanette, biography 216
Great Depression 65, 91, 93, 121–2, 125–6, 175
Great Songs of the Māori 29
Green, Boyd 107
Grey, George 196–7

H

Hadfield, Octavius 197
Haight, David B. 190
Hamilton Stake 45
Hamilton Technical College 91–2
Hamilton Temple 52, 96; construction of 27–8, 43; marriage in 166; Ben Couch and 161–2, 164; Doug Martin's service at 188, 192; Garry family's service at 97–8; Palmer family at 108; Pateriki Te Rei and 83; Visitors Centre 153–4
Hamilton Ward 96, 187–8
Hamon, Henare 3
Hands, Brian 205
Hapi, Joe 63–4
Harris, Boy 82
Harris, Kelly *80*
Harris, Marie 80
Hart, Charles 174
Hart, William Leslie 173–4, 176
Te Hau, Mere 22
Te Hau Ki Tūranga 207
Haukawakawa 23
Hauraki region 5, 7–8, 14, 61, 70
Hawaii: Doug and Wati Martin in 180–1; James Elkington in 30; Paewai family in 125; Palmer family in 117; Polynesian Culture Centre in 202
Heperi, Hohepa 3
Hetariki, Bree *134*
Te Heu Heu, Timoti 204
Hinckley, Gordon B. 190–1
Hippolite, Frank 24
Hoby, Wi Katene 198
Holland, Sidney 43
Holyoake, Keith 58, 66, 71, 124
Home Sunday School 108–9
Hongoeka 86, 197
Horomona, Ringi 26
Hotunui 6, 60
Hoturoa 6, 20
Hughie, Vaughn 83
Hui Pariha 130, 219
Hui Tau: Doug Martin baptised at 179; and Elkington family 21, 23–4, 26, 28; Katene family at 201–2; Pateriki Te Rei at 79–80
Hunter, Thomas 145

I

Ihimaera (Smiler), Pera 3
Independence, MO 97
Inter-Parliamentary Union 70
Iwi Transition Authority 169

J

James D. Moyle Oral History Programme 44, 54
Jenson, Andrew 14
Johnson, Gordon Wills 166
Johnson, Matt 21
Johnston, Norma (Roberts) 35, 37–41, *38*, 44, *49*, 52–5, *53*, 99
'Join Together' 204–5
Jones, Collins 188
Jones, Pei Te Hurinui 85, 204
Josephs, Di John 82
Jury, Whatahoro 2

K

Kaa, Hone 86
Kaikohe 28, 131, 134–8
Kaipara Dairy Company 89
Te Kairangi, Amiria 195, 198–9
Te Kairangi, Atanatiu 195
Te Kairangi, Hareti 198–9
Kaitoki Māori Cemetery 139
Te Kākākura, Wi Parata 197
Kamau, Maraki 181
Kāpiti Island 20, 199
Kapua, Hinganga 78–9
karakia 85–6
Karauria, Wi 79
Te Karere 27–8, 200
Katene, Te Arohi (Rose) Maraea 196
Katene, Bill 208
Katene, Callum, biography 216
Katene, Frederick 199
Katene, George ix–x, 200, *201*
Katene, Hari 199
Katene, Kaaro 81
Katene, Manu 199
Katene, Ngaronga 199
Katene, Te Oti Kerei 195–6, 198–201, 208
Katene, Te Puoho 2; childhood of 199–201; church service of 202–3, 208–9; community service 206; legacy of 209; and Māori Chorale 205–6; and Māori Theatre Trust 204–5; and Takapūwāhia Marae 206–7; whakapapa of 195–6; *see also* Mackie, Frances Anne
Katene, Rangi 199
Katene, Selwyn, biography 217
Katene, Taku 199
Katene, Wikitoria *201*
Kauae Cemetery 84, 87
Kauhoe, Arta 80
Kaye, Danny 202
Kennedy, David 167
Kimball, Spencer W. 45–6, 51–2, 98–9, 113, 115–16, 166, *167*, 190–1
Kingi, Lou 186
Kīngitanga movement 8, 71, 85
Kiribati 114
Kirikiri 11–13, 60–2, 68; churches at *13*
Kirikiri Valley 8–9
Kirk, Norman 58, 64, 71
Knox College 127
Te Kohu, Riripeti 6
Kohunui 158, 161, 164
Koroneihana 85
kōwhaiwhai 207
Kuranui College 161

L

labour missionary programme 27–9, 43, 82–4, 96, 151, 180–1, 186, 210n19
Labour Party 66, 69, 84–5, 165
Lambert, James Needham 121
Laurenson, John 174
Lee, Harold B. 108–9
Leeds, England 52
Liahona Moleni, Rangi 23, 27, *28*, 30–1
Lilburn, Douglas 202
Los Angeles Temple 99
Lundius, Ada Jeannette (Garlick) 141–7, 149–50, 152
Lundius, Per Emil Henrik 142
Lundon, David 142
Lundon, Matilda Maud 142

M

Te Maari, Heke 158
Te Maari, Piripi 158

MAC (Māori Agricultural College): earthquake at 26; James Elkington at 21–2; Nireha Paewai at 123; Pateriki Te Rei at 79; Steve Watene at 63–4
MAC Old Boys Association 24, 26
Mackie, Frances Anne 202, 209
Madsen, Julius V. 23
Mahuta, Tonga 67
Makirikiri 122, 133
Manaia 77–9, 81
Manuirirangi, Te Akapikirangi 81
Manuirirangi, Turake 3
Manuirirangi family 79
Manurewa Stake 152–3
Māori, LDS beliefs about origins of 29
Māori All Blacks 64, 159
Māori Battalion 200–1, 204
Māori Community Centre, Auckland 67
Māori Education Foundation 69
Te Māori exhibition 85
Māori High Priests 24
Māori Land Court 37, 64, 66–7
Māori language *see* te reo Māori
Māori music 206
Māori Pioneer Battalion 199
Māori renaissance 204, 207, 211n27
Māori Women's Welfare League 85
Marquis, Tony 41
Martin, Craig Tainui 183–4
Martin, Douglas James 2, 96, *174*, *178*, *184*; children of 182–5; church leadership 186–92; and Couch family 161, 164, 169; genealogy of 173–6; at Ian Garry's funeral 100; legacy 192–3; marriage and conversion 176–81; at Plastic Products 182, 185–6; *see also* Crawford, Wati; Ferris, James
Martin, Douglas Jonathan (Jr.) 183–6, *184*, 190, 192; biography 217
Martin, George *174*, 175
Martin, Jessie *174*, 175
Martin, Sydney 183, *184*
Matai Whetu Marae 63
Mataira, Alice Halbert 3
Mātaiwhetu Marae 11
Matauri Bay 77–9, 86
Matenga, Paratene 158
Matenga, Whakahe 3, 95
Maxwell, Neal A. 165
McCarthy, Farina 95

McCready, Allan 58
McDonald, Jack 153
McRae, Nira 83
McRae, Peti Maylia (Te Rei) 79–80, 82–4, *83*, 87
Meha, Arapata 22
Meha, Hineapa 132–5, *133*, *134*, 138–9
Meha, Huitau Mere (Elkington) 20, *22*, 23–6
Meha, Kahu 83
Meha, Stuart 3, 24, 132–3
Melchizedek Priesthood 48, 108, 160
Mendenhall, Wendell B. 42, 96, 188
Metekingi, Mark 203
Methodist Church 37
MIA (Mutual Improvement Association) 43, 95
Mitchell, Tai 82
Molony, Arthur James 102
Molony, Gertrude Amy 102
Monson, Thomas S. 152, 189
Mormon Tabernacle 97, 202–3
Morris, Ivory Te Pora 132
Morris, LeRoy 148–9
Morrison, Howard 206
Mount Wellington Borough Council 68
Muldoon, Robert 165–7
Munro, Donald 203
Murphy, Jack 91
muttonbirds 24

N

Naera, Te Weringa 160
Napier Earthquake of 1931 79, 175
Nash, Walter 68–70
Nathan, Bill 58
National Māori Rugby League Tournament 65
National Party 104, 164–5
Native Affairs Department 66–7
Nauvoo, IL 97, 99
Nelson, Russell M. 51, *54*, 98, 114–15
Nepia, George 21, 63–5
New Zealand Co-operative Dairy Company 90, 94
New Zealand Division (World War Two) 38–9
New Zealand Kiwis (rugby league team) 66, 71
New Zealand Māori Chorale 205–6
New Zealand Māori Council 69, 157, 164
New Zealand Māori Health Committee 135
New Zealand Māori Theatre Trust 204–5

New Zealand Opera Company 203
New Zealand Rugby Football Union 157, 169
New Zealand Society for Music Therapy 206
New Zealand Symphony Orchestra 205
New Zealand Temple *see* Hamilton Temple
New Zealand Waterside Workers Union 68
Te Ngā, Matene *see* Rutatenga, Matene
Ngā Purutanga Mauri 86
Ngā Ruahine 77
Ngāi Tahu 158
Ngaruawāhia 20, 79, 90–3, 96–8, 189
Ngata, Apirana 71, 82, 207
Ngāti Hauā 7
Ngāti Huia 78
Ngāti Kahungunu 22, 121–2, 158
Ngāti Koata 20, 77
Ngāti Korokī 7
Ngāti Kura 77
Ngāti Maniapoto 85
Ngāti Maru 5–8, 11, 60–1, 70
Ngāti Muturangi Māori Club 67
Ngāti Rakaipaaka 22, 122
Ngāti Rangatahi 195
Ngāti Rangiwhakaewa 122–3
Ngāti Raukawa 86, 158, 160
Ngāti Tama 20, 196
Ngāti Toa 20, 81, 87, 158
Ngāti Toa Rangatira 77, 86, 207; confiscation of lands 197–8; James Elkington and 20; migration of 196–7
Ngāti Whakaue 79
Ngawaka, Raihi 2
Nicholson, Iwikatea 87
Nohorua 20, 78, 80
Northcote, Auckland 35–7; Volunteer Fire Brigade 36

O

O'Conner, Alice 90
Ōpotiki High School 63
oratory 63–4, 80, 85
Te Oriki, Te Teira 122
Ōtaki Māori Boys College 158
Ottley, Sidney J. 28, 80, 149, 180

P

Packer, Boyd K. 190
Paerata, Kaiser 64
Paerata, Te Rawhiti 3

Paewai, Alice 123
Paewai, Api Te Rina 217
Paewai, Hepa 124
Paewai, Kamilla *134*
Paewai, Lui 125
Paewai, Manahi *123*, *134*
Paewai, Manahi Nitama 2, 121–2, *123*, *129*, *130*; childhood 124–6; church service 128–31; community service 131–2, 134–6; family 132–4; later years 138–9; at medical school 126–7; sporting achievements 128, 159; whakapapa 122–4; work and thrift ethic 136–8; *see also* Meha, Hineapa
Paewai, Mavis 122
Paewai, Nireaha 122–3, 125
Paewai, Pearl 123
Paewai, Punga 124, 137
Paewai, Rachel 123
Paewai, Ringa 124
Palmer, Ann 104, *105*, 115–16
Palmer, Brian 108, *111*, 112
Palmer, Frederic and Elizabeth 102
Palmer, Jennifer 104–5, *111*, 118; biography 217–18
Palmer, Kenneth Moloney 2, *105*, *111*; church service 107–12; conversion 106–7; death and legacy 118–19; early life 102; genealogy of 101; glasshouse operation with Garlicks 152; managing Distribution Centre 50; marriage and family 104–5; missions 112–18; war service 102–4; *see also* Garlick, Jill Beeban
Palmer, Kevin *111*, 112–13
Palmer, Lynn 104, *105*, *111*
Palmer, Mark 108, *111*, 112
Palmer, Michael 108, *111*
Palmer, Mike 112
Palmer, Stephanie *111*, 112–13
Palmer, Truda 102
Palmyra, NY 97
Panmure Ward 151–2, 188
Paora, Joanne 69
Te Papaiouru Marae 85, 87
Parahi, Gooch 159
Parker, Vic 69
Peckham, Harry 189
Pere, Baden 137
Perriton, Alan 188
Perriton, Robert 188

Petone Borough Council 69
Petone Rugby League Club 69
Philippines 136, 184, 191–2
Piper, Hugh 91
Pirinoa 158–9, 161–2, 164
Plastic Products 182, 185–6, 188, 190
Te Poari 11
Pōkarekare Ana (album) 205
'Pōkarekare Ana' (song) 205–6
Pomare, Maui 71
Porgy and Bess 203–4
Porirua City Council 206
Potae, Henare 3
Potter, Tony 166
Presbyterian Church 26, 95, 177
Programme of the Church of Jesus Christ of Latter-day Saints 41
Provo, UT 118
Te Puea Herangi, Princess 20
Te Puke 102, 104, 107, 152
Pukerua Bay 198–9
Te Puoho Ki Te Rangi 196
Puriri, Rangikawea 3

Q

QEII Arts Council 203
Quorum of the Twelve Apostles 26, 41, 45–7, 50, 114, 166–7

R

Raiātea 86–7
Ranfurly Shield 159
Te Rangihaeata 196–7
Rangitāne 22, 122–3
Rangitāne o Tāmaki Nui a Rua 121
Rangiteapake, Pātara 6
Rangitoto ki te Tonga *see* D'Urville Island
Rata, Matiu 66
Rātana movement 66, 69
Te Rauparaha 196–7
Te Rauparaha, Tāmihana 197
Te Rei, Ariana 78–9
Te Rei, Arta Kauhoe 80, 84
Te Rei, Ihaka 77–80
Te Rei, Irlene Miriama *80, 82, 83*
Te Rei, Marie, biography 218
Te Rei, Marie Waiata 80, *83*, 84
Te Rei, Matiu Nohorua 80, *83*, 84, 87
Te Rei, Ngatere 81, *83*
Te Rei, Otere Ihaka 80
Te Rei, Pateriki 2, *80, 83, 86*; adult life of 79–81; Air Force service 81–2; and te ao Māori 85–7; community and church service 82–4; legacy of 87; political activism 84–5; whakapapa of 77–8; *see also* McRae, Peti Maylia
Reid, Sanitorium 159
Relief Society 26, 81, 96
te reo Māori 85, 153, 166
Returned Services Association (RSA) 82
Reweti, Kuku 60–1, 63
Richards, Legrand 47–8
Riwai, Hinerua 158
Riwai, Mere Ngautanga 158
Riwai, Tahana Jack 158
Riwai-Couch, Manuera Benjamin *see* Couch, Ben
RLDS (Reorganised Church of Jesus Christ of Latter-Day Saints) 23
Roberts, Jennifer *see* Palmer, Jennifer
Roberts, John 39, *49*, 51
Roberts, Michael 39, *49*, 50, 53; biography 218
Roberts, William vii, 2, 35–6, *38, 46, 53, 54, 55*; in Auckland Stake 44–7, 152; and Church Construction Programme 43; conversion 40–1; early life of 36–7; end of life 52–4; and Kenneth Palmer 114; as New Zealand Temple President 52, 99; as regional representative 48–52; in World War Two 38–9; *see also* Johnston, Norma
Roberts, William Parry 36, 55n2
Rogers, Messines and Janet 82
Romney, Marion G. 44, 52, 187–8
Romney, Orson D. 21
Rosenvall, Albert E. 188
Rotary 126, 135
Rotorua Ward 84, 109
rowing 91
Rudd, Glen L. vii–viii, *46*, 118–19, 191, 193
rugby (union): Ben Couch and 159–60; Geoff Garlick and 146; Ian Garry and 90–1; and James Elkington 21; Martin family and 178–9, 183; Nitama Paewai and 125, 128, 136; Pateriki Te Rei and 82; Steve Watene and 59, 62–5; and William Roberts 37; *see also* All Blacks; Māori All Blacks

rugby league: Ian Garry and 90; Pateriki Te Rei and 82; Steve Watene and 59, 65–7, 69, 71–2
Rukutai, Phyllis May (Watene) 57–8, 60, 65–6, 72
Rukutai, Puhipi James 74n39
Ruruku, Pene 30
Ruruku, Roma Hoera 20–1
Ruruku, Turi 21, 23, 30
Rutatenga, Matene 2, 5–6, 61; conversion 12–14; war experience of 7–8; whakapapa of 6; see also Apikera; Te Kohu, Riripeti

S

Sabar, Joe 159
Sabbath observance 24, 108
sacrament meetings 82–3, 109, 118, 128, 149
'Sailing Away' 205–6
Salt Lake City 26; Doug Martin in 184–5, 189–90; Garry family in 96–7, 99; Geoff Garlick in 152–4; Kenneth Palmer in 110, 112, 115
Samoa 49–51, 114, 192
Saunders, Carl 160
Savage, Benjamin Boscawen 60
Savage, Benjamin Tangihia 61
Savage, William Taiwhanake 61
Sayers, David 96
Scott, Earnest and Norman 82
self-reliance 136–7, 153
Senior Aaronic Priesthood Programme 48
Sheffield, Gary 107
Simpson, Robert L. 99, 114, 150, 189
Smith, Brian 134
Smith, Eldred G. 189
Smith, George Albert 42, 79
Smith, Kurei 134
Smith, Nahi 134
Smith, Niki 134
Snow, Brian 111
South Africa 36, 89, 122, 128, 136
Southern, Keith 204–5
Southern Māori electorate 164
SS Arawa 36
St George, UT 154
St John's Ambulance 41, 135
Stafford, Elizabeth 173–6
Stafford, Eric see Martin, Douglas J.
stakes, organisation of 44

Steve Watene Memorial Trophy 65
Steven, Evan 29
Stokes, Gwen 154
Stott, Ani Tipare 181
Swendiman, Fred 98

T

Tahiti 49, 86, 192
Tainui 6, 60, 67, 160
Takapūwāhia 195; Elkingtons at 25–6; Katene family at 199–200; Kauhoe Arthur at 81; Ngāti Toa Rangatira at 196–8
Takapūwāhia Marae 86, 196; and Pateriki Te Rei 87; renovation of 206–8
Tanner, N. Eldon 51, 112, 117, 167
Tapsell, Peter 84–5
Tatana, Ritimana 78
Te Tatu o te Pō Marae 58
Taumatawīwī, battle of 7
Taupiri 91, 93
Taurima, Tommy 204
Taylor, John 179
Taylor, Malcolm 188
Taylor, Vaughan Milton 179
temple clothing 96, 166, 181
Temple View, Hamilton 43, 97, 99: Doug Martin at 180, 186; Elkingtons living in 30; Mission Training Centre 118; Syd Crawford at 181; see also Hamilton Temple
Temple View Stake 208
tennis 37, 59, 63, 65, 82, 93
Terina, Api 134
Thames High School 63
Thames Kopu Native Primary School 63
Thompson, April (Garlick) 106, 146, 150, 151, 152–4
Thoms, Miriama Te Wainokenoke 77
tikanga 64, 85–6
Timu, Alice 176
Te Tiriti o Waitangi (Treaty of Waitangi) 7, 70, 198
tithing 44, 108–9, 160, 177
Toa Rangatira meeting house 198, 208
Tom French Cup 129
Tonga 27–8, 49, 81, 192
Te Tōtara Pā 5, 7, 14
translation 49, 112
Tribole, Hinauri 70